Nigel Nicolson was born in London in 1917, the younger son of V. Sackville-West and Harold Nicolson, and was brought up at Knole and Long Barn, and after 1930 at Sissinghurst Castle, where he still lives. He was educated at Eton and Balliol College, Oxford, and served in the Second War in Africa and Italy under the command of Field Marshal Alexander, whose biography he wrote. He entered publishing as George Weidenfeld's partner in 1947 and politics as MP for Bournemouth East in 1952. He has written several books on architecture and social history, and edited the three-volume editions of his father's diaries.

'The most extraordinary revelation of human relationships since THE WELL OF LONE-LINESS. But unlike Radclyffe Hall's tortured tale PORTRAIT OF A MARRIAGE is non-fiction and wholly true . . . The world's most outspoken book.' – *The Bookseller*

'Mr. Nicolson explains how he spent a long and agonizing decade pondering the question of publication . . . His decision is to be applauded . . . His mother's day-by-day description of her contradictory emotions under the stress of the wild, irrational love is perhaps the most affecting, vivid and perceptive thing she ever wrote.' – *Financial Times*

'His tact throughout is delicate, his perceptions acute. He defines his book as "a panegyric of marriage". Not only is it that but it is one of the most absorbing stories, built around two very remarkable people, ever to stray from Gothic fiction into real life.' – *Times Literary Supplement*

'Marvellous story, moving and funny.' – *Spectator*

'Those who have read the three volumes of Sir Harold Nicolson's diaries and letters must have high expectations of his son's new and more ambitious venture. These expectations will be amply fulfilled . . . The marriage he presents was about as unconventional as could be. However, it worked . . . miraculously. And the admirable point of Mr. Nicolson's book is not to elicit a gasp of surprise but to compile an affectionate account of how the miracle occurred . . . Mr. Nicolson's editing is beyond praise.' – *Times Literary Supplement*

'The perfect complement to the DIARIES AND LETTERS, in terms of filial love and editorial skill Mr. Nicolson has equalled his earlier achievement.' – *The Times*

PORTRAIT OF A MARRIAGE

Also by Nigel Nicolson

PEOPLE AND PARLIAMENT
LORD OF THE ISLES (*Lord Leverhulme*)
GREAT HOUSES OF BRITAIN
GREAT HOUSES
ALEX (*Field Marshal Earl Alexander of Tunis*)
DIARIES AND LETTERS OF HAROLD NICOLSON (3 vols *Edited*)

Nigel Nicolson

Portrait of a Marriage

Futura Publications Limited
A Contact Book

A Contact Book

First published in Great Britain in 1973
by Weidenfeld and Nicolson

First Futura Publications edition 1974
published in association with
Weidenfeld and Nicolson

Copyright © 1973 by Nigel Nicolson

Cover design Patrick Mortemore

ISBN 0 8600 7091 3

Printed in Great Britain by
Cox & Wyman Ltd
London, Reading and Fakenham

Futura Publications Limited
49 Poland Street, London W1A 2LG

To S.A.

Foreword

When my mother, V. Sackville-West, died in 1962, it was my duty as her executor to go through her personal papers. She was careful about such things, and had filed everything of importance, including all her letters to and from Harold Nicolson during the fifty years of their engagement and marriage, and all her own diaries and the diaries of her mother, Lady Sackville. In the forty pinewood drawers of a large Italian cupboard I found hundreds of letters from the friends who had meant most to her since her childhood. At the time I read very little, making a mental note that while all the material existed for a full record of her life, it should be allowed to simmer.

I took a final look round her sitting-room in the tower at Sissinghurst (a room which I had entered only half a dozen times in the previous thirty years), and came upon a locked Gladstone bag lying in the corner of the little turret-room which opens off it. The bag contained something – a tiara in its case, for all I knew. Having no key, I cut the leather from around its lock to open it. Inside was a large notebook in a flexible cover, page after page filled by her neat pencilled manuscript. I carried it to her writing-table and began to read. The first few pages were abortive drafts of a couple of short stories. The sixth page was headed '23 July 1920', followed by a narrative in the first person which continued for eighty more. I read it through to the end without stirring from her table. It was an autobiography written when she was aged twenty-eight, a confession, an attempt to purge her mind and heart of a love which had possessed her, a love for another woman, Violet Trefusis.

The simplicity of it, its candour, the extraordinary sequence of events which it unfolded, her implicit plea for forgiveness and compassion, for the strength to resist further temptation, stirred me deeply. I had long known the barest outlines of the story (but not from her) and here was every detail of it, written with scarcely an erasure or correction at a moment when the wound was still fresh and painful. Although her narrative began uncertainly with a rambling account of her childhood, when she came to the heart of her problem it grew in power and intensity, sharpened by a novelist's instinctive variation of mood and speed, almost as if it were not her own experience that she was describing but another's.

I never showed it to my father, although in the first paragraph she wrote that he was the only person whom she could then trust to read it with understanding. My mother's death had shaken him so dreadfully that this reminder of the crisis of their marriage might have increased his misery intolerably, and I feared that he might destroy it, or it him. When I quoted in the Introduction to his published Diaries a few innocuous passages from the autobiography describing her childhood at Knole and their early married life, he never asked to see the rest of it. Now I think that I should have shown it to him when the agony of her loss had been transmuted into numb acceptance of it. He might well have agreed with me that this was a document unique in the vast literature of love, and among the most moving pieces that she ever wrote; that far from tarnishing the memory of her, it burnished it; and that one day, perhaps, it should be published.

Let not the reader condemn in ten minutes a decision which I have pondered for ten years. In Harold Nicolson's lifetime, and in Violet's, no question of publication could arise. He died in 1968; Violet in 1972. I consulted several people, above all my brother Benedict, and Violet's close friend and literary executor, John N. Phillips, to whom I acknowledge my debt for his sympathetic attitude and for copies of certain letters. Both agreed to publication in the form which I suggested. A few of my parents' friends expressed misgivings, but most confirmed my growing conviction that in the 1970s an experience of this kind need no longer be regarded as shameful or unmentionable, for the autobiography was written with profound emotion, and has an integrity and validity of universal significance.

It is the story of two people who married for love and whose love deepened with every passing year, although each was constantly and by mutual consent unfaithful to the other. Both loved people of their own sex, but not exclusively. Their marriage not only survived infidelity, sexual incompatibility and long absences, but became stronger and finer as a result. Each came to give the other full liberty without inquiry or reproach. Honour was rooted in dishonour. Their marriage succeeded because each found permanent and undiluted happiness only in the company of the other. If their marriage is seen as a harbour, their love-affairs were mere ports-of-call. It was to the harbour that each returned; it was there that both were based.

This book is therefore a panegyric of marriage, although it describes a marriage which was superficially a failure because it was incomplete. They achieved their ideal companionship only after a long struggle which was still not ended when Vita Sackville-West wrote the last words of her confession, but once achieved it was unalterable and life-long, and they made of it (as I wrote in the Introduction to my father's Diaries, without revealing the extent of their difficulties) one of the strangest and most successful unions that two gifted people have ever enjoyed.

Although V. Sackville-West left no instructions about her autobiography, and as far as I know had never shown it to anybody, I believe that she wrote it with eventual publication in mind. It assumed an audience. She knew that I would find it after her death, but did not destroy it. She wrote it as a conscious work of art, in such a way that it would be intelligible to an outsider, and her use of pseudonyms is itself an indication that she expected, even hoped, that other eyes might one day read it, by this device safeguarding the reputation of her friends while risking her own. There are passages in the manuscript which suggest that the writing of it was for her much more than an act of catharsis.

She refers to 'possible readers' of it. She believes that 'the psychology of people like myself will be a matter of interest' when hypocrisy gives place to 'a spirit of candour which one hopes will spread with the progress of the world'. That time has come now, more than fifty years after she wrote those prophetic words, and I do not believe that she would deplore the revelation of her secret, knowing that it could help and encourage those similarly placed today.

However, to present the autobiography unexplained and without its sequel would do my parents less than justice, for it was written in the eighth year of a marriage which lasted forty-nine. I came to two conclusions: that it should be published as the first, though main, section of the complete story; and that because it is a story so exceptional, it needed confirmation and amplification, for which all the material existed in the Italian cupboard and the files. The events which V. Sackville-West recounted could be retold as they appeared to other main actors in the drama – Harold Nicolson, Violet Trefusis, Lady Sackville – and to secondary characters like Rosamund Grosvenor, Denys Trefusis and Orazio Pucci, and in retrospect to myself, her son, who was only three years old when the climax was reached in a hotel at Amiens in February 1920. The contemporary letters and diaries throw a new light upon certain incidents and reveal others of which she was ignorant, but they utterly substantiate the truth of what she wrote. Her memory of these cataclysmic events was exact.

The story is told in five parts, two by her, three by myself. Parts 1 and 3 are her autobiography verbatim, altered only by its division into two separated sections (for reasons of balance and intelligibility), and by the substitution of real names for pseudonyms, which are given only when they first occur. Parts 2 and 4 are my commentaries upon it, to which I add essential new facts and quotations from letters and diaries. Part 5 is the justification of the whole book and of its title, for it summarizes the remaining years of her marriage, and shows, particularly in the context of my mother's brief love-affairs with Geoffrey Scott and Virginia Woolf, how my parents' love for each other survived all further threats to it, and made out of a non-marriage a marriage which succeeded beyond their dreams. If it does not show that, the book is a betrayal.

Nigel Nicolson

Sissinghurst Castle, Kent
April 1973

Part One

BY V. SACKVILLE-WEST

Of course I have no right whatsoever to write down the truth about my life, involving as it naturally does the lives of so many other people, but I do so urged by a necessity of truth-telling, because there is no living soul who knows the complete truth; here, may be one who knows a section; and there, one who knows another section: but to the whole picture not one is initiated. Having written it down I shall be able to trust no one to read it; there is only one person in whom I have such utter confidence that I would give every line of this confession into his hands, knowing that after wading through this morass – for it is a morass, my life, a bog, a swamp, a deceitful country, with one bright patch in the middle, the patch that is unalterably his – I know that after wading through it all he would emerge holding his estimate of me steadfast. This would be the test of my confidence, from which I would not shrink. I would not give it to *her* – perilous touchstone!, who even in these first score of lines should teach me where truth lies. I *do* know where it lies, but have no strength to grasp it; here am I already in the middle of my infirmities.

I start writing, having spent no consideration upon this task. Shall I ever complete it? and under what circumstances?, begun as it is, in the margin between a wood and a ripe cornfield, with the faint shadows of grasses and ears of corn falling across my page. Unkernelled nuts hang behind me, along the fringe of the wood; I lie on green bracken, amongst little yellow and magenta wild-flowers whose names I don't know. I lie so close to the ground that my only view is of tall corn, so crisp that in the breeze it stirs with a noise like the rustle of silk. All day I have been in a black temper, but that is soothed away. There is no place, out here, for temper or personality. There is only one personality present: Demeter.

Yesterday I was on the sea in a sailing-boat; it was very rough, and at moments I was extremely frightened, but I wished I wasn't frightened, because theoretically I enjoyed seeing the ship put her nose down into the waves, seeing the spray break over the deck, and then feeling my face all wet and tasting the salt water on my lips. The world of the sea is quite a different world. There is a whole different set of noises – the wash of the waves, the wind in the rigging, the banging of the blocks, the shouts of the crew – and one has a whole different set of wishes and preoccupations – the wish that the boat would keep still, if only for five minutes, as a rest from the perpetual balancing, the preoccupation as to whether the wind will get up, or go down, whichever it is; the immense, the overwhelming importance of weather, both as regards one's comfort and one's progress.

I realize that this confession, autobiography, whatever I may call it, must necessarily have for its outstanding fault a lack of all proportion. I have got to trust to a very uncertain memory, and whereas the present bulks enormous, the past is misty. I can't remember much about my childhood, except that I had very long legs and very straight hair, over which Mother used to hurt my feelings and say she couldn't bear to look at me because I was so ugly. I know that I wasn't a physical coward in those days, because I can remember doing dangerous things on a bicycle and climbing high trees – and yet, stop, I do believe I must have been a coward already, because I can remember thinking a great deal about whether I should be brave the next day when I went out riding, and I was too much fascinated by seeing other people do things which I knew I shouldn't dare to do myself. I never realized this until this moment. Anyway, I wasn't so much of a coward, and I kept my nerves under control, and made a great ideal of being hardy, and as like a boy as possible. I know I was cruel to other children, because I remember stuffing their nostrils with putty and beating a little boy with stinging-nettles, and I lost nearly all my friends in that kind of way, until none of the local children would come to tea with me except those who had acted as my allies and lieutenants.

I don't remember much more about myself as a child than that. I remember more about outside things. I don't remember either my father or mother very vividly at that time, except that Dada used to take me for terribly long walks and talk to me about science, principally Darwin, and I liked him a great deal better than Mother, of whose quick temper I was frightened. I don't even remember thinking her pretty, which she must have been – lovely, even. My impression of her was that I couldn't be rough when she was there, or naughty, and so it was really a great relief when she went away. I remember very vividly terrible scenes between her and Dada – at least, she made the scene, he usually said nothing at all, or very mildly, 'Oh, come, dear, is that quite accurate?' Her statements rarely *were* accurate; I realized this, very, very slowly, but was incredibly obtuse over it; in fact I didn't really grasp it until a comparatively short time ago. (Evening is coming on, and I shall soon have to stop writing; thank God I am alone tonight.)

When she and Dada went away, I was left alone with Grandpapa. He was very old, and queer, and silent. He hated people, and never spoke to the people who came to the house [Knole]; in fact, if he got the chance he used to go to London for the day when he knew people were coming, and I used to be left alone to entertain them. It amused me later on, when sometimes I was had downstairs to make fourteen, to see him sitting quite mute between two wretched women who were trying to make conversation to him, or else crushing them into silence: 'You have lovely gardens here, Lord Northwood [Sackville].' 'What do you know about gardens?', he would snap at them. But at the same time he was always shrewd in his estimate of people, and never liked those who were not worthy of liking, or disliked those that were. Mother used to get furious when in about six words he demolished her friends, but Dada used to laugh, and then she turned on *him*. But I suppose she was really very devoted to Grandpapa, in her own way, because underneath everything her ideas of duty are sound, and although the most incomprehensible, she is certainly the most charming person upon earth, whom I adore.

Grandpapa liked children and believed in fairies. Every night after dinner he used to fill a plate with fruit and put it ready for me to fetch early next morning; he used to put it in a drawer in his sitting-room, labelled Diana's [Vita's] Drawer, in very elaborate lettering in coloured chalks that he had done himself. He always amused himself in shy, secret ways like that; he used to spend hours whittling little bits of wood into queer shapes, and polishing them with sandpaper till the surface was like velvet, and he had a set of little remarks that he invariably made when the occasion turned up: 'Nice fresh taste', he used to say over the first asparagus; and 'Poor old Cox', whenever anything went wrong with anybody; but I never discovered the origin of that. To go back to the fruit, it was a regular ritual, which nothing would have induced him to forgo, and which I never knew him to forget, even, poor old man, at the beginning of his last illness, while he was still downstairs; even if there were twenty people to dinner he heaped the plate for me just the same and carried it to the drawer, and if ever I forgot to fetch it in the morning he would make a grievance that lasted until it turned into a joke, and so became mellow instead of bitter.

In the same way he minded very much if I didn't go down to his room after tea and play draughts with him. It upset his habits, and also I think he must have been fond of me; he liked having children in the house, and later on he liked Charles [Edward Sackville-West], who was my cousin ten years younger than I, and was a genius, and could play Wagner when he was four. (He was very delicate, always passing from critical illness to critical illness, so that he was always brought downstairs wrapped in an enormous white Shetland shawl, in which he sat at the piano, with his puny little legs dangling, as unable to touch the pedals as his tiny hands were to span an octave.) Grandpapa liked children and he liked flowers, but he didn't care a rap about the house, and when people asked him questions about it, or about the pictures or silver or furniture, he used to refer them to Mother.

Mother made all the capital she could out of the house; to hear her talk about it you would have thought she had built it, but she had no real sense of its dignity, as Dada had, who worshipped it in his bones, but would sooner die than say so. I think it must have been very hard for him then, living in the house as Grandpapa's heir, but being only the nephew, not the son, and having no word to say in the management either of the house, the gardens, or the estate, and hearing Mother make up legends about the place, quite unwarrantable and unnecessary – the place was quite good enough to stand without legends, heaven knows! – and hearing her get all the credit for everything, because she was the kind of person who always came in for a lot of flattery from everyone. That was what came of her being ruthless and completely unanalytical, and having a charm that exacted flattery; and of his being so sensitive and modest. There certainly *was* something ruthless about Mother, and one of the things that has left the strongest and cruellest impression upon me was a horrible little dialogue I overheard once in London, as I lay in bed in the dark next door. She was alone with Grandpapa, and was evidently very much annoyed over something, for I heard her telling him how much in the way he was, with that sort of *flick* in her voice that to this day makes me shudder; and he was moved to protest – he, who never said a word! – and I heard his old voice saying piteously. 'But what do I do? I never even ring a bell.' I wish I could forget that little dialogue, but I can't; it burnt. Mother didn't soften, any more than she would soften towards me when I cried; yet she can soften marvellously if you only touch the right chord – I have noticed this in other people. It is really a sort of sentimentality that is moved emotionally, whether by something real or something unreal – usually the latter.

That was Grandpapa, with his odd little tricks, of always flinging his cap down with extreme violence in exactly the same place, of balancing himself endlessly and maddeningly from one foot to the other; with his dislike of people, his shyness of servants (he spoke the truth when he said he never rang a bell!), his funny jerks and phrases, that sometimes made him seem rather like an old goblin – that, at any rate, was Grandpapa on the surface, though what he was like underneath heaven alone knows. Of all human beings, he was surely the most inscrutable. I lived with him for sixteen years, and had I lived with him for yet another sixteen I have no doubt that he would have remained just as much of an enigma. One might have ended by putting him down as truly insensible, but in contradiction of that theory comes the most surprising fact about him, which I have kept for the end: during his middle youth he lived illicitly with a very beautiful Spanish dancer, by whom he had seven children in, I think, as many years.

This old story, this 'Romance of the Peerage' (*vide Daily Mail*), is so well known that in talking about it I feel as though I were talking about something which happened to some other family than my own. The 'Romance of the Peerage' label is enough to make me feel that. 'Who's who in the story', and then the personages: Asuncion Ramon [Pepita], a beautiful Spanish gipsy, living with Lord Sackville, then Lionel Strangways [Sackville-West], as his wife, calling herself Countess West (poor thing, isn't it pitiful, that title?), Gloria [Victoria] (my mother), their beautiful daughter, now married to the present Lord Sackville, Baptiste [Henry], their son, now claiming the title of Sackville and estates of Knole, and then the leading article on Knole, concluding in triumphant journalese, 'Too homely to be called a palace, too palatial to be called a home'. (Oh my lovely Knole, how right he was, that nameless journalist in his horrible jargon! I stand at the corner of the wall, and look down on you in the hollow, your grey walls and red-brown roofs, and hear myself saying the well-

24

worn phrase, 'You get rather a good view of the house from here. . . .')

The only time I remember Grandpapa breaking out through his reserve was one morning when I followed Mother into his sitting-room holding on to the end of her long, long plait. I can remember him jumping up and saying, 'Never let me see that child doing that again, Victoria.' It sounds an improbably melodramatic phrase, written down like that, but that was precisely what he said. It appears that Mother was in the habit, when a little girl, of walking about holding on to her mother's hair in such a fashion. I have got two photographs of my grandmother, which show clearly how beautiful she must have been; truly beautiful of feature and expression, not merely pretty, although they are ugly faded photographs taken at Arcachon about 1870. She was the illegitimate daughter of a gipsy and a Spanish duke; the gipsy, her mother, had been a circus acrobat, and was no doubt descended from a line of such, and the duke descended from Lucrezia Borgia. I think my maternal ancestry is hard to beat for sheer picturesqueness. It accounts for much in Mother, who at times is pure undiluted peasant.

But Grandpapa! *Qu'allait-il faire dans cette galère?* How did he, the man of silence, set about absconding with the dancer, who was at that time quite respectably married to someone else? I would give my very soul for a fly-on-the-wall peep backwards into one of the scenes between them. And think of their establishment – singing, happy-go-lucky, in the midst of a puddle of tiny children, he, an English diplomat, scion of the most correct old English family, heir to Knole, and given his own elusive character! Of course I knew nothing about this when I was small. My first inkling of anything wrong in my mother's birth was one whose snobbishness I am ashamed to record: some people used to address her letters as the Honble. Mrs Sackville-West, and others didn't; I, from some obscure instinct that resented any aspersions being cast upon my mother, always did.

Pepita died when my mother was nine, leaving Grand-papa with five small children (two of the others had merci-fully died), three girls and two boys. He stuck the girls into a convent [in Paris]; I don't know what happened to the boys; I suppose they went to school. My mother was heartbroken, and to this day can hardly talk about her mother's death without tears; also from being the spoilt favourite, she now led a harsh convent life, seeing her father two or three times a year, and spending even her holidays in the convent. Here she remained until she was seventeen, when she was sent to another convent in England to learn English. When she was eighteen a great family clamour arose: should she and her sisters be sent out to join their father, who was now British Minister in Washington? (Washington having since then been made into an Embassy, Mother now always speaks of him as British Ambassador, as she thinks that sounds more impressive.) It was finally decided that they should go, so Mother – eighteen, a vision of loveliness, imperious, cap-ricious, and speaking broken English with a strong French accent – was sent over to America with her two younger sisters.

I reconstruct all this from the unvarying evidence of eye-witnesses. Released from convent rule, she seems to have bounded upright at once like a sapling that had been bent down, to have taken Washington by storm, and left her sisters nowhere in the background. I expect strong seeds of resent-ment were sown in their minds, that sprouted later in the succession case.

I am getting tired, and all this does not really concern my own lamentable muddle. But it was all there for me, in the background, and as a child I realized dimly that a vinegary spinster aunt [Amalia] lived with us for some years at Knole, and annoyed Mother by giving me preserved cherries when Mother asked her not to, also that there was a person called Henry who from time to time came to the entrance and de-manded to see Grandpapa, but was not allowed to. I suppose I overheard servants' gossip. It is a little difficult to disen-tangle what I actually knew at the time from what I have learnt since. But there certainly was always something, some mystery in the background.

Evening has nearly fallen; sunset-light on the hill opposite has turned the yellow corn-fields rose-pink. I have dined out on the terrace, writing this all the while on my knee. I do love the summer and always dread Midsummer Day as the watershed of the year. Midsummer Day used to be one of Grandpapa's jokes; after it was past he used to say regularly, 'Days drawing in now', and now it has for me yet another significance. I have heard from Robin [Harold Nicolson] this evening that he will not return from Paris for another five days; I had expected him tomorrow. Shall I, by then, have brought this recital up to the lamentable present, I wonder? I am dreadfully tired. Everything is so hushed, and I feel secluded and serene – not melancholy tonight. The country is too lovely for that. How lucky for me that I live in this fruitful and tender country: it *soaks* its serenity into one. Moors and crags would kill me, I think. The Weald is an antidote – alkali on acid, or whatever it is. I must go to bed.

LATER

I have had a bath, and am in bed, and feel less tired. My head swirls with this writing. (I am an incredible egoist, that's the long and short of it.) I keep on thinking of tales, and personages, and places: my old Nannie, whom my Mother sent away after fifteen years because she took it into her head that Nannie had eaten the quails; Lilian [Rosamund Grosvenor], four years older than I, who was brought over to Knole for three days to console me when Dada went to the South African war, and who even in those early days (I was six and she was ten) was always clean and neat whereas I was always grubby and in tatters; my dogs, absorbingly adored; my rabbits, who used to 'course' in secret with my dogs, and whose offspring I used to throw over the garden wall when they became too numerous; the trenches I dug in the garden during the war; the 'army' I raised and commanded amongst the terrorized children of the neighbourhood; my khaki suit, and the tears of rage I shed because I was not allowed to have it made with trousers – no, not so much as a proper kilt; my first play, whose rehearsal was remorselessly scattered by Mother after all my pocket-money had gone in art-muslin: all these, I suppose, made my childhood very much like that of other children, but to me it stands out now, so vivid, that I see myself in the garden, feel the familiar cut of my pocket-knife into the wooden table in the summer-house where I did my lessons, see the little cart into which I used to harness three ill-assorted dogs, see myself, plain, lean, dark, unsociable, un-attractive – horribly unattractive! – rough, and secret. Secrecy was my passion; I dare say that was why I hated companions. Anyhow, it's a trait I inherit from my family. So I won't blame myself excessively for it. I forgot to say that two or three times I tried to run away, but was always brought back, and once Mother made me kneel down while she prayed over me.

25 JULY, 1920

I was happy last night. I lay awake thinking about this writing, and watching the patterns that the moonlight, shining through branches and lattices, made upon my bed. This morning I woke up to wonder whether it was worth while going on with a bald egotistical statement; it keeps me from *Soap* [*The Dragon in Shallow Waters*] which I ought to finish. I got a rather sad letter from Harold this morning. As a rule he does not allow me to see when he is depressed. His sadness never fails to touch me to the quick. He is the only person of whom I think with consistent tenderness. I can say with truth that I have never, never cherished a harsh thought about him; at the most I have been irritated, but then he has always known it. I would not allow myself to be irritated against him while he remained unconscious, or when he was not there. I can say this with absolute truth. He has complete power over my heart, though not over my spirit. It is real tenderness I feel for him, it is a constant sense of 'Tread gently, for you tread upon my dreams'. I think with tenderness of Dan [Benedict] sometimes, of Basil [Nigel] very rarely, of Chloe [Violet Trefusis] never. I am so harsh to her that I could put almost any strain of suffering upon her without feeling a qualm of pity – could, and have. All this makes the whole thing so agonizing and so puzzling.

I had got to where Mother went out to Washington and captivated everybody in the place, including a Red Indian chief and the President of the United States. She was more or less the queen of Washington, I gather, and it must have been a gratifying alternative for a girl who had been destined to be a governess. (She had got her diploma as a qualified governess from the convent, but I can't believe that she would have remained a governess long! I have seen the diploma. It describes her as José Sackville-West, by which name she had up till then been known, but now that she figured as the Minister's daughter it was changed to her first name of Gloria [Victoria] – a name which suits her so admirably well. Glorious Gloria [Victorious Victoria] as somebody named her.) She didn't marry in America. When Grandpapa succeeded to Knole and, simultaneously, got turned out of the diplomatic service for indiscretion, she and her two sisters came back with him and lived at Knole. The second sister didn't stay there long; she married a Frenchman, and later got divorced and went on the music-hall stage as a dancer. They were very poor at Knole, but Mother, although wildly extravagant in bouts (fairly continuous bouts, I must say), is a good manager in everyday life. I don't know how long she lived there unmarried, but sooner or later she met Grandpapa's nephew, the heir, and married him, and I was born two years later [1892]. She says she would have drowned herself sooner than have another child, so I suppose her love of self-indulgence was rampant already.

She loved me when I was a baby, but I don't think she cared much for me as a child, nor do I blame her. My principal recollection of her then is that I used to be taken

29

to her room to be 'passed' before going down to luncheon on party days, when I had had my hair crimped; and I was always wrong and miserable, so that parties used to blacken my summer. Our common hatred of them was a great link between me and Grandpapa, and we used to have secret jokes about the people while luncheon was going on. I don't mean to imply that Mother neglected me, or wasn't good to me, but simply that she figured more as a restraint than anything in my existence.

I believe she and Dada were very happy at first, especially after the spinster aunt had finally departed in hostility, but I know nothing of their relations except what she herself has told me, and that isn't in the least reliable. She says he began to flirt with other women, and I know that she herself imported a new personage into Knole when I was six or seven; this was a person we all called Seery, a nickname invented by me in early stages. Seery [Sir John Murray Scott] stood six-foot-four, and weighed twenty-five stone. Once I measured him round where his waist ought to have been, and it was five feet. He had a round pink face like a baby, and white mutton-chop whiskers, and soft fluffy grey-white hair which Mother used to rumple. He was the best humoured, most lovable, genial and generous man imaginable; everybody loved him, even Grandpapa, who behind his back would say, 'Good fellow, Johnny', although they never called each other anything but 'Sir John' and 'Lord Sackville' most punctiliously. Seery was always laughing, when he wasn't asleep – laughing, and saying 'Shoo! pshoo!' to the swarm of flies that was for ever buzzing round his fat face in summer, and at which he used to flick perpetually with an enormous silk pocket-handkerchief. He prided himself on being a very good organizer, and very methodical, but as a matter of fact he muddled every arrangement, and mislaid all his possessions, in spite of the innumerable drawers and leather cases in which he used to put things away. When I think of Seery I see him sitting before an immense writing-table, rattling a bunch of keys and trying every key in every lock in turn, with his spectacles pushed up on to his forehead, and stopping to say 'shoo' to the flies. Then when he had got a drawer open, Mother would come and make a pounce at his stamps, and he would cry, 'Go away, you little beggar', or 'you little Spanish beggar', but of course he worshipped her and let her have whatever she wanted. (At times she wanted a good deal.) I see him like that, or else I see him dropping asleep in his chair after lunch, till the lighted tip of his cigar touched the tablecloth and Mother woke him up crying, *Voyons, voyons, Seery!*, when he always started up and said, 'I wasn't asleep – I was thinking.' He used to go to sleep too on his shooting-stick out in the turnip-fields, while the birds streamed over his head, for he was very gallant about being so fat, and would always go out shooting or fishing with Dada and the younger men, sometimes riding a pony like a young carthorse that ended by having a permanent curve in its back.

Mother became absolutely the light and air of his life. She bullied and charmed him, fought with him, bewitched him, until he simply could not exist without her. If he had lost her, I really believe he would have pined away and died – or at any rate got thin, which seems even more difficult to believe. I don't know whether one ought to call that being in love. Somehow it seems too grotesque, the idea of anyone so fat being in love in the ordinary sense of the word. She was just life to him, that's all. She used to tell me that he was in love with her, and came whenever possible to importune her at her bedroom door at night; and she arranged with me that, in the event of his falling into a fit outside her bedroom, which might be compromising, she would come to wake me and between us we would bump him downstairs to his own bedroom, she would take his shoulders and I his feet, and she thought that by slipping him from step to step we would manage to shift that enormous mass without waking anybody. I was so accustomed to Mother that it never occurred to me that there was anything odd about this arrangement – on the contrary, I thought she was very clever to have so much foresight. She used to tell me this, I say, but I rather doubt whether there was much truth in it, as during all the years I spent with them (and during the later years I wasn't particularly unobservant, although not particularly sharp either) I never saw anything to corroborate it.

Poor Seery! she *did* lead him a life. But at least it wasn't the deadly stagnation of the life he had led up to then, between two old sisters and a crew of harpy brothers, one more middle-class than the other. Seery wasn't middle-class by nature, although he was by birth. I never knew anyone so grand, or so openhanded. He was very rich. He had been the secretary and adopted son of a famous collector [Sir Richard Wallace], who had died leaving him his whole fortune, much of his collection, and quite a lot of houses. Two of these houses were in Paris. We used to stay with him there every year after I was eight. Most of the house [2 rue Lafitte] was let, and we lived in an apartment on the first floor; it was lovely, in its own way as lovely as Knole, so that I never knew what it was to live in ugly rooms. One could stand at one end of the apartment and look down a long vista of rooms opening into one another, with an unbroken stretch of shining parquet floor, and all the rooms were panelled with cream-white and gilt Louis xv *boiserie*, or else with faded old green silk. All the furniture was French, with rich ormolu mounts, and there were hanging chandeliers in every room, and sconces on the walls, and, in the big gallery, priceless Boucher tapestries. The big gallery was in a hopeless confusion when we first went there, but Mother soon rearranged that. All the servants were very old and very magnificent; the butler had long white whiskers, and there were about six other old footmen, who all wore white gloves. There were endless fat horses and carriages, all equally antediluvian; there were no women, except the cook, who was the butler's old wife and a regular *cordon bleu*, and the *lingère*, who did nothing but look after the linen, and very necessary she must have been, for every sheet was like the finest cambric pocket-handkerchief. Seery kept up a tremendous *train de maison* there; every flower, fruit and vegetable seemed to be out of season, and larger than they would have been anywhere else *in* season. But it wasn't in the least ostentatious; it all seemed perfectly fitting and natural. I loved being there; that is to say, I loved the apartment, where I could wheel myself from room to room in an invalid's chair that I had discovered in a corner of the gallery, but I didn't enjoy the shops much, where I had to sit on a high stool for hours while Mother bought fiddling things that didn't seem to me to matter.

In the evenings they sometimes went to plays, and I was left alone, unless Grandpapa was there, and then he and I used to play a game at the window, of who could see the funniest sight down on the boulevard. When Grandpapa wasn't there I used to light all the candles in all the rooms and prowl about by myself; I liked that. Sometimes I used to go into the big gallery and cry bitterly over a stuffed spaniel in a glass case that I imagined was like a spaniel of mine that had died. I had orgies of sorrow over that spaniel. When Mother rearranged the gallery she did away with it, and I hid it in a cupboard where I could get at it whenever I wanted an excuse for tears, and I remember writing out my prayers and putting them under the spaniel. I must have been very sentimental, but, as I never let anybody know, it didn't matter.

Seery had another place near Paris [Bagatelle], in the Bois. That was a gem of a place, built for Marie Antoinette, and standing in a big garden of the *jardin anglais* sort. The house was empty, but we went there for picnics. There was the statue of a nymph in a grotto, bathing her foot in the water and I used to deck her with leaves. Years later Seery sold this statue, and one day when I was with Mother in a big dealer's shop in London I saw it there, and not being very old burst into floods of tears; they hadn't dared tell me it had been sold. This episode and the spaniel sound as though I was always crying then, but as a matter of fact I wasn't. I was really rather defiant; only I had loved the nymph so much. I wish Seery could have left her to me in his Will instead of the diamond necklace he did leave me.

Besides going to Paris we went to Scotland with Seery every year. He was nearly always with us, or we with him, which his family didn't relish at all. We had a place in Aberdeenshire, and I have a diary which I was made to keep there in French as a punishment for wrestling with the hall-boy. Next year we had a nicer, wilder place [Sluie], where I ran wild for three months; it was on the Dee, among lovely heather hills and little trout-lochs. I knew really every inch of the hills, and was exactly like the Scotch farm-children with whom I used to play. I was eleven then. The farmer's son was a year older than me, and in the course of long days spent by the river or on the moors he told me a great many things he oughtn't to have told me; but I honestly hadn't got a mind like some children, and as I had always lived in the country I took most things quite for granted, and was neither excited nor interested by them. I practically lived at the farm, where I built myself a shanty. I was happy there. Mother was sensible about me. I was always out, either with the guns, or with the farmer's boys, or by myself with the dogs (I had an Irish terrier then who could jump like a greyhound). Oh God, oh God, I wish I was back there – those lovely, lovely hills, those blazing sunsets, those runnels of icy water where I used to make water-wheels, those lovely summer evenings fishing on the loch, those long days when I often walked fifteen miles or more with the guns and gillies, I *was* young, I *was* healthy, I *was* simple, my eyes smart with tears to remember it. I had a kilt and a blue jersey, and I don't suppose I was ever tidy once, even on Sundays. Mother was happy too; she used to pound up and down the same level bit of road, singing to herself, and she started an open-air craze which has never abated since, but which has provided every door in every room at Knole with a door-stopper.

I said I was eleven then. We went there every autumn until I was fifteen or sixteen, from early August till late October. When I was about twelve I started to write. (It was *Cyrano de Bergerac* that first initiated me to the possibilities of literature!) I never stopped writing after that – historical novels, pretentious, quite uninteresting, pedantic, and all written at unflagging speed: the day after one was finished

34

another would be begun. I think that between the ages of thirteen and nineteen I must have been quite dreadful. I was plain, priggish, studious (oh, very!) totally uninspired, unmanageably and lankily tall, in fact the only good thing that could be said of me was that I wouldn't have anything to do with my kind. Seeing that I was unpopular (and small wonder, for a saturnine prig), I wouldn't court popularity. I minded rather, and used to cry when I went to bed after coming home from a party, but I made myself defiant about it. I don't mean this to sound in the least pathetic; I wasn't unhappy, only solitary, but I don't pretend that I minded solitude, I rather chose it. (Looking back, I think I maligned myself rather by calling myself totally uninspired: I had flaring days, oh yes, I did!, when I thought I was going to electrify the world; it was like being drunk, and I can find traces of it now in the margins of all those ponderous, interminable books I wrote – two little letters, v.e., which stood for 'very easy', and I look at them now, and re-read the leaden stuff which they are supposed to qualify, and take upon trust that I found those now forgotten moments full of splendour.)

These years are tedious to write about – tedious, and very uncertain. I mean the years from thirteen to nineteen. Things happened, of course, things that made an impression and changed me – not that I changed much, or grew any more sophisticated. What happened? Let me try to remember: there is writing, always writing, and moroseness, and periods of real hard work and proficiency at the daily school to which I went every autumn and winter term in London. I set myself to triumph at that school, and I did triumph – I beat everybody there, sooner or later, and at the end-of-term exams I thought I had done badly if I didn't carry off at least six out of eight first prizes. I think I was quite self-conscious over this: if I couldn't be popular, I would be clever; and I did succeed in getting a reputation of being clever, which was quite unmerited, for I am distinctly *not* clever, but which like all reputations has died hard. I don't believe it is quite dead yet – people say, 'Oh yes, she writes

35

doesn't she?', implying that one must be clever in order to write. I wasn't hated at that school, at least I don't think so; I think they quite liked me. But I really cared not a scrap whether they liked me or not. Those were my most savage years! I worked very hard, and became more pedantic than ever. I've got a scholarly turn of mind, let me face that damning truth.

Other things happened too. I acquired a friend – I, who was the worst person in the world at making friends, closed instantaneously in friendship, or almost instantaneously (to be exact, the second time we saw each other), with Violet [Keppel, later Trefusis]. I was thirteen, she was two years younger, but in every instinct she might have been six years my senior. It seems to me so significant now that I should remember with such distinctness my first sight of her; we met at a tea-party by the bedside of a mutual friend with a broken leg, and she made to me some little remarks about the flowers in the room. I wasn't listening; and so didn't answer. This piqued her – she was already spoilt. She got her mother to ask mine to send me to tea. I went. We sat in a darkened room, and talked – about our ancestors, of all strange topics – and in the hall as I left she kissed me. I made up a little song that evening, 'I've got a friend!'. I remember so well. I sang it in my bath.

I long to stop over Violet – to tell how much I secretly admired her, and how proud I was of the friendship of this brilliant, this extraordinary, this almost unearthly creature, but how I treated her with unvarying scorn, my one piece of really able handling, which kept her to me as no proof of devotion would have kept her – but I am going to tell other things first, because all the present is filled with Violet, and during the past she appears constantly too. I will stop only to say that from the beginning I was utterly sure of her; she might be elusive, she might be baffling, she might even be faithless, but under everything I had the rather insolent (but justified) certainty of her keeping to me. I listened to stories about her with a superior and proprietary smile. I would have remained for ten years without hearing a word from her, and at the end of those ten years I would have held the same undamaged confidence that we must inevitably re-unite. There isn't a word of exaggeration in these statements – nothing, for that matter, in the whole of this writing is to be exaggerated or 'arranged'; its only merit will be truth, but truth as bleak as I can make it.

(My writing has been broken here by Violet telephoning to me; I scarcely knew whether it was the Violet of fifteen years ago, or my passionate, stormy Violet of today, speaking to me in that same lovely voice.)

There were other happenings in those years. I went to Italy, to Florence. Violet was there, in fact I went to join her. (See how she comes in again immediately!) That was the first time I had been anywhere except to Paris, and it opened my eyes thoroughly. And Violet – how well did I know her then? My dates are so uncertain and I have no papers to guide me. I must have known her very well – it is coming back to me by degrees – for I had learnt Italian with her in London, and we had been together in Paris, and had acted part of a play I wrote in French in five Alexandrine acts, about the Man in the Iron Mask, and in those days we rather ostentatiously talked to one another in French in order to *tutoyer* one another and so show what great friends we were. It all comes back to me. Her mother [Alice Keppel] was the King's mistress (which added a touch of romance to Violet), and often when I went to their house I used to see a discreet little one-horse brougham waiting outside and the butler would slip me into a dark corner of the hall with a murmured, 'One minute, miss, a gentleman is coming downstairs', so that I might take my choice whether it was the King or the doctor. Often Violet would be sent for to come down to the drawing-room, when we said, 'Oh bother!', much as we did when I was sent for in my own house to see Seery. I took one as much for granted as the other.

Before she went away to Florence, she told me she loved me, and I, finding myself expected to rise to the occasion, stumbled out an unfamiliar 'darling'. Oh God, to remember

37

that first avowal, that first endearment! Then we didn't meet till Florence, and she gave me a ring there – I have it now, of course I have it, just as I have *her*, and I should bury my face in my hands with shame to remember our childish passion for each other (which was too fierce, even then, to be sentimental), were it not for the justification of the present.

I feel I am doing all this part very badly, very confusedly; it is very difficult to do, because I am afraid of taking too seriously what would, normally, have begun and ended as the kind of rather hysterical friendship one conceives in adolescence, but which had in it, I protest, far stronger elements than mere unwholesome hysteria. There *is* a bond which unites me to Violet, Violet to me; it united us no less than it unites us now, but what that bond is God alone knows; sometimes I feel it is as something legendary. Violet is *mine*, she always has been, it is inescapable. I knew it then, albeit only through my obscurely but quite obstinately proprietary attitude; she knew it too, less obscurely, and took all the active measures to make me realize it. That I left them unseconded, yet without any fear of losing her, proud and mettlesome as she was, only goes to prove how certain I was of my hold upon her. She was *mine* – I can't express it more emphatically or more accurately than that, nor do I want to dress up an elemental fact in any circumlocution of words.

That autumn [1908] I stayed with her in Scotland. I was sent to Scotland to stay with Seery and his sisters because Grandpapa was ill, and I suppose Mother and Dada knew he would die and wanted me out of the way. My parting with him makes me sad to remember now. He got me into his little sitting-room and asked me to kiss him. I said I hoped he would be better when I came back, but he only shook his head. He died while I was staying with Seery. One of Seery's sisters – the big one, whom her family called the Duchess – came to my room before breakfast with the telegram; she had on a pink flannelette dressing-gown, and no false hair, and I remember noticing how odd she looked. She kissed me in a conscientious sort of way, but I wasn't very much moved over Grandpapa's death just then; it only sank in afterwards. I changed my red tie for a grey one, and tried to pray for Grandpapa, but couldn't think what to say. Then I went downstairs to Seery's room, and never to my last moment shall I forget the sight he presented, sitting at his dressing-table perfectly oblivious, the twenty-five stone of him, dressed only in skin-tight Jaegar combinations, and, dear warm-hearted old Seery, crying quite openly over the telegram. I felt I ought to be crying too, if Seery, who was about sixty to my sixteen, could cry, but I was too much overwhelmed by Seery's appearance

I went to stay with Violet after that, rather proud of my new mourning, and I am afraid I forgot to sorrow much while I was there. I remember various details about that visit: how Violet had filled my room with tuberoses, how we dressed up, how she chased me with a dagger down the long passage of that very ancient Scotch castle [Duntreath], and concluded the day by spending the night in my room. It was the first time in my life I ever spent the night with anyone, though goodness knows it was decorous enough: we never went to sleep, but talked throughout the night, while little owls hooted outside. I can't hear owls now without recalling her soft troubling presence in my room in the dark.

Then I went to London, where I found Mother in deep black, and for the first time I realized Grandpapa's death when Mother told me how much he had suffered and had died saying my name. (I was gratified by that.) We couldn't go to Knole except unofficially, because Mother's brother was bringing a lawsuit against Dada, claiming succession. We were very poor then, because all the money was kept in Chancery. I was taken to the law-courts for a minute while the case was going on, and saw all Mother's Spanish relations sitting there in the well of the court; the case collapsed and Dada, Mother, and I had a triumphant return to Knole, pulled up in the carriage by the fire-brigade with ropes, under welcoming arches.

I saved up my pocket-money to go back to Florence next spring [1909]. I was seventeen then, and less plain (still very plain, though), and an Italian [Orazio Pucci] fell in love with me and wanted me to marry him, which made me feel very grown-up. He followed me to Rome, and then to Paris, where I refused to see him, but I found him waiting for me on the quay at Calais when I crossed to England. In the autumn of that year I went with Mother and Seery to Russia. Oh how I loved it! I don't know whether to give an account of it, or to pass it by. We stayed with a Pole owning an estate 100 miles square between Warsaw and Kieff. At the frontier between Austria and Russia Mother refused to get out of the train to go to the Customs, till they sent two soldiers with rifles to fetch her, and in the grey dawn she was marched between them down the platform, saying to everyone she met, by way of protest, '*Ich bin eine grosse Dame in England*', the only German phrase she could evolve. We finally got to the local station, where we were met by an immense yellow motor and taken in it for fifty miles across atrocious country (no road, nothing but pits and bumps – Seery kept on saying between his bumps, which were more considerable than anybody else's, that Napoleon ought to have made decent roads across Russia, and Mother and I laughed so much we were nearly ill, what with bumps and laughter), until we came to a very elaborate French Château [Antoniny] looking very incongruous in the middle of the steppes. Here we found, besides our host and hostess, about twenty Poles we had never seen or heard of before, but they were all very friendly, and the life there was magnificent. There were eighty saddle-horses, a private pack of hounds, carriages-and-four, Cossacks attached to one's particular service and sleeping across the threshold of one's door, hereditary dwarfs to hand cigarettes, a giant, and Tokay of 1740. Not the least part of it was the host, who had a European reputation as a gambler before he forswore cards; he had teeth like a wolf (in fact he was not unlike a wolf altogether), and when he danced the Mazurka, as he did invariably after the 1740 Tokay, they snapped, and seemed to increase in size, number and prominence.

I found a sort of rhapsody I wrote after that; it is written in Italian (for secrecy), but I translate: 'How much I loved Russia! those vast fields, that feudal life, that illimitable horizon – oh how shall I ever be able to live in this restricted island! I want expanse.' It goes on: 'I am happier this winter. I hope the terrible times of sadness are over. At heart I am still sad, and always shall be.' There is more of it, but that suffices. I must have been suffering from a bad attack of *Weltschmerz*, and indeed I had just finished a play on Chatterton of quite unequalled gloom.

Florence again in the spring, with the Italian still faithful. I saw very little of Violet at this time; the two years between us were a barrier. I 'came out' – a distasteful and unsuccessful process – but the death of the King [Edward VII] saved me many festivities. Thus can the tragedies of great Kings be turned to the uses of little people.

26 JULY [1920]

It was just then, however, that I first met Harold. He arrived late at a small dinner-party before a play, very young and alive and charming, and the first remark I ever heard him make was, 'What fun', when he was asked by his hostess to act as host. Everything was fun to his energy, vitality, and buoyancy. I liked his irrepressible brown curls, his laughing eyes, his charming smile, and his boyishness. But we didn't become particular friends. I think he looked on me as more of a child than I actually was, and as for myself I never thought about people, especially men, under a very personal aspect unless they made quite definite friendly advances to me first; even then I think one wonders sometimes what people are driving at.

I was eighteen then and he was twenty-three.

That summer [1910] I caught a heaven-sent attack of pneumonia, and as a consequence of my being ordered abroad we spent the whole winter from November till April in the South of France near Monte Carlo. My illness revived my intimacy with Violet – I have the panic-stricken letter she wrote me, after hearing an exaggerated account of my being ill – and I suppose I saw something of her that autumn, because I can remember driving round and round Hyde Park with her one night after going to a play, a day or two before she left for Ceylon, and the end of that motor-drive was one of the very rare but extremely disturbing occasions when she kissed me. If I had gone to Ceylon with her, my life would probably have turned out very differently. But oh Lord! What's my miserable life? It only bulks large because these pages covered with pencil happen to be a history of it.

Well, we had an enormous white villa at Monte Carlo [Château Malet], where I lived in a perfection of happiness for those six months. Harold came to stay, and he and I fell into a rather childlike companionship, and I was rather hurt when he said goodbye to me without any apparent regret. I missed him – he was the best actual *playmate* I had ever known, and his exuberant youth combined with his brilliant cleverness attracted the rather saturnine me that scarcely understood the meaning of being young. Later I used to call him 'the merry guide', which name best describes him:

> And in the dews beside me
> Behold a youth that trod
> With feathered cap on forehead,
> And poised a golden rod,
> With mien to match the morning,
> And gay delightful guise . . .

That was Harold to the life. 'Gay delightful guise . . .' I cannot, *cannot*, bring sorrow into those eyes.

Violet returned from Ceylon in the spring, bringing me rubies, and we spent a day or two at San Remo. She also came to see me at our villa. How little we thought, as we stood under the olive-trees in the wild part of the garden (I remember admiring to myself the thick plait of her really beautiful hair), how little we thought of the next time we were to be together in that same place! When I went to her

42

at San Remo, we saw an acrobat with no arms or legs. We had written to each other copiously during the whole winter, and now when she went to live in Munich, we continued to write, and she kept urging me to go and stay with her there, but I never did.

Harold meanwhile was in Madrid, and, but for an interlude when I dragged a plaintive but self-sacrificing Mother to Florence in the spring, the rest of the year was a repetition of the experience of being 'out'. But now something else happens – something which, I would like to emphasize, started in complete innocence on my part. I want to be frank. I have implied, I think, that men didn't attract me, that I didn't think of them in what is called 'that way'. Women did. Rosamund did. I have mentioned Rosamund as being the neat little girl who came to play with me when Dada went to South Africa. She had come out to stay at Monte Carlo – invited by Mother, not by me; I would never have dreamt of asking anyone to stay with me; even Violet had never spent more than a week at Knole: I resented invasion. Still, as Rosamund came, once she was there, I naturally spent most of the day with her, and after I had got back to England, I suppose it was resumed. I don't remember very clearly, but the fact remains that by the middle of that summer we were inseparable, and moreover were living on terms of the greatest possible intimacy. But I want to say again that the thing did start in comparative innocence. Oh, I dare say I realized vaguely that I had no business to sleep with Rosamund, and I should certainly never have allowed anyone to find out, but my sense of guilt went no further than that.

Anyway I was very much in love with Rosamund.

Harold came back from Madrid at the end of that summer [1911]. He had been very ill out there, and I remember him as rather a pathetic figure wrapped up in an Ulster on a warm summer day, who was able to walk slowly round the garden with me. All that time while I was 'out' is extremely dim to me, very largely I think, owing to the fact that I was living a kind of false life that left no

43

impression upon me. Even my liaison with Rosamund was, in a sense, superficial. I mean that it was almost exclusively physical, as, to be frank, she always bored me as a companion. I was very fond of her, however; she had a sweet nature. But she was quite stupid.

Harold wasn't. He was as gay and clever as ever, and I loved his brain and his youth, and was flattered at his liking for me. He came to Knole a good deal that autumn and winter, and people began to tell me he was in love with me, which I didn't believe was true, but wished that I could believe it. I wasn't in love with him then – there was Rosamund – but I did like him better than anyone, as a companion and playfellow, and for his brain and his delicious disposition. I hoped that he would propose to me before he went away to Constantinople, but felt diffident and sceptical about it.

In January [1912] I went away with Dada to stay in a large country house [Burghley] for a hunt-ball, and when I woke up on the morning after the ball, in a great barn of a room, with the piercing cold freezing my nose and knees, I read with a shock a letter from Mother beginning thus: 'Darling child, I did not wire to you the very upsetting news of poor Seery's death. . . .' I was horrified, and very, very sorry. It was difficult to think of that mass of good-humour and kindliness as being dead. I was dreadfully sorry – and also rather doubtful as to whether Harold and I would be allowed to go away next day to another country ball [at Hatfield] as we had intended. This sounds a selfish thing to have thought of then, but he was leaving for Turkey for at least six months directly after, and I wanted to know.

Well, I went downstairs as soon as I was dressed, and found Dada helping himself to kidneys in the dining-room, and I seemed to stand between two contrary factors – poor Seery lying dead, so much of him too – and the burning question of Harold. I didn't dare to ask Dada whether I would be allowed to go or not. It seemed too ironical that the two things should coincide in that way. After breakfast Dada and I went back to London by train through the snow, and all the time I sat staring out of the window wondering whether I would be allowed to go with Harold. When we got to London we drove straight to the hotel (we lived in a hotel that winter, for the sake of economy), and found Mother there, who had on a thick black veil and had evidently been crying. Quite soon afterwards Lady Blanche [Lady Constance Hatch], a stringy, wispy, French-music-hall-Englishwoman, with whom Dada had been for years most inexplicably in love, arrived and immediately burst into tears, which seemed to me silly, because although she had known Seery very well and had stayed with him and us a lot, both in Paris and in Scotland, she couldn't really have minded his death to that excessive extent. Mother went away then into her own bedroom. I kept struggling to make myself feel things as being real, and not as though we were all on the stage. Harold came next; he was very grave. I felt rather important, being the only person having access to Mother's bedroom, and I liked being asked by the others how she was. Mother did not cry; she always tries not to cry, because it gives her a headache. Then we went down to luncheon, Dada, and Mother, and Harold, and I, and I was all the time dreadfully afraid that Mother would break down in the restaurant; however she didn't. It had been settled by then that Dada and Harold and I were to go to the country after luncheon as arranged. I was glad, but rather apprehensive, because by then I was sure that Harold meant to propose to me and I knew I should say yes. He had never kissed me, and I wondered whether he would.

1 AUGUST [1920]

He had never even made love to me – not by a single word – and I only knew he liked me because he always tried to be with me, and wrote to me whenever he had to go away. Besides, people had put it into my head. I had always thought they were wrong, but they weren't, and that night at the [Hatfield] ball he asked me to marry him, and I said I would. He was very shy, and pulled all the buttons one by one off his gloves; and I was frightened, and tried to prevent him from coming to the point.

He didn't kiss me, but we sat rather bewildered over supper afterwards, and talked excitedly though vaguely about the flat we would have in Rome. I had on a new dress.

Only two or three days remained before he had to go away to Constantinople. I went up to London next day and told Mother I was engaged to him, but we were forbidden to write to one another except as ordinary friends, because we were too young, and also there was the question of money. We spent those two or three days together at Knole, and my impression is that we walked the whole time at a great speed through wet grass. Then he went away, and I got ill and was very depressed and miserable. Mother used to come to my room once or twice a day holding a little green bottle of disinfectant to her nose, and saying that there were three hundred steps between her room and mine, and what a bore it was feeling one had to go and see someone who was ill and waiting for one, so that after she had gone away again I used to sob with depression.

When I got better I also got more cheerful, and the Rosamund affair deepened. It was rather ironical that that affair should have started in the same house [The Grove, Watford] as where I spent the night of Harold's proposal. I went to Florence with her that spring, where, with an absurd old governess who had a mump on one side of her face and was always saying, 'Oh my dears, do consider your illustrious names', we shared a three-roomed cottage. I really was innocent over the Rosamund affair. It never struck me as wrong that I should be more or less engaged to Harold, and at the same time much in love with Rosamund. The fact is that I regarded Harold far more as a playfellow than in any other light. Our relationship was so fresh, so intellectual, so unphysical, that I never thought of him in that aspect at all. It was rather his own fault, after all, from the over-respectful way in which he had always treated me. I can best express what I mean about him by saying that he stood at the absolutely opposite pole from the lover-type of

46

man. Some men seem to be born to be lovers, others to be husbands; he belongs to the latter category. Rosamund wasn't exactly jealous of him then; he was too far away, and our engagement was too vague, and she knew that although I was very fond of him I was passionately in love with herself – I use the word 'passionately' on purpose. It was passion that used to make my head swim sometimes, even in the daytime, but we never made love.

Harold came back on leave in August, and we spent most of the next two months together at Knole, but our engagement was still kept a secret and our behaviour was irreproachable. Rosamund was jealous of him then. I wish I could remember things better. All that year Seery's Will remained unproven, but it was known that he had left Mother all the contents of the Paris house and £150,000 as well, but that his family were furious and meant to dispute the Will, so there could be nothing definite about Harold and me. I wasn't particularly anxious to have it settled; I was quite happy as I was. One evening when we were out in the wet garden after a rainy day, he kissed me for the first time, and rather characteristically called me his wife. Looking back, I see how characteristic it is that he should always have thought of me in that way, but I must say I was thrilled then. After that we made a fuss and obtained that we might write to one another as though we were engaged. Rosamund minded dreadfully – as much from envy as from jealousy, I think. In October she, Harold and I, all three, went to Italy, travelling as far as Bologna together, and there Harold left us to go on to Constantinople by the Orient Express, while Rosamund and I went on to Florence.

I hate writing this, but I must, I must. When I began this I swore I would shirk nothing, and no more I will. So here is the truth: I was never so much in love with Rosamund as during those weeks in Italy and the months that followed. It may seem that I should have missed Harold more. I admit everything to my shame, but I have never pretended to have anything other than a base and despicable character. I seem to be incapable of fidelity, as much then as now. But, as a sole justification, I separate my loves into two halves: Harold, who is unalterable, perennial, and *best*; there has never been anything but absolute purity in my love for Harold, just as there has never been anything but absolute bright purity in his nature. And on the other hand stands my perverted nature, which loved and tyrannized over Rosamund and ended by deserting her without one heartpang, and which now is linked irremediably with Violet. I have here a scrap of paper on which Violet, intuitive psychologist, has scribbled, 'The upper half of your face is so pure and grave – almost childlike. And the lower half is so domineering, sensual, almost brutal – it is the most absurd contrast, and extraordinarily symbolical of your Dr Jekyll and Mr Hyde personality.' That is the whole crux of the matter, and I see now that my whole curse has been a duality with which I was too weak and too self-indulgent to struggle.

I really worshipped Rosamund then. We motored all over Italy, and I think it was our happiest time. Meanwhile the growl of the [Scott] lawsuit came closer and closer, and the date was finally fixed for June [1913]. I didn't go to Italy that spring, I went instead to Spain, which I looked on as partially my own country, and where in three weeks I picked up Spanish with comparative fluency. I loved Spain. I would give my soul to go there with Violet – Violet! Violet! How bloodless the Rosamund affair appears now under the glare of my affinity with Violet; how seraphic and childlike my years of marriage with Harold, when that side of me was completely submerged! I am so frightened of that side sometimes – it's so brutal and hard and savage, and Harold knows nothing of it; it would drive over his soul like an armoured chariot. He has blundered upon it once or twice, but he doesn't understand – he could no more understand it than Ben could understand algebra.

Things began to rush, after I came back from Spain. The delay over my engagement began to irritate me, and one day I wrote to Harold saying we had perhaps better give up the idea. He sent me a despairing telegram in reply, and then I scarcely know what happened inside my heart: something snapped, and I loved Harold from that day on; I think his energy in sending me a telegram impressed me, just as I was impressed when he came after me in an aeroplane when I ran away. Anyway, I wired back that everything was as before, and the letter which followed the telegram touched me greatly, for I saw by it how much he truly cared. But I continued my liaison with Rosamund. I say this with deep shame.

The lawsuit was the next thing. It lasted for a fortnight, and had for immediate result a new worship for Mother, which had been incipient for several years. I couldn't bear her to be attacked, and I adored her for looking so lovely in the witness-box and for completely charming the judge, the jury and the audience, and for baffling the opposing counsel and making a fool of him till he scarcely knew whether his head was on his shoulders or off them. Of course she won her case, and we were all very triumphant, except Dada to whom it must have been torture, but I didn't realize that at the time, which just shows how young I was for twenty-one in the ways of the world. He had by then got rid of his stringy, wispy Lady Constance, and from now dates his friendship with another woman, Rebecca [Olive Rubens], who with her husband spent a lot of time at Knole.

Harold came back before the case was finished, and came down to the court with me during the last days. It was funny going there and seeing all Seery's family, whom I had known so well, especially his sisters, one of whom had broken to me the news of Grandpapa's death. I used to long for Seery to appear miraculously in court and tell them all what he thought of them, especially when they said that Mother and I had destroyed an unfavourable will of Seery's. I was frantic over that, and tried my best to show it when my turn came to go into the witness-box.

I ought to say that Violet was now back in England since a year, and I had seen her sometimes, but not very often, because Rosamund was even more jealous of her than of Harold and prevented me from going near her. So I really only saw her when she came to Knole for parties, but then I was always conscious of the same old undercurrent, and for that reason I never mentioned Harold to her; he was something separate. Once she came to my room in the middle of the night and asked me if I were in love; but that was some time before, and I could say No quite truthfully. She always came like that when she had the chance, and she usually kissed me then – on my mouth, I mean – but we never did, even ordinarily, at other times. Violet was very amusing then and a terrible flirt, throwing over first one man and then another; she used to do all kinds of parlour-tricks, which I never saw, as she stopped immediately I came into the room, and if ever we met anywhere accidentally she would turn white to the lips. I used to amuse myself by taking her unaware in this way, and Dada in the innocence of his heart used to say, 'Did she turn pale?', as a joke.

Well, after the case was over Mother said we could be engaged and married in the autumn, so it was announced. Rosamund was miserable. She used to cry all night and every night, as I very well knew, because her bedroom was next door to mine at Knole, but as I had ceased to care for her and thought only of Harold, I was only exasperated by her tears and tried to stop them by getting angry, not by being sympathetic. I was cold as ice to her, and I see now what a beast I was, and how pathetic she was, because she really did adore me, and added to the misery of knowing that I cared for someone else, she must have felt that she had no one who cared two straws for her – except an obscure sailor whom she didn't like. It was rather a relief to get away from Knole to Switzerland [Interlaken] with Mother and Harold and an elderly millionaire [W. W. Astor] whom Mother had in tow. She was feeling the strain of her two days in the witness-box, when everything that she said, although truthful in the letter, was certainly misleading in the spirit, and when one had to remember very carefully what one had said the day before, or even the hour before. She was, however, serenely happy in Switzerland, and as for Harold and me, we simply lived in heaven.

When we came back to Knole life became a jumble of letters, wedding-presents, and clothes, the whole being plentifully watered by Rosamund's tears. I have seldom seen anyone in such despair, but it didn't touch me. Mother lavished jewels on me. Harold and I grudged an hour spent away from one another. I hurry over this part, because it is the same for everybody. On the 1st of October [1913] we were married in the chapel at Knole, decked out like a theatre by me. Mother, who doesn't like being *émotionée*, stayed in bed. I had cried bitterly the evening before at the prospect of leaving Knole and giving up my liberty, but I had cried away all my regrets and had none left when the day came. Rosamund survived my wedding-day somehow, and rather splendidly rose to the occasion of hiding away her own sorrow; she is really rather splendid in some ways. Violet didn't come. I never told her anything about my engagement, and she learnt it through the papers and wrote me sarcastic letters through which I could read her anger.

That was my wedding.

We went away for three days to the country, and then came back to London for one night, which I spent with Mother and Dada while Harold went to his parents. I saw Rosamund, and said goodbye to her, which bored me very much, as I couldn't live up to the level of her emotion. Next morning early Harold came to fetch me in a motor and we left for Florence, where we lived in the little cottage I had shared with Rosamund eighteen months before. That is one of the things I am most ashamed of in my life. It was horrible of me. Besides being disloyal to Rosamund, it was a dreadful *manque de délicatesse*.

For sheer joy of companionship I should think the years that followed were unparalleled or at least unsurpassed. One side of my nature was so dormant that I believed it would never revive. I was really gentle, self-sacrificing, chaste; I was *too* good, if anything, because it made me intolerant of the frailties of other people. (Now, I feel I could forgive anyone anything.) We were a sort of by-word for happiness and union. We never tired of one another! How rescued I felt from everything that was vicious and violent! Harold was like a sunny harbour to me. It was all open, frank, certain; and although I never knew the physical passion I had felt for Rosamund, I didn't really miss it. This lasted intact for about four and a half years.

After a month spent in Italy and Egypt, we lived in Constantinople, and I found out there that I was going to have a child. I was pleased, but Harold was most pleased. His slightly medical attitude was the only thing that annoyed me, and I tried to counteract it by forbidding him to tell anyone except his own parents and mine. He wrote a letter to my mother about it which I tore up in a fury, which he couldn't understand at all. But on the whole I was very *bien-pensant* about it, as indeed about everything else – stagnantly *bien-pensant*! I don't think I regret myself as I was in those days; at least, I regret that the person Harold married wasn't entirely and wholly what he thought of her, and that the person who loves and owns Violet isn't a second person, because each suits each.

The correct and adoring young wife of the brilliant young diplomat came back to England in June. I remember a divine voyage by sea from Constantinople to Marseilles, through the Aegean, a second honeymoon. We met Mother in Paris, and both thought that she was going off her head, as she was obviously in an extraordinarily unbalanced state of mind. Then we went to Knole. War was declared on the 4th of August, and Ben was born on the 6th. Scenes immediately began with Mother over his name, and they culminated in our taking a house in London as it was impossible for us to remain with Mother. We spent the winter in London, and I became quite sociable, I was, in fact, thoroughly tamed. I hardly ever saw Violet (who, at her own sarcastic request, was Ben's godmother), partly because she was jealous and partly because I was altogether too well tamed for her. That was the only period of my life when I achieved anything like popularity. I was no longer plain, I took adequate trouble to make myself agreeable, Harold was loved by everyone who met him – we were, in fact, a nice young couple to ask out to dinner. Oh God, the horror of it! I was so happy that I forgot even to suffer from *Wanderlust*.

And then, and then, those years: let me think. All that winter Mother was dreadfully and impossibly quarrelsome and queer, and no one could do anything with her. We thought she was going to Rome, but the day before she was due to start she said she wouldn't go. We were all frankly dismayed, having looked on Rome as a heaven-sent solution. Mercifully Dada was with his regiment, so he didn't suffer much from it all. She went at last to a nerve doctor who did her worlds of good. What else? We bought a country cottage [Long Barn] where we spent the summer and Harold went up to London every day. If he had to spend the night in London we thought it a tragedy. We had once been parted for three days while he went yachting – never more. Domesticity could go no further. Ben grew apace, and we were to have a second child at the end of September.

The nightmare of that September and October remains with me. Dada left for Gallipoli in September, and I waited and waited for the baby. I waited all October, and the days grew shorter and wetter; Harold had a fortnight's leave, which was the only bright spot. The baby was not born until the first week in November, and then it was born dead, and I was very ill myself, after two nights and days in which I seemed always to be watching the candles in the room grow paler in the light of the dawn.

As soon as I could be moved, we went away to London. I minded horribly about the baby, and it got worse instead of better. I never knew why it all happened like that, but I think it was owing to a shock I had had months before: there was a terrible gale raging, and we were all at dinner [at Knole], with screens round us to keep off the draughts, and the carpet rising gustily on the floor, and I for one was convinced that something would happen. (I was always, and still am, nervous about Harold.) Sure enough, the butler came in suddenly and said there had been an accident to the car. The car was bringing Rosamund from the hospital where she worked, and Harold from the station. I grabbed a coat and rushed out, but it was impossible to walk against the wind, and the night was black as pitch. I waited at the door, nearly dead with fright. Presently two men came, supporting Rosamund between them; she was covered in blood, her nose was pushed broken half across her face, and she was talking nonsense. There was no sign of Harold. For an hour I didn't know whether he had been in the motor or not; the chauffeur was carried in badly injured and Rosamund was completely out of her senses. However, after an hour he appeared, having walked from the station through that hideous night. It made a great impression on me, both my anguish about Harold and the really dreadful apparition of Rosamund, and I am sure that was responsible for the baby.

I want to get on, I want to finish those years that might have been the life of another person. I want to get to the present.

There are so few events in those years, except war events. In our personal life there was nothing except moving to London for the winter, to the cottage for the summer, watching Ben grow and learn to speak, and for me, writing. I should think it was hardly possible for two people to be more completely and unquestioningly happy. There was never a cloud, never a squabble. I knew that if Harold died, I should die too; it all made life very simple. I saw Violet from time to time, but she was more alien from me than she had ever been, and yet in a way our friendship was on easier terms; that strange undercurrent had never made itself so little felt.

She is very proud, and a first-class dissimulator.

In the winter [1917] Nigel was born, and shortly after that Rosamund's mother died of cancer. I was with Rosamund during the operation (which was only for appendicitis), and with her too when the surgeons told her with revolting details that they had discovered cancer. She left a letter for me, bequeathing to me the care of Rosamund. I have not fulfilled this trust.

We spent that summer in the country again, with Ben and

Nigel. That was the last of our untroubled summers, but I didn't know it; there was nothing to foreshadow events. The war went on, and weighed on everyone; but no one could have been less affected than we were, except for Dada who had been out ever since 1915.

Chronology

1827 'Old' Lionel Sackville-West born

1830 Pepita born in Malaga

1852 Lionel meets Pepita in Paris

1826 SEPTEMBER: Their illegitimate daughter, Victoria
    born in Paris

1871 Pepita dies at Arcachon

1873–80 Victoria in Paris convent

1881–8 Victoria in British Legation, Washington

1886 21 NOVEMBER: Harold Nicolson born in British
    Legation, Teheran

1888 SEPTEMBER: The Murchison letter ends 'old'
    Lionel's career

    OCTOBER: Mortimer dies, and 'old' Lionel becomes
    Lord Sackville

1890 JUNE: Victoria and 'young' Lionel marry at Knole

1892 9 MARCH: Vita born at Knole

1894 JUNE: Violet Keppel born

1897 Victoria meets 'Seery', Sir John Murray Scott

1904 Vita meets Violet Keppel

1905–8: Vita at Miss Wolff's school, London

1906–10; Her early novels and plays

1908 MAY: Vita's first visit to Florence, with
    Rosamund and Violet

    3 SEPTEMBER: 'Old' Lionel Sackville dies

1909 APRIL: Vita meets Pucci in Florence

    AUTUMN: Vita goes with her mother and Seery to
    Russia

1910 FEBRUARY: Legitimacy case decided in Sackvilles'
    favour

    APRIL–MAY: Vita in Italy with Pucci again

    JUNE: Vita 'comes out'; she meets Harold

NOVEMBER: Vita in Monte Carlo with Lady
Sackville and Rosamund until April 1911
1911 JANUARY: Harold and Pucci visit her in Monte Carlo;
Harold goes to Madrid Embassy
CHRISTMAS: Harold at Knole
1912 17 JANUARY: Seery dies
18 JANUARY: Harold proposes to Vita at Hatfield ball
24 JANUARY: Harold leaves for Constantinople
APRIL–MAY: Vita in Florence with Rosamund
AUGUST: Harold home on leave
OCTOBER–NOVEMBER: Vita returns with Rosamund
to Italy.
1913 APRIL–MAY: Vita goes to Spain and Italy
18 MAY: 'Crisis' telegrams between Vita and Harold
24 JUNE: Scott case begins
3 JULY: Harold returns to England
7 JULY: Scott case decided in Sackvilles' favour
5 AUGUST: Vita's engagement to Harold announced
MID-AUGUST: Interlaken
1 OCTOBER: Vita and Harold married at Knole;
honeymoon in Italy and Egypt
AUTUMN: Vita and Harold in Constantinople
until spring 1914
1914 21 JUNE: Vita and Harold arrive back in England
from Constantinople
4 AUGUST: Outbreak of war
6 AUGUST: Benedict (Ben) born at Knole
28 DECEMBER: Accident to Rosamund at Knole
1915 MARCH: Vita and Harold buy Long Barn
3 NOVEMBER: Vita's second son born dead
1916 JANUARY: Vita and Harold buy 182 Ebury Street
in London
1917 19 JANUARY: Nigel born at Ebury Street
1919 19 MAY: Lady Sackville leaves her husband and
Knole for ever

Part Two

BY NIGEL NICOLSON

My mother (whom I shall now call Vita, except occasionally) was understandably hazy about her own mother's
origins, and it was only in 1936, when she read the contemporary documents for her book *Pepita*, that the facts
replaced in her mind the legend on which she had been
brought up. Pepita was not the illegitimate daughter of a
gipsy and a Spanish duke. Both Vita and her mother would
certainly have preferred it that way, and in a further dramatization of the legend, the duke was named as the Duke of
Osuna. Nor was Catalina Ortega, Pepita's mother, an ex-
acrobat. There was certainly gipsy blood in her, but she was
happily married to a barber of Malaga, Pedro Duran, and
after her husband's early death supported her family by
patching and selling old clothes. Pepita was born in Malaga
in 1830, and there was a younger brother, Diego. Her early
career was not a great success. Her first contract, in Madrid,
was cancelled, the ballet master saying in later evidence:
'In my opinion she was no artist at all as regards dancing,
but no doubt her personal charms might fascinate the public
abroad. She might perhaps be good enough for Germany,
but not for Spain.'

One must take Pepita's beauty on trust. There is no
photograph of her in her prime, and the oleographs which
advertised her performances throughout Europe do scant
justice to the 'Star of Andalusia', whose face and figure remained stamped on the memories of all who saw her. At the
age of twenty, she married another Spanish dancer, Juan de
la Oliva, but the marriage broke up in quarrels a few months
later, and she was free to take as her lovers whomsoever she
chose, and she chose many. Lady Sackville sometimes gave
the story an extra twist by claiming Prince Yousoupoff as
her natural father, and it could have been so, if the date of

her birth, 1862, had corresponded with the dates of that brief affair, for her birth-certificate recorded that she was '*fille de père inconnu*', leaving her parental options enticingly open. However Lionel Sackville-West, who much against his will was obliged by the lawyers to leave the full facts on record, acknowledged his paternity of Pepita's three daughters and two sons, and of two other children who died in infancy.

Lionel and Pepita had first met in Paris when he was on leave from his diplomatic post at Stuttgart, and from that moment onwards, with some intermissions, they remained lovers until Pepita's death. They never lived in England, though Pepita once danced at Her Majesty's Theatre in London, but took a series of villas at places on the Continent which lay conveniently equidistant between Lionel's various legations and the cities which Pepita's charms were subduing one by one. She retired to Arcachon in southern France, and died there in 1871, giving birth to her seventh child, who lived only six days.

Vita's mother was christened Victoria Josefa Dolores Catalina, and she bore her father's surname, Sackville-West. Soon after Pepita's death he was appointed British Minister in Buenos Aires, and Victoria was sent with her sisters, Flora and Amalia, to the Convent of St Joseph in Paris, where she remained seven years, friendless, retarded and miserable. Her brothers, Maximilien and Henry, were sent first to Stoneyhurst and then to learn farming in South Africa. Victoria was not told of her illegitimacy until she was moved from the Paris convent to another in London in 1880, and it was then that she also heard for the first time that she had an uncle called Mortimer, Lord Sackville, who lived in a huge house called Knole, another uncle Lord De La Warr, and two aunts, the Duchess of Bedford and the Countess of Derby. It was quite a shock. She knew nothing of the world. She could hardly speak English. She regarded herself as a waif, fit only to be a governess like Jane Eyre, and it was this waif whom her father suddenly proposed to translate to Washington as his hostess at the British Legation, where she would occupy the leading position in diplomatic society.

During his infrequent visits to Paris, Lionel must have seen in his eldest daughter latent qualities which convinced him that she would succeed in this alarming task, for the risks to his career were immense. He was obliged to admit officially what had long been common gossip, that although a bachelor he had five children; that his intended hostess was one of them, and she a totally inexperienced girl of nineteen. Queen Victoria gave her amused consent to this odd arrangement on condition that no objection was raised in Washington itself, and a Ladies' Committee was formed there to discuss it, headed by the President's wife, Mrs Garfield. 'A letter had come from Lady Derby, stating the situation,' said one member of this tribunal subsequently, 'and that Mr Sackville-West was fond of his daughter and requested that she be received. The decision was that she should be received cordially as her father's daughter.' Victoria arrived in December 1881, alone, for Vita's autobiography is at fault in saying that her sisters went with her. Flora and Amalia did not join her until several years later, and their addition to the Sackville-West *ménage* America thought 'a bit too much', according to the same witness, but by then Victoria had won for her family a position immune to censure. They loved her.

My grandmother often spoke to me about her seven years in Washington as the first and greatest triumph of her life, and her boast was fully justified. I thought that she must be exaggerating when she told me that the second proposal of marriage which she received was from the President of the United States himself, President Arthur, a widower (Garfield having been assassinated before her arrival), but I have since discovered that it was true enough for an official denial to be issued by the President's brother: 'The story that the President is engaged to Miss West is absurd and without foundation, and the President has no idea of marrying now.' My grandmother said that she refused him late in the evening after her first banquet at the White

House. 'I burst out laughing,' she wrote in her Book of Reminiscences when she was aged sixty, 'and said, "Mr President, you have a son older than me, and you are as old as my father."'

What is beyond dispute is that she captivated Washington from the start. Contemporary Press comments could be merciless about other people – even about her father, who was described retrospectively as 'reserved and taciturn, and people who did not like him called him dull. He had at any rate an unusual power of silence.' But about Victoria they were unanimous. 'She has become the reigning belle. Her beauty and intelligence are alike remarkable. About both those rare qualities there is something exotic, which give both an added charm.' 'She is most pleasing in manner and appearance. She has the graceful figure of a very young girl and a most piquant face with large appealing dark-blue eyes.' 'She made an enormous impression by her beauty, charm, modesty, grace, clothes and taste.' 'The dignity of a woman with the unconscious sprightliness of a child.' On her unusual origin the Press remained gallantly dumb. Lionel was described as a widower, and the only reference to Pepita was that 'Miss West's harsh English angles are rounded off by the graces of her Spanish mother'.

Another quality soon developed – her efficiency. She took in hand the large staff of the Legation, diplomatic and domestic, and knowing exactly what she wanted, would tolerate no argument or disobedience. She was a natural organizer and hostess, gracious to the distinguished and, lacking all shyness herself, thoughtful for the shy. In the convent, dancing and deportment had not been taught, but she seemed to know it all, instinctively. In her first season she presided at five balls, with five hundred guests at each, and began to change the conventions and even the protocol of such occasions, to the delight of the young ensigns and attachés who flocked around her, first as a novelty, and soon as the leader of their improvisations. Finding that the Highland reel was unknown in Washington (she herself having first heard of it only six months before), she held classes in the Legation to which an invitation was an honour and a command. As the most popular of all the girls she found no difficulty in putting an end to the custom of 'bunching', by which young men were obliged to send to their partners bouquets which they could ill afford. She played tennis; rode horseback; shot rapids in a canoe; went fishing; discussed his campaigns with General Sherman; hunted with Red Indians; visited many parts of the United States; and spent two months every winter in Canada, where she broke another dozen hearts. For all that, she was a girl whom it was difficult to know well. When she drove out each evening in a stylish two-horsed carriage, attended by her coachman and footman, she was sometimes accompanied by her father or a girl-friend, never by young men. Any who attempted the mildest flirtation were brought up short: 'Please go away. I do not like this kind of conversation.' She was totally innocent until she married, and she remained all her life fastidious and proud.

The indiscretion which ended Lionel's career in 1888 is known in diplomatic history as the affair of 'the Murchison letter'. A man calling himself Charles F. Murchison, a former British citizen living in California, wrote to the Minister asking his advice on the forthcoming presidential election. Lionel was foolish enough to reply that he favoured the return of President Cleveland for a second term. His letter was published under such headlines as 'The British Lion's Paw Thrust into American Politics', and his recall was demanded by the State Department. Fortunately his brother Mortimer died a month later, and he was able to return to England with the excuse that his new responsibilities as Lord Sackville obliged him to retire. Victoria now exchanged the management of the Legation for that of Knole, the largest house in England still in private hands.

She chose from among her many suitors her first cousin Lionel, and married him in June 1890. Their only child, my mother, was born at Knole on 9 March 1892. She was christened Victoria Mary, but was known even before her birth as Vita, to distinguish her from her mother who shared the same name, Victoria Sackville-West, as did her father and grandfather, both Lionel Sackville-West and later Lord Sackville. To make clear the relationship between the two Victorias and the two Lionels, and as a key to the famous legitimacy case which followed, a simplified family-tree will be found useful:

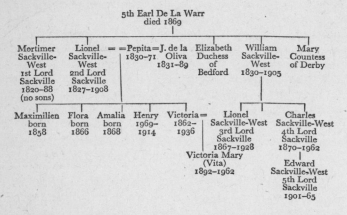

Victoria's marriage to her cousin was not welcomed by the family, except by her father, who saw in it an unexpected opportunity to keep his favourite daughter beside him at Knole and in a sense 'legitimize' at least one of his children, and by Lady Derby, who adored her niece. The others shook their heads at the extension of the family scandal into a new generation, deploring the perpetuation of the 'bad Spanish blood', and dreading the terrible progeny which this marriage might beget. They did not dare say these things to the two Lionels, but pointed out the unsuitability of cousin marrying cousin, their difference in age (she was twenty-seven, he twenty-three), and the disadvantage of a Protestant's union with a Roman Catholic. The latter difficulty Victoria boldly overcame by defying an edict from the Pope himself that any children of the marriage must be brought up in the Catholic faith. For this disobedience, she later claimed with pride, for it added another facet to her story (*'Quel roman est ma vie!'*), she was excommunicated by Cardinal Manning, with whom she had a stormy interview.

Vita, both in her autobiography and in *Pepita*, drew portraits of her parents which do too much honour to her father and too little to her mother. She emphasized her mother's eccentricity to the detriment of her truly remarkable personality and gifts. When she wrote the autobiography, she was still frightened of her; when she wrote *Pepita*, she was anxious to link the two halves of her story by arguing that the gipsy strain in her grandmother persisted in her mother, leading to wild fluctuations of generosity and parsimony, affection and selfishness, determination and incompetence. In fact Victoria Sackville was a woman of strong will softened by charm and over-sweetened by sentimentality. She was master as well as mistress of Knole, both in her father's day and in her husband's. 'Old' Lionel was uninterested in the house and carelessly indifferent to his financial affairs, while young Lionel lacked bite and grasp. Victoria began her long régime at Knole by a programme of modernization – introducing electricity, central-heating and bathrooms, rearranging the furniture, and substituting cars for carriages; and when she found that her decisions on these matters went unchallenged, she began slowly to take over the management of the estate and its finances. She had her feet firmly on the ground. She was the family's strategist. When money was short it was she who speculated successfully on the Stock Exchange, she who opened in London a shop called Spealls for the sale of lamp-shades and stationery which became highly lucrative, she who was in constant consultation with the lawyers on the intricacies of the two great lawsuits, she who won both, she who saved Knole.

At first she was very much in love with her husband. He was the only man whom she ever loved absolutely. 'Lionel was perfect to me in those days,' she wrote in her Book of Reminiscences. 'He gave me ten years of the most complete happiness and passionate love which I reciprocated heartily. I adored him, and he adored me.' Not until 1905 is there a word of criticism in her diaries of his growing neglect of her.

Vita worshipped her father, seeing in him all the attributes of a country gentleman, of whom little was required but good manners and an interest in country pursuits. But she would have admired him less if he had not been her father and the current bearer of the Sackville title. For her that was enough: he *must* be good. For us grandsons he seemed invested with every *droit de seigneur*. Subsequently I have come to see him differently. He was certainly gentle and unostentatious, but he was a man who lived for pleasure, a snob (the prisoner as well as the beneficiary of his rank and times) who cast an indifferent eye at the labouring Midlands as he hurried northwards in his first-class carriage to shoot and fish. His duties on the Kent County Council he carried out without enthusiasm. It was only in his two wars that he discovered the dignity of achievement. For the rest of his life he amused himself. Vita writes that for years he was 'inexplicably' in love with Lady Constance Hatch. To me it is not inexplicable at all. He became increasingly off-hand with Victoria to whom he owed so much, uninterested in her pursuits, bored by her clever friends. He preferred an uncritical, undemanding society woman to the wife who was always asking necessary but uncomfortable questions about the estate, and who was growing stout with middle age. The eventual collapse of their marriage was as much his fault as hers. Of Vita he was fond, but he never began to understand her complicated personality, and discouraged all her wide-eyed enthusiasms as a girl. 'I wish,' he was always complaining to Victoria, 'I wish that Vita was more *normal*.'

For years Victoria tolerated her husband's gallivanting and sullenness as she tolerated her father's taciturnity and rudeness. Gradually she began to form her own circle of more stimulating and attractive companions. There were no women among her intimates, and no younger men. She made a corner in millionaires and lonely elderly artists. The list of her conquests dispels the impression left by *Pepita* that she was nothing but a scatter-brained charmer, for men like Sir John Murray Scott, Pierpont Morgan, Kipling, Lord Kitchener, W. W. Astor, J. L. Garvin, Auguste Rodin, Sir

Edwin Lutyens, Lord Leverhulme, Henry Ford and Gordon Selfridge would not have sought her company again and again after a first meeting unless she had as much to offer them as they to her. Even in her fifties she still had a great physical appeal. One of her old admirers, Cecil Spring-Rice, wrote to her: 'I tell you, you are charming, fascinating, heaven knows what. There is no end to your perfections . . . You are an accomplished mistress in love. You play with it and use it and manage it, like a seagull the wind, on which he floats but is never carried away.' She throve on the unpleasant Edwardian convention of the touch of a finger from an old flame, and a bunch of orchids next day. She enjoyed adulation, but in her middle age was repelled by physical lust. She craved luxury, and was not too proud actually to beg. She loved power, but it must be given to her; she would not impose it. She could be cruel. She was both tender and fierce, quick to tears and quicker to sharp repartee.

Several of her new friends fell deeply in love with her, among them Pierpont Morgan, Astor and Rodin, but her diary, which is frank enough about their advances, is reticent about her response. She kept all her letters from William Waldorf Astor in an envelope marked, significantly (for, yes, she was vain), 'For Vita to read after my death', and in them he left little to the imagination: 'A woman in the flower of her prime needs a romantic attachment. It is the knowledge that someone is thinking of you, desires you, longs for the touch of your beautiful body, that keeps the heart young. Sweetheart, goodbye.' Of one meeting with Pierpont Morgan in 1912 she wrote in her diary: 'He holds my hand with much affection and says he will never care for me in any way I would not approve of, that he was sorry to be so old, but I was the one woman he loved and he would never change.' Undeterred by this, she invited him to Knole the following week: 'He has a wonderful personality. I have never met anyone so attractive. One forgets his nose entirely after a few minutes. He said he would be seventy-five next April.' She herself was then fifty, and weighed twelve stone. As for Rodin, it is quite clear from his letters, the extravagant compliments which he paid her in his studio (every one recorded at length in her diary) and his marble bust of her, that he was for several years infatuated with her. She permitted him liberties but not licence. There is something distasteful about this side of her character. Lionel's flirtations with pretty young women were to be preferred.

Of all her admirers the most permanent was Seery, Sir John Murray Scott. Vita had described him so fully in her autobiography and in *Pepita*, that there is no need to labour the point that he was Lady Sackville's devoted companion from 1897 until his death in 1912. Constantly quarrelling, they could not bear to be apart, and when they were, wrote to each other twice a day. They both had something of the Latin in them, she by birth, he by long residence in France. It was fun to duel, and even more fun to make up. They were a couple of aristocratic curators, she of Knole, he of half the Wallace collection, buying, selling, speculating, arranging, valuing – and knowing that there was money enough, his money, to purchase anything which either of them really wanted. They shared his purse: to buy for her was like buying for himself. Of course she liked Seery for his money: if he had been penniless half the fun would have been missing. His wealth gave him grandeur – and what a *pied-à-terre* was the rue Lafitte, what a country cottage Bagatelle, what a playground Sluie! In London they were always in and out of each other's houses, and he a constant visitor to Knole. At Sluie she had long hours alone with him, while old Lionel slept, young Lionel shot and fished, and Vita wrestled with the hall-boy on the moors.

That was the open side of their relationship. The hidden side was not physical love, for I accept my mother's verdict that it never existed apart from a little hand-patting, but his steady financial subsidy to Knole. All the facts came out after Seery's death. The Knole estate had an income of £13,000 a year, and this was enough to maintain the fabric of the house, and pay the staff of sixty indoor and outdoor servants and the household bills. But it did not pay for

Victoria's improvements, her large house in Hill Street, sporting expeditions, their constant weekend parties, her extravagance in clothes and bibelots, and the enormous expenses of the legitimacy case (£40,000 in lawyers' fees alone). The estate was heavily in debt. When Seery came to hear of their difficulties, he volunteered help, first by loans and then by converting loans into gifts, and promised Victoria that by his Will he intended to set her free from all financial worry. In his lifetime he gave her and young Lionel £84,000. She never directly asked for it, but never refused it, and was careful to let Seery know of her embarrassments. Lionel encouraged her. 'I have had many unpleasantnesses with my dear old Seery,' she wrote in her diary for 1904, 'but Lionel advises me to be very diplomatic and put up with his humour. He says I must think of the future.' She knew that Seery could afford to help her and that it gave him pleasure, and she persuaded herself that it was not to her that he was being so generous, but to Knole, which he loved. Seery's family, watching his fortune melt away to a woman whom they regarded as an interloper and an adventuress, were not so charitable. They called the Sackvilles 'The Locusts', even before they knew about the Will.

It was against a background of impending crisis that Vita grew up. There were three threats to her future: Grandpapa might have secretly married Pepita, as Vita's uncle Henry claimed, and if he could prove it, he would inherit Knole, not her father; secondly, her mother might one day quarrel so irrevocably with Seery that he would cancel his Will; thirdly, even if he did not, the Scott family might successfully dispute it. Vita gradually became aware of these family secrets, for they were endlessly discussed over the dinner-table, but her childhood, though lonely, was otherwise unruffled.

The surviving evidence supports in general her sketchy account of her earliest self. She was fractious with other children, though not so brutal as she suggests. When she was five, Lady Winchilsea wrote to her mother complaining that 'Vita was rough with little Mountjoy'; and six years later Victoria reproves her: 'Dada was telling me lately that he was afraid you had become a little abrupt and rough, so you must try, my very dear child, to copy Mama and remember that it gives people pain if they are not treated very kindly and thoughtfully. But Victoria's attitude to Vita could be indulgent: 'She is extremely intelligent, and such a sweet child'; 'She is a very good child'; 'She speaks French so well, and is making good progress with her German.' Vita preferred the blacker picture of her childhood. Describing for Harold in 1912 what she was like ten years earlier, she wrote: 'I was an unsociable and unnatural girl with long black hair and long black legs, and very short frocks and very dirty nails and torn clothes. I used to disappear for hours up high trees, and they couldn't find me until I threw eggs out of the birds-nests on to their heads.' Violet Trefusis, then Keppel, recollected in her autobiography, *Don't Look Round*, her first impression of Vita:

She was tall for her age, gawky, most unsuitably dressed in what appeared to be her mother's old clothes. We were both consummate snobs, and talked chiefly about our ancestors. I essayed a few superior allusions to Paris. She was not impressed. She digressed on her magnificent house in the country, her dogs, her rabbits. I thought her nice but rather childish. Vita at that age was stolidly, uncompromisingly, British. In her deep stagnant gaze there was no dawning Wanderlust.

Among the earliest documents in Vita's handwriting is a Will which she drew up in 1901, aged nine, and it confirms the impression of her exceptional tomboyishness:

To Mama: A quarter of my bank money and my diamond V [a brooch in that shape].

To Dada: A quarter of my bank money. My pony and cart. My cricket set. My football.

To Seery: My khaki. My miniature. My claret jug. My whip.

To Bentie [her governess]: My pearl V. Half my bank money. My ships.

To Ralph [Battiscombe, a Sevenoaks boy]: My armour. My swords and guns. My fort. My soldiers. My tools. My bow-and-arrow. My pocket money. My target.

Ralph Battiscombe, apparently her residuary legatee, since the last three items were added in pencil as she acquired them, disappear from this story, but his existence shows that Vita was not entirely without favourites of her own age. '*Hier les Battiscombe sont venu prendre le thé*,' she wrote to her mother in 1903. '*Nous avons joué au cricket, et après le thé, Ralph et moi, nous avons pris le fusil-à-air et pendant que Sylvia et Queenie se promenaient avec Fie* [Vita's new governess, after Bentie was sacked], *nous* stalked them.' One reads in her mother's diaries of nursery parties at Knole of up to twenty other children, and Vita was made presentable enough to be allowed downstairs each evening, and to attend, aged twelve, a banquet in the Great Hall at Knole for the West Kent Yeomanry, in which her father was an officer. She was twice a bridesmaid, at the weddings of her Uncle Charles and the Duke of Westminster.

Other sides of her nature soon began to appear. '*Je suis très contente de ne pas être à Londres*,' she wrote to her mother, a sentiment which she was to echo throughout her life. 'Vita,' wrote Victoria, 'is busy gardening, and cultivates mostly salads and vegetables for her Grandpapa', and her first garden was a large V in cress. In 1904, at Sluie, 'I had to scold Vita severely for being so thoughtless when I give her any little commission to do. She forgets and dawdles terribly. She sobbed last night, a thing she rarely does. She minds me very much [Victoria never learnt to speak English faultlessly], is very obedient, but so absent-minded and careless and untidy.' A picture begins to form: Vita was tamed by her mother when with her, untamed when not, loving the country and its sports, pampered by nannies, very much the daughter of the house, with a streak of stubbornness and a yearning for solitary adventure. There is no mention in her

73

mother's diaries of the 'two or three times I tried to run away', so the attempts cannot have been too serious. She was happy at Knole, which was certainly no prison. On the night before her wedding she looked back on her childhood:

Pictures and galleries and empty rooms,
Small wonder that my games were played alone;
Half of the rambling house to call my own,
And wooded gardens with mysterious glooms. . . .
This I remember, and the carven oak,
The long and polished floors, the many stairs,
Th' heraldic windows, and the velvet chairs,
And portraits that I know so well, they almost spoke.

Through Knole and her preferred solitude she discovered the joy of writing. The diary which she starred in 1907 begins disconcertingly: 'R zn gl ivhgliv gsv uligfmvh lu gsv uznrob.' It is a code touchingly simply to crack, for it consisted in nothing more than substituting z for a, y for b, and so on, throughout the alphabet. When decoded it reads, 'I am to restore the fortunes of the family', having received that morning £1 for a poem published in the *Onlooker*, the first money she ever earned. The diary continues (transliterated): 'Mother scolded me this morning because she said I wrote too much, and Dada told her he did not approve of my writing. I am afraid my book will not be published. Mother does not know how much I love writing.' The book was *The King's Secret*, a novel of seventy-five thousand words about Knole in the time of Charles II. It contains a description, unmistakably autobiographical, of her boy-hero at the same occupation as herself:

In a little arbour situated in the garden at Knole, a boy muffled up in a blue scarf was busy scribbling something in a ponderous book. The arbour was furnished only with a wooden seat and a table, and its sole occupants were the boy and a big hound who lay at his feet. His pen flowed rapidly over the paper. Outside the snow lay thick on the ground. The floor of the arbour was of stone, and the

74

boy's foot tapped impatiently on it when he was in difficulties ... Never having been much with older children,
in whose company he did not find himself at home, he had
made his own thoughts his companions. He feared the
shots of ridicule which might be fired at him did he air
any of his opinions, so he held his tongue and committed
his thoughts to paper only. He wrote from morning till
evening.

In little over four years, between 1906 and 1910, Vita
wrote eight full-length novels (one in French) and five plays,
and nearly all the manuscripts survive at Sissinghurst. Her
plots lay ready to hand, in the story of Knole and the
Sackvilles. *The King's Secret* was not the first. She began her
literary career at eleven years old with ballads in the
Horatius manner,

> The good Queen Bess was wond'ring
> What noble she could send
> To take to Mary Queen of Scots
> The tidings of her end.
> When up rose Thomas Sackville,
> A doughty man and true ...

continued with a bloodthirsty dramatization of the story of
Ali Baba (the scene transferred, of course, to Knole), and
then wrote *Edward Sackville: The Tale of a Cavalier*, a novel
of sixty-five thousand words penned in a clear childish hand
as easy to read as print, with scarcely a correction. Her
fluency was remarkable. She taught herself the techni-
ques of narrative and dialogue by careful observation of
what she read, since she had no literary mentor and was yet
to go to school. One can spot the strong influence of
Cyrano. The Sackvilles, who were on the whole a modest
family given to lengthy bouts of melancholia, were transformed by Vita into troubadours who played the most romantic roles at the most dramatic moments of English
history, and behaved in every situation with the utmost
gallantry. Here is Lord Dorset talking to his son:

'Never did I think', said the proud old Earl sadly, 'that I should have a son who would bring disgrace on our house. Tell me your name.'

'What mean you, my Lord?'

'What is your name?'

'Buckhurst,' his son answered with surprise.

'I mean your full name. How are your letters super-scribed?'

'To Richard Sackville, Lord Buckhurst.'

'And you can bear that name, the name of Sackville, and yet commit a disgraceful action? Out on you, my son, do you not blush to own it? Nay, but I blush myself for shame of you! Seek your own chamber. I will have no more of you.'

Buckhurst went without a word and threw himself on his bed, but sleep would not come to him. His father's words rang in his head. He had committed a disgraceful action; he who was a Sackville.

The disgraceful action was that he had been caught flirting with his cousin.

When Vita went to France and Italy, the novels and plays were about Richelieu and Robespierre and the Medici, but in every country and at every epoch her characters spoke the same nineteenth-century version of seventeenth-century English dialogue. The only novel left unfinished was *The Life of Alcibiades*, which she abandoned when even she realized that Periclean Athens must have been a rather different place from Cromwellian Knole. The novel bears no signs that she had yet read the *Symposium*. Alcibiades in his youthful manhood was firmly saddled with a wife.

At seventeen, having had her gloomy *Chatterton* privately printed at Sevenoaks, she attempted something more ambitious. It was a novel of 120,000 words called *Behind the Mask*, set in modern times. Her style had not yet matured. The book begins: 'The Baroness d'Arquailles owned a magnificent castle in the heart of the mountains of Auvergne. Far from any other house, far distant even from a large town, she might pace her ramparts like the fair lady of some brave knight of old'; but, as she made progress with her story, her wings grew stronger. It is a love-story of unbelievable austerity, in which the key sentence reflects her contemporary attitude to men: 'She liked him for his respectful attitude of deference towards her, mingled with the cool authority of future possession.' Then this: 'It is better for us to live apart and love each other all our lives, than to marry and quarrel after a few months. Love is too tolerant. Love admits of no imperfections.' The moral is clear: you must never marry the person you love, for fear of spoiling it; you must marry someone you don't love, for then there is nothing to spoil. Again, 'There was no vulgar passion. Their love was too pure for that.' She says to him: 'I love you absolutely, completely and entirely, so much that I can renounce you without a pang.' He says to her: 'And I love you so much that I obey, and go.' It is a wildly romantic and foolish book.

At Knole in 1907 four people closely related to each other and linked by common forebodings, but totally different in character, were slowly moving apart. Victoria's diary gives this glimpse of their outwardly placid, inwardly uneasy, existence:

I should like Vita to be more open. She seems indifferent: it is her life as an only child which is the cause of it. She is so wrapped up in her writings that it is apt to make her forget things. She is a very good child on the whole, but with a tendency to be too sure of herself, and a little bit hard. She has changed enormously since her 'things' have come on. If only she would become warmer-hearted. It has been rather hard to live all my life with Papa and Lionel who are both so cold on the surface, and now I find the same disposition in my child. I like my old Seery because he is so *sympathique* and I want that so much, with my Spanish nature. I hate flirting and trifling with men, and Lionel knows it well enough. I have given up the hope of making him more outspoken; he is a dear, gentle, quiet nature, but he never takes the initiative or the lead, and is frightfully reserved. Papa is also hopeless in that way.

Next year, in September 1908, old Lord Sackville died, and the abscess which had been gathering for years burst suddenly. Henry produced his carefully accumulated evidence that he was his father's legitimate son, the rightful heir to Knole. The case was heard in the High Court in February 1910. The story, for newspaper readers, had everything. A family which belonged to the highest Edwardian society were quarrelling publicly about inheritance – the inheritance of one of the most historic houses and titles in England, and a large sum of money – all because a young diplomatist had fallen in love with a Spanish ballerina sixty years before, and made her his mistress. Best of all, the new Lady Sackville was obliged to dispute her brother's evidence, and avow, openly and emphatically, that she and all her father's other children were bastards. If Henry could prove his legitimacy, she and her husband would be dispossessed of Knole and left destitute.

The weakness of Henry's case was that he could not show conclusively that Lionel and Pepita were ever married, and even if they had been, the marriage would have been invalid, because Pepita was already married to Oliva. There had been a separation but no divorce (and could not have been, in nineteenth-century Spain), and Oliva had outlived Pepita by eighteen years. Its strength was that Lionel had on several occasions legally claimed Pepita as his wife and five of her seven children as legitimate, including Henry himself. About Victoria no such claim was ever made ('*fille de père inconnu*'), nor about the eldest son, Maximilien, who had entered the world as 'son of Oliva and Pepita', a statement which was admitted by both sides to be untrue. All the others were described on their birth and baptismal certificates as children of 'Lionel Sackville-West and his wife Josefa (*Pepita*) Duran'. In 1869 old Lionel had signed a declaration before the Mayor of Arcachon to the same effect, and on Pepita's death-certificate she was again named as his wife. When the girls were married, they were all described as the daughters of Lionel, without qualification. Fortunately all this evidence was known before old Lionel's death, and in 1897 he had put his name to a long *démenti*, beginning, 'I am a bachelor', and affirming that he had made these false declarations 'simply and solely to save the reputation of Pepita, and at her earnest request'. After her death he saw no reason to perpetuate the lie, for it now involved a considerable fortune, a peerage, and the laws of his own country – and he held a very senior position in the British Foreign Service. He wrote to Henry before leaving for Washington, telling him unequivocally: 'I never married your mother, and consequently you, as well as your brothers and sisters, are my illegitimate children.'

In face of this repudiation of the evidence by the man who should know best, and who could have had no other motive for depriving his son of the inheritance in favour of a nephew, Henry turned to fraud. He produced in court an alleged copy of Amalia's birth certificate, to which the words 'Parents married in Frankfurt-am-Main' had been added in a later hand, but the words did not appear on the original, and no record of such a marriage could be traced at Frankfurt. Secondly, he or his agents (but the handwriting experts said it was Henry) tampered with the register of the church in Madrid in such a way as to suggest that no marriage between Pepita and Oliva had ever taken place. Unluckily for Henry, many witnesses to the wedding were still alive, and it had been separately recorded in four other official registers which he had overlooked. His case collapsed. On the third day of the hearing he dismissed his Counsel, Sir Edward Clarke, for 'mishandling his testimony', and appeared, lamentably, in person, beginning his address to the Judge: 'If your Lordship will give me time, I will go on with this case myself. I know I shall lose it, but I will have a good try.' By the fifth day Henry had had enough: 'I can do nothing more, my Lord. I am done. I cannot defend myself any further. I retire my petition.' Judgement was given

79

against him, with costs. To this day it is not known how Henry, an unsuccessful farmer, raised the money to fight his case, but it was probably financed by speculators who hoped to profit from his victory. The Sackvilles' costs were never paid.

The now undoubted Lady Sackville and her husband and daughter were greeted on their return to Knole by a welcome more suited to someone who had just established her legitimacy instead of its opposite. The day was declared a public holiday in Sevenoaks. The horses were taken from their traces at the approaches to the town, and the local fire-brigade pulled the carriage through the streets and park to the very doors of Knole, under triumphal arches and between cheering crowds. Bands preceded the embarrassed cortège, and at intervals the carriage was halted for the presentation of illuminated addresses and bouquets of flowers. Vita says that she rather enjoyed it, but the photographs of the occasion are better evidence: she looked despondent and ashamed.

That was 'The Case'. It was followed three years later by 'The Other Case', which was even more dramatic, and the two in combination made the Sackvilles temporarily the most notorious family in the country, and Vita, to her dismay, the darling of the crowds. The nickname 'Kidlet', by which Seery had called her, was for several years enough to identify her in a headline, and the publicity and gossip which subsequently attended her activities and the publication of her early books went far beyond her wishes or youthful deserts. I shall describe the Scott case ahead of its proper chronological place in order to clear away from the narrative of Vita's personal life a massive landslide which could have wrecked it.

Seery died on 17 January 1912, collapsed in a chair at Hertford House. In his Will he left to Lady Sackville £150,000 in cash 'in gratitude for all your affection and kindness to me', and the contents of the house in the rue Lafitte, of which the value was estimated to be £350,000.

To Vita he left a diamond necklace, and the 'expectation' that her mother would wish to pass on to her the bulk of his fortune when she died. These bequests were to be duty-free, the duty to be paid out of the residue of his estate, which he divided among his brothers and sisters, for he was a bachelor, together with his London house and its contents. Seery's family disputed the Will on the grounds that Lady Sackville had used undue influence to alienate their brother's affection from them, and to secure for herself a wholly disproportionate part of his property. The defence was that Sir John had every right to leave it to whomsoever he wished and that being of sound, indeed agile, mind until the day of his death, he was quite capable of resisting any influence of that kind and could have changed his Will at any moment. His affection for Lady Sackville was simply that of a connoisseur for a charming companion who shared his tastes, and he wished to relieve her and Knole of financial anxiety after his death.

The case went on for nine days, starting on 24 June 1913. It attracted even larger and more glittering crowds than the Pepita case, for the two stars of the contemporary Bar, Sir Edward Carson and F. E. Smith, were appearing respectively for the Sackvilles and the Scotts, and the material was even juicier, being more recent and involving even large sums of money and even greater scandal. The ladies in the public gallery dressed as if for Ascot, and brought with them cushions to ease the unaccustomed hardness of the benches and picnic-hampers to avoid vacating during the luncheon interval seats which might be filched by disappointed latecomers.

F. E. Smith's opening address lasted nine hours. He drew a picture of a grasping woman who would stoop to any device to lay her hands on Sir John's money. He recounted incident after incident during the fourteen years of their friendship to demonstrate how she had gradually edged the Scotts out of her way. She began by humiliating them under the guise of helpfulness. She arranged the furniture in their houses; she asked her own friends to Seery's dinner-parties 'to make them more lively'; she then suggested to Seery that only one sister at a time, and later none, need attend these parties, 'for people don't come to meet your sisters'; she introduced their guests to each other 'because the sisters don't know who anyone is'; she acted as hostess at rue Lafitte when King Edward came to lunch, and the sisters were told to eat in a hotel; she chose the music for their soirées; she borrowed the Scotts' carriages without asking, and Seery's chef for Knole; she kept the brothers away from Sluie. But it went much further than that. She flattered Seery, 'mesmerized' him, wheedled money out of him during his lifetime and more or less dictated his Will, working with her feminine strength upon his masculine weakness, not because she liked him (oh no, she found him rather boring), but because she was mercenary and he 'was a very innocent man, easily influenced'.

When the Scotts entered the witness-box one by one to corroborate these charges, the contrast between them and the lovely woman sitting in the body of the court was so apparent that Lady Sackville's case was won almost before she or her Counsel had uttered a word. She was like a yacht among a crowd of fishing-smacks. It was quite evident that the only reason why Seery had preferred her company to theirs was that they were dull and she delightful. It was quite true that she had thrown them into the shade, but they were shadowy people already, and their jealousy rendered them even more unattractive to him. She had remodelled his social life in the way that he most desired, and in doing so she could not help but expose his sisters' deficiencies. She let a ray of originality into his humdrum life, and he showed his gratitude to her in the best way he knew. Besides, it was not Scott money, nor family heirlooms, which he was leaving to an outsider: it was Wallace money and the Wallace collection (or the half of it which was not already in Hertford House). Had Seery gained that inheritance by 'undue influence' over Sir Richard and Lady Wallace? The sisters had certainly never said so during the many years when they had benefited from it. Yet it had come to him for exactly the same reasons as those which led him to leave part of it to Lady Sackville – because they had been fond of him, and he was fond of her. He was not cutting his brothers and sisters out of his Will; he was providing for them generously, as he had during his lifetime, allowing them to share his house and its superb contents, which were now bequeathed to them. If he had married and had children, they would have been fortunate to inherit anything from him at all.

These were the arguments which Carson put forward day after day, and his star witnesses were Lady Sackville and Vita. Lady Sackville's cross-examination by F. E. Smith is one of the classics of English legal history. It lasted two whole days. It was not so much her tart repartees ('How dare you say that to me?' 'You don't seem to realize, Mr Smith, that Knole is bigger than Hampton Court') which impressed the jury, as her reasonable answers to brutal questioning about her private life, her most intimate letters, even her husband's friendship with Lady Constance. It was a performance equal to her triumph during her first few months in Washington, and it was based on inner calm, strong nerves and an acute memory for dates and figures, and (as Vita remarks) for 'what she had said the day before, or even the hour before'. Not once did she falter.

Vita considered that her mother's evidence. 'although truthful in the letter, was certainly misleading in the spirit'. I believe that this is putting it too strongly. In her constant quarrels with Seery, Lady Sackville had never been the first to make peace, threatening time after time to leave him, and never more so than during the last years of his life, when her interest in preserving friendly relations was greatest. He held the Will over her like a threat, but she never capitulated. A few months before Seery died, she wrote to him: 'It would be much better if you refrained from reprimanding me and asking me constantly to make amends. I cannot and will not submit to it.' Six weeks later, when he renewed his threat to leave all his possessions to the Wallace Collection, she retorted: 'Well, make up your mind, and then we won't have any more talk about it. I will fill the gap by Spealls [her shop].' This was not the language of a sycophant or schemer. She certainly wanted his money, but on her own terms. 'You old silly,' she would call him. 'You little rascal,' he would reply. But neither meant it. The most that could be said against her was neatly put by the *Pall Mall Gazette* at the time: 'Sir John was ready to give, and Lady Sackville scrupled not to receive.'

Vita's part in the case was mainly concerned with the evidence of the most bizarre witness on the Scotts' side, a Major Arbuthnot, who testified that on a particular evening he had called on Seery at his London house, and opened by mistake the door into the library:

> There were two ladies in the room, and they were going through the drawers of Sir John's desk, evidently searching for papers. I stepped back, and one of the ladies said 'Now!', and Lady Sackville came out followed by Miss Sackville-West, and they went down the passage on tiptoe hanging their heads down as if not to be seen. Miss Sackville-West put her hand up like that [*indicating*] as she went out. After dinner I told Sir John what I had seen. He looked dazed and wrung his hands. He said, '*Ah mon Dieu, c'est incroyable.*'

The clear inference was that they were searching for a Codicil which radically altered the Will. When Vita was asked about this incident, she was able to show by the evidence of her own diary and her mother's that she had been ill all that day, and Lady Sackville had stayed with her. Nor was there any mention of it in Seery's meticulous journal, and no servants came forward to support the Major's statement. It was as much Vita's appearance and manner in the witness-box – 'a tall dark girl, very young and very nervous, in a demure grey hat trimmed with cherries, and a deep white *fichu*' – as what she said, which convinced the jury that she could have had no part in such a ridiculous stratagem, and her mother, even if she were guilty of it herself, would have had more sense than to take with her so innocent a child. At the end of Vita's evidence, the Judge

(Sir Samuel Evans) asked her kindly: 'Who gave you the name Kidlet?' 'I do not remember. I think it was Sir John.'

Sir Samuel's summing-up was strongly in the Sackvilles' favour. 'If it was the influence of friendship,' he told the jury, 'the influence arising out of a community of tastes, out of the affinity of natures . . . it was perfectly legitimate, and you ought to say so in your verdict.' They did. They conferred for only twelve minutes, and decided for the Sackvilles.

Lady Sackville was now a rich woman. She sold the contents of the rue Lafitte for £270,000, and this was perhaps the only shameful part of the affair, for Seery (as she well knew) had hoped that she would use his 'fine things' to enrich the Knole collection, not sell them to provide her with pocket-money.

Among those who gave evidence for the Sackvilles in the Scott case was Rosamund Grosvenor; and among those who heard Vita give hers were Violet Keppel and Harold Nicolson.

Rosamund was the daughter of Algernon Grosvenor, a relative of the Duke of Westminster, and until 1908 they lived at Sevenoaks. Daily she came to Knole to share Vita's lessons, though she was four years older, and old Lionel composed a little saying about her, 'Rosamund Grosvenor got nearly run over', which bothered Vita because she could not see how he got it to rhyme properly. Rosamund stayed frequently at Knole for weekends, and went twice to Sluie, and once to the rue Lafitte. Vita's early references to her in her diary are very tepid: 'She is likeable enough, but very ordinary.' 'She has no personality – that's all.' Rosamund's letters could not have been less suited to Vita's mood in what she calls in her autobiography 'my most savage years'. They began 'My sweet darling' and ended 'Your little Rose'. Even during their brief but intense love-affair, her letters never failed to strike the wrong note of deference, cloying sentimentality, possessiveness and mock anger. 'I do miss you, darling, and I want to feel your soft cool face coming out of that mass of pussy hair.' 'My poor little head begins to ache. I was miz, but I *do* forgive you.' 'How unspeakably lucky I am to possess you. I shall think of *you, you, you* and nothing else, tomorrow, next day, and Sunday and Monday, and every day and hour and moment!'

Violet was two years younger than Vita, but to pick up one of her childhood letters after Rosamund's is like handling rockets after sparklers. Take this, written when she was fifteen, in English for once, perhaps because it suited the Gothic theme, describing Vita's visit to Scotland after her grandfather's death the year before:

I arrived here yesterday [Duntreath Castle]. I have also arrived at the conclusion that I love this place almost better than anywhere else. Do you remember it at all well? Do you remember the peacocks stalking round the house in the small hours of the morning uttering penetrating but unmusical cries, the gorgeous flaming sunsets that set the hills a-kindling for all the world like *cabochon* rubies? Do you remember the staid and stolid girl – a remote connection of mine – whose birthday we celebrated at a place called Lennox Castle? Do you remember the enforced exercise *à travers pluie et tempête* which I considered it my duty to inflict on you? And the secret staircase and Sonia's threats to accompany us although she had no clothes on to speak of? And Willie's violent infatuation which he really considered incurable at the time? And the haunted room and the dumb Laird behind the dining-room screen? And the 'Viper of Milan', and the deluge of Deucalion which inundated us all whenever we set foot out of doors? Don't you remember the purposeless incessant tick-tock of pigeon feet upon the roof, and the jackdaws flying from turret to window, and the desultory cries of the night-owls?

This next letter, translated from her exquisite French, was written in October 1910, when Violet was sixteen:

I love you, Vita, because I have had to fight for you so hard. I love you because you never gave me back the ring

I lent you. I love you because you will never capitulate. I love you for your fine intelligence, for your literary ambition, for your innocent flirtatiousness. And I love you because you never seem to doubt my love. I love in you what I know is also in me, that is, imagination, a gift for languages, taste, intuition, and a mass of other things. I love you, Vita, because I have seen your soul.

Here is Violet at seventeen:

Ah Vita, je suis toute triste quand je songe combien nous ressemblons à deux joueurs, avides de gain, dont l'un ne voudrait hasarder une carte qu'à condition que l'autre avançât la sienne au même moment! Tu ne veux pas me dire ' Je t'aime' parce que tu crains à tort, la plupart du temps, que, d'un élan simultané, je ne te le dise aussi!
[Oh Vita, it makes me so sad when I think how like to two gamblers we are, both greedy to win, one of whom will not risk throwing a card unless the other simultaneously throws his! You will not tell me that you love me, since you fear (wrongly, for most of the time) that I will not make the same declaration to you at the same moment!]

Finally this, in translation, a month later, anticipating so much of what was to follow:

I would like to tear you away from your Italy, slap you on both cheeks and take you on a pleasure-trip with me far away, far from everything which could act like a narcotic on a nature which appears from your last two letters to be half-asleep. My God, my God, how can I shatter this Olympian calm which obliterates my purple and scarlet memories of you! First we must go to Spain, you as my pupil, I as your Cicerone. I will show you Manzanares with its winding lanes; Irun, overshadowed by the Pyrenees, with its lovely cruel girls; Pamplona, flanked by eroded mountains; Burgos, sad and archaic. Follow me everywhere! I will show you eyes of dark velvet, the fandango, undulating bodies, the throbbing castanets, the magpies strutting between the olives, the sad plains, a fluttering mantilla. Follow me, follow me! I will force you to see a hand poised to strike, blood shed in secret, the calculated vendetta which is pitiless and has never been heard to speak of pardon. I will show you treason, infamy, women without scruple, without shame. I will show you madness, Vita (madness, do you hear?), which cracks from the fingers of a woman who saw her husband disembowelled last Sunday in the bull-ring!

Vita first met Violet Keppel in 1904 when she was twelve and Violet ten. She was the elder daughter of George and Alice Keppel and had one sister, Sonia, who was six years younger. Like Vita she had no friends until they met each other at a tea-party in London. They went to the same school in South Audley Street, Miss Helen Wolff's, where Vita carried off all the prizes, and met again in Paris, where they performed together Vita's interminable play *La Masque de Fer* before an audience of sleepy servants at the rue Lafitte. In 1908 Violet and Rosamund were Vita's companions on her first visit to Florence. 'It became quite clear,' wrote Violet in *Don't Look Round*, 'that Vita's reaction to Italy was exactly what mine had been to France. She was bowled over, subjugated, inarticulate with love. She would wander from church to church, picture to picture.' They stayed at the Villa Pestellini, an ochre-coloured house with loggias and terraces and a cottage in the garden, and descended each day to the city, sightseeing with a rapture that few tourists have experienced. On her return, Vita poured her love of Italy helter-skelter into her current novel:

It is a sense almost physical, so strong is it, a feeling of desire, saved from vulgarity by its very mysticism, the intoxicating repletion of beauty, in the mode of calm and sumptuous repose; it is the brilliant, mysterious, resplendent soul of the Renaissance, hovering still, infinitely sad beneath its peacock colours, in its unprobed depths.

She had suddenly grown up.

On her second visit to Italy, next year, she met Marchese Orazio Pucci, son of one of the oldest Florentine families, and he fell immediately and inconsolably in love with her. Vita, aged seventeen, was a little taken aback, but delighted to find that the Pucci name opened every door which had previously been closed to her, starting with the Palazzo Pucci itself. When she left Florence for Rome, Pucci followed next day, uninvited; on the Channel steamer when Vita and her mother were returning home, there was Pucci again. Lady Sackville liked him ('He is such a self-possessed and real gentleman,' she noted in her diary. 'I feel so sorry for him, as I am sure he loves Vita and knows it is hopeless') and invited him to Knole. There he becomes 'Poor little Pucci . . . He took heaps of photographs of Vita in her summer-house and at her writing-table. I let him see in a lot of little ways that he could never marry her. She does not in the least want to marry him; she knows that he would be too masterful for her, and the life too quiet.' At dinner that night he put on his uniform, 'to please Vita . . . I don't think she was touched at all, poor little chap.' Next year, Pucci tried again, when Vita went to Florence for the third year in succession. She was still disconcerted by such homage, but now accepted it more easily, and they spent every day together, motoring through Tuscany and Umbria, with her old governess Fie as a chaperone. Vita's diary reveals her slightly warmer response:

There is a difficulty with *il devotissimo O.*, who wants madly to come to Venice with us and is not allowed to. However, he and Fie make it up, and he can come as far as Bologna tomorrow. I suppose I ought not to have come here [Florence], because of him: he has got it really badly! This year he has made no secrets, but plunged into declarations the very first evening. I like him well enough, *en ami*. So I told him, which does not suit him at all.

He followed them to Venice nevertheless, but was ordered by Fie to stay at a separate hotel and made no further progress with his suit. He wrote to Vita constantly; she seldom replied. At Monte Carlo, in 1911, he finally gave up. He proposed again; she refused ('My God, how unhappy I would be with him!'), and on the following day, 'He says he will go to Africa. He is quite changed. He spoke coldly and seemed ill, lowering his eyes.' She next heard from him that he was in Tripolitania sublimating his love in desperate combat with the Senussi. I do not believe that they ever met again. He married happily and devoted the rest of his life to caring for the buildings of Florence. When I saw him there in 1944, he asked kindly after my mother, without mentioning his early adoration for her, but I felt his eyes upon my back as I left the room.

At eighteen Vita was more than just 'less plain'. She was lovely. The Laszlo portrait of her, painted in January 1910, confirms exactly the impression which she made upon Violet on her return from a long absence in Ceylon and Germany:

> I expected a representative Englishwoman, perpendicular, gauche, all knobs and knuckles. No one had told me that Vita had turned into a beauty. The knobs and knuckles had disappeared. She was tall and graceful. The profound, hereditary Sackville eyes were as pools from which the morning mist had lifted. A peach might have envied her complexion. [*Don't Look Round*]

She was still secretive, and her friends remarked that she could hate as passionately as she could love. She was unpredictable, giving with both hands and then shutting her fingers tight into her palms. She was easily hurt by an unkindness, and nervous that she would be laughed at for failure, being desperately eager to excel. Although she tried to hide her feelings as much as possible, she had a craving for sympathy. With her parents she became increasingly reserved, and like them sought companionship elsewhere. She feared most her father's ridicule, because she loved him most, and would never allow him to read her books or accompany her to Italy, while he regretted (as he wrote to Lady Sackville) that 'Vita doesn't like more normal or ordinary things, but I see that it is no good trying to force her, and I am very much afraid that she will end by marrying a soul', by which he meant anyone with the slightest interest in the arts or general ideas.

Vita did her duty as the daughter of Knole and went to parties, sometimes to four balls a week and luncheons every day, and she enjoyed them if they were the sort of parties at which powdered footmen announced duchesses. Like both her parents she was a snob, in the sense that she attached exaggerated importance to birth and wealth, and believed that while the aristocracy had much in common with working people, particularly those who worked on the land, the middle class (or 'bedints' in Sackville language) were to be pitied and shunned, unless, like Seery or Lord Leverhulme, they had acquired dignity by riches. When she was twelve years old, she could write to her mother, 'The little Gerard Leghs are not bedint, are they?', and, 'Yesterday we had a Sevenoaks girl to tea: she was rather nice, but a little bedint of course', and she never quite rid herself of this complex; her most famous novel, *The Edwardians*, written in 1930, was strongly influenced by it. She was a conforming rebel, a romantic aristocrat. The two sides of her character, the gipsy and the grandee, are well illustrated by the account she gives in her autobiography of her visit to Russia in 1909, and by a letter which she wrote to Harold during their engagement, describing a party at the American Embassy in London:

Cambon and Imperiali [the French and Italian Ambassadors] sat on either side of me and made elaborate foreign compliments and said I ought to be an ambassadress. I said, No, I ought to live in a garret and be poor, and they threw up their hands and said, '*Ah mon Dieu, quelle horreur!*' Then we went down the white marble staircase, and I felt a magnificent house wasn't to be despised. I liked it because it was so rich and unbedint and ambassadorial; and because I am a snob enough to love long dinner-tables covered with splendid fruit and orchids and gold plate, and people whose names I can find in the *Daily Mail* sitting all around. I get on with them so much better than with little dancing things in ballrooms. Except souls. I do like souls. They are amusing and easy and not heavy to talk to.

The little dancing things were the young men of noble birth whom her mother and father dangled before her. At least two of them were worth more than that description, Lord Lascelles and Lord Granby, each heir to one of the most magnificent houses in Britain, Harewood and Belvoir. Lascelles was much in love with her, but gossip had it that she would marry Granby. I do not believe that she was ever tempted. Her real friends were souls, but souls who had some breeding and a gun, who could make a fourth at bridge and knew the difference between claret and burgundy, young men like Robert Vansittart, Patrick Shaw-Stewart, Alex Cadogan, Duff Cooper, Archie Clark-Kerr, Philip Sassoon, the Grenfell brothers, Gerald Wellesley. It was the world in which Harold Nicolson had already found a natural place – with a significant difference: he had no gun; he could not play cards; he could not even dance.

Vita and Harold first met in the summer of 1910, at a dinner-party given by Anne Stanley before a Sherlock Holmes thriller, *The Speckled Band*. He was invited to Knole in June, as Lady Sackville's guest more than Vita's, and sat in the pouring rain to watch Vita's performance as Portia in an open-air Shakespearian masque. They met once or twice more in London during the season, but it was not until the autumn that she showed him any special favour:

Knole, 5 November 1910
My dear Mr Harold,

I have been asked to 'ask a man' to dine on Thursday and go to a dance, so would you like to come! I promise you shan't be made to dance! Do come.

Yours very sincerely,
Vita Sackville-West

P.S. Mr Vansittart is here.

Harold was nearly twenty-four, Vita eighteen. His father was Sir Arthur Nicolson, recently British Ambassador in St

Petersburg, and now Permanent Under-Secretary of State at the Foreign Office; his mother was a sister of the former Vicereine, Lady Dufferin. After an unhappy boyhood at Wellington College, Harold had suddenly blossomed at Balliol, and, to his father's astonishment, had succeeded in winning one of the coveted vacancies in the Foreign Office only the year before. Vita's first impressions of my father are given in her autobiography, and at this stage little need be added. His remarkable nature will gradually appear as this narrative progresses. He was immensely companionable, active, intelligent, very well-read, an undoubted soul and had charming looks and excellent manners. Lady Sackville immediately took to him, but this was no recommendation to her daughter, for she had taken with equal warmth to Pucci and Lord Lascelles.

As Vita admits, her friendship with Harold developed slowly. In her diary (which for the next five years she kept in Italian, because her mother could not understand it) she recorded in January 1911 his departure after a brief visit to Monte Carlo as *cosa tristissima*, for she had found his company more than pleasing, and once, when they were playing draughts and she beat him, he said, '*As-tu un franc?*', which thrilled her because he had *tutoyé*-d her. There is no further reference to him in her diary and no letters were exchanged between them, until September, when he came home from the Madrid Embassy and spent a weekend at Knole. He returned there for Christmas and the New Year, and it was then that he fell in love with her. Lady Sackville, who had a sharp eye for such things and their likely consequences, noted in her diary: 'I suspect the dear boy is very much in love with Vita; they have the same tastes and ideas – but where is the money to come from?' In his letter of thanks to Lady Sackville, Harold hinted at what she had already guessed, and in the manner which would most please her: 'No, I shan't find anyone in Constantinople [he had just been posted to the Embassy there]. I fear that I have an unfortunate faculty for admiring people who are far above me, and whom I can't marry. Perhaps it is lucky that I am going abroad.' He was to leave England on 24 January 1912. He had three weeks in which to prove to himself that his pessimism was unjustified.

Vita was whirled away from him by another round of parties to which he was not invited. 9 *January:* Queen Anne's Mead, Windsor, Lady Arran's house. Other guests: Diana Manners [Cooper], Patrick Shaw-Stewart, Lord Lascelles, Lord Nugent. 10 *January:* Ball at Taplow – Lady Desborough. 12 *January:* Eridge Castle. 14 *January:* Ball at Tonbridge. Vita wrote to her mother:

> I enjoyed Taplow much more than any of the others. There were masses of people I knew, so many that I couldn't dance with half of them, though we stayed till 4! It was a shock to realize afterwards that I had danced almost the whole time with souls. What would Dada say? Lady Desborough was very amiable to me, and I like her son, Mr [Julian] Grenfell, who is enormously tall and danced with me and took me into supper.

On 16 January she went to stay with the Exeters at Burghley for the Stamford ball, and next morning Seery died. Vita heard the news from Lady Sackville on the eighteenth, and has described her quick dash to London and her relief that her own plans for that night were not cancelled, 'because by then I was sure that Harold meant to propose to me and I knew I should say yes'. Together they travelled down to The Grove, Watford, and changed there for the Salisburys' ball at Hatfield. Her diary gives a version of what happened different to that in the autobiography. Translated from the Italian, it reads:

> Until midnight I scarcely saw Harold, who then asked me to dance, and then we went up to the second floor where there was almost nobody. He asked me to marry him. I asked him to wait at least a year, because I am not yet sure. I seem to have dreamt it. For in the bottom of my heart I know that I *shall* marry him, and that we are virtually engaged. After having so much hoped that he

94

would speak out before he went abroad, my only idea was to prevent him from speaking.

Lady Sackville's diary leaves little doubt that Vita did not 'say she would'. 'V. did not refuse him: but said that she would not give him any answer now. . . . Kidlet sat on my bed and talked by the hour about it all. She asked Lionel to let Harold come down to Knole for a last interview, as he is leaving for Constantinople at once.'

Harold came to Knole on 20 January. It was the day of Seery's funeral. Vita wrote that night: 'We said goodbye as ordinary friends, in front of Dada and Lady Connie [Lady Constance Hatch]. I don't understand it. I am quite dazed. Words are empty and faces expressionless.' Lady Sackville, as usual, took command:

> I told H. there can be no possible engagement for $1\frac{1}{2}$ years. Vita must be left absolutely free. He can come back and see her in July, and they can write to each other, not more than one letter a week each, but they must not correspond as engaged people, and no words like Dearest or Darling must be used. I discussed ways and means if the marriage comes off. He would like V. poor and to love him for himself, but I shall see to all that if I get poor Seery's money.

On 24 January Harold left for Constantinople. On the same day the Scotts began disputing the Will.

Well, were they engaged or weren't they? Harold thought they were, more or less. Vita couldn't remember exactly what she had said. Her mother was quite firm that they were not. Her father tried to pretend that nothing unusual had happened.

At the root of her parents' lukewarm response was disappointment that this was not a match good enough for their Vita, the only child of a famous family, despite herself the débutante of her year, a beauty, a scholar, and now (unless the Scotts upset the Will) an heiress. Even the Sackvilles could not pretend that the Nicolsons were bedint, for although they were descended from a long line of Edinburgh solicitors and an occasional rear-admiral, in their remoter ancestry were some robber-barons of Skye, which was a little better, and Sir Arthur was the holder of a baronetcy dating back to Charles I. He had reached the very peak of his exclusive profession, and was soon to be created Lord Carnock. But the Nicolsons did not move in society. Lady Sackville had never met Lady Nicolson in any of the drawing-rooms and country houses which she frequented, and Sir Arthur was too busy, and too crippled by arthritis, to fish or shoot. And they had no money beyond Sir Arthur's salary. Phrases like 'a penniless Third Secretary' began to circulate when the gossip spread.

Lady Sackville, however, was not entirely selfish about it, even in the privacy of her diary:

> Vita telephoned Harold before he left London to say that I am not angry with him. Of course I am not, as I know she cares for him and he for her. She is such a difficult girl to please where men are concerned. It is not at present a good marriage, although he has a brilliant future before him as a diplomatist, and he is very attractive, and so intelligent and such a gentleman. But there is no money, and above all it is terrible for me, as she must live abroad if she takes him. My life will be very lonely, now that Seery has gone, if she goes too. I dread my talk with Lionel on the subject.

Lionel was less generous. He said that she saw only the sentimental side. 'Naturally he is very disappointed that she is not making a great match with a great title', when Lascelles and possibly Granby were offering her the historic names of Harewood and Rutland. But to Vita 'Dada was very sweet, though it is clear he had other dreams. He said that if in a year's time I still thought of nobody else but Harold, he would not make difficulties.'

Thus it was left. There could be no announcement of any engagement, for there was no engagement. Harold, exiled to Asia for at least six months, must attempt by infrequent and impersonal letters to maintain his tenuous hold on Vita, while she was courted by every little dancing thing in London, the two noblemen, the souls, and (did he but know it!) a girl, Rosamund Grosvenor, with whom she was passionately in love. All depended upon Vita, and Vita was now panic-stricken. On the very day when Harold left England, she wrote in her diary: 'I don't remember ever having been so unhappy. Only today have I begun to understand that I do not love him. He went to Constantinople this morning. I was in bed all day and have had time to think.' What he never understood was that his chief rival, even more possessive than Rosamund, even grander than Harewood, was Knole: 'I am all alone here, and all this big house is mine to shut up if I choose, and shut out all the rest of the world by swinging the iron bars across the gates . . . It is so peaceful, and my little court so lovely in the moonlight. With its gabled windows it looks like a court on a stage, till I half expect to see a light spring up in one window and the play begin with me for sole audience.'

Lady Sackville, knowing nothing of Vita's reservations, and of course nothing of the true situation concerning Rosamund ('She is such a nice companion for Vita'), began to enjoy herself, censoring 'their cold and reserved little letters', and flirting with Harold in the very way she denied her daughter. Harold was astute enough to spot the loophole. He could write to Lady Sackville from Constantinople all the things he was forbidden to write to Vita:

Of course I am terribly jealous of Granby and all of them, but I hardly own this even to myself, and I ride alone over these beautiful hills and feel I could sing with happiness over what has happened and may happen. But then, in the evening, there are bad times when I go to parties here, and think she is at parties elsewhere, with eligibles all around her. And here I am, supremely ineligible, buried away in the Orient. But then my wiser self says it is better thus in the end, if I *do* win her, as then I shall feel that she does it with her eyes open.

To Vita he sent boxes of Turkish delight, and letters beginning Dear Vita and ending Yours Harold. For three months, until it became unendurable, he kept the rules.

In April 1912 Vita went with Rosamund to Florence, and they stayed in the cottage at the Villa Pestellini. From there she wrote to Harold: 'We went to pay a call on some people I used to know called Pucci [Orazio was still fighting in Tripoli]. . . . I've been so happy here, it is hot and the *grilli* [crickets] sing, and I love Rosamund, and somewhere in the world is you, and that is an undercurrent through everything else. I ought not to tell you so.' He did not read into the reference to Rosamund anything that he was not supposed to read. Not in this: 'Rosamund knows about you and me. She is a very dear and sympathetic person, though she may not be particularly clever, and I am very fond of her. And she is a perfect tomb of discretion.'

Vita was suffering from the acute strain of what she euphemistically calls her dual personality. In love with Rosamund, she was teaching herself, willing herself, to love Harold too. She was playing for time, half-hoping that his ardour would cool, half-hoping that it would not. 'This is the first time I have lived at all and begun to make friends,' she wrote to him, 'and if I let you take me away this year, it will all end. After all, I am only twenty. Let me be selfish for myself until next June [1913], and I'll spend the rest of my life being unselfish for you.' And then, a little more definitely and breaking the rules: 'Do you want quite dreadfully to see me again? I don't know why I ask. It is a wild person you are going to marry.'

When Harold returned home on leave in August, the situation had scarcely changed since he had left in January. There was still great uncertainty. They met at Knole almost as strangers, partly because Lady Sackville ordained complete discretion, and partly because Vita was still in two minds (oh how literally!). When both Harold and Rosamund went away for a few days, he to visit parents, her diary recorded '*Sono triste senza R.*', with no mention of him. But on 29 September: 'H. and I went through the show-rooms. In the Venetian Ambassadors' Bedroom he kissed me! He kissed me! I love him. *Io l'amo tanto, tanto* . . . But I so much want to see R. again.' At the same time Lady Sackville's enthusiasm for Harold was beginning to wane:

> V. is not suited to diplomacy and taking trouble about a lot of bedints. She ought to be a *grande dame*, very rich, where she could do what she likes and not have to do anything against the grain. She told me yesterday she would like to live alone in a tower with her books, and then she threw up her arms and said, 'Oh Mama, I really don't know what I want.' Poor child, of course she does not, and it is my duty to keep off the evil day of her marriage as long as I can, as she is not ready yet.

At the end of his leave, Vita and Rosamund went with Harold as far as Bologna, where he left them and continued to Constantinople. Although this was the moment when she was 'never so much in love with Rosamund', Vita could write to her mother, 'Oh Mama, I am so unhappy. I want Harold back so much. I can't believe I shan't see him come in at any moment', and at twenty such emotion cannot be feigned. But when she returned alone to Knole, only her diary received her secret: 'How I long to be back in Florence. This sporting life here bores me to tears. And I miss R. every moment, unbelievably.' When Rosamund did return: 'I talked to her very frankly about H. I do not think I love him enough to marry him [*non credo che l'amo abbastanza per sposarlo*]. Before talking to her like that, I had not really understood my own mind. But for a short time, I'll let things slide. Perhaps something will happen.' On 18 December 1912, he wrote: 'I ask myself if it would not have been better if Harold had married someone else. I can see nothing in the future but boredom and pain. I cannot, I cannot, leave everything for him – at least, I don't think I can. He will come back in April, and it makes me shiver. Oh why did he come to the Hatfield ball, and why didn't I refuse him at once? But he is so nice, so young, and he loves me, and we should be happy together.' 26 December: 'I spoke to Rosamund about H. She is the only person who knows the truth. Tonight I think I can never do it.'

It was almost a relief to her when the Balkan War temporarily stopped postal communication between Turkey and England, and when it was resumed, she wrote to Harold letters which gave no hint of her dilemma. She skirted the central problem by teasing him about diplomacy: 'Of course I shall hate the diplomatic life. After a few years when we get tired of solitude *à deux*, as we must, there will remain – what? Rio de Janeiro, boring old diplomats, no English friends.' But on occasions she could write to him as if she had reached an unalterable decision to marry him:

> If I don't seem to care much about all the others, you know why. If I leave my beautiful Knole which I adore, and my Ghirlandaio room which I adore, and my books and my garden and my freedom which I adore – it is all for you, whom I don't care two straws about. Now you deny a word of all that! But I want to sit on the arm of your chair and read your despatches over your shoulder, and rumple your curls which will make you cross. And I want to give dinner-parties in *our* house, when we will be so bored with the people because we would rather be alone.

To her diary she still spoke with her other voice:

> Harold has written that his father is probably going to be made Ambassador in Vienna, and that we shall go there too. The very idea of Vienna has appalled me. Am I to pass all my life abroad? I can't do it. I let Mama see how I felt, and this was the first indication she has had of my change of mind. I could see that she was delighted. I simply can't leave Knole for Vienna!

In March 1913 Harold began to sense that something was wrong when her letters became shorter, less affectionate and very intermittent, but he failed to diagnose the seriousness of his situation because he had no inkling of its cause ('I walked three times round the park with Violet. She was crazy. She embraced me as she never has before, talking to me like a lover. Rosamund doesn't know that I was with Violet tonight.') He wrote:

No letter from you for ten days. This is dreadful for me. You can't be too lazy to write to me, and if you are, it means that you don't care one fig ... Is this a foolish letter to write? But it is only because my eyes are stinging with disappointment, and my heart is sore, sore, and you are so far away and I don't know what is happening. I can't bear it. You out there laughing with strange people – people I don't know, people who may have a power over your mind – and sometimes, before dinner, you write me a letter while Rosamund is having her bath, and it is written so lightly, and it goes so far. Oh Vita, *il pleure dans mon coeur comme il pleut sur la ville*.

She wrote to console him, 'Sometimes I think you are quite happy there with your friends and your wars, and that I am not all-important to you, and then I don't write ... Of course I love you', and much else, which produced a telegram in which one can sense his schoolboy relief, 'A ripping letter from you'. But worse was to come.

Vita went to Spain, and from Spain to Italy (*O Italia mia adorata!*), and returned to England in May 1913 drunk with the freedom she had tasted. The shallowness of her social life, the insipidity of Rosamund, had been exposed by contrast with the gipsies and bull-fighters with whom she had consorted in Seville, with the fishermen at Sorrento. How could she now tie herself to a husband, and tamely wait for him at a chancery door? 'I am happy to be in my old Knole,' she wrote in her diary, 'but I am in a bad humour. I have a half-wish [*quasi-voglia*] to marry Harold this summer and finish with it ... Oh God, how will it end? And he returns at the beginning of July. I have no idea what to do. Today I wrote him a letter which will make him jump.'

This was the crisis. Her letter to Harold has not survived: he may have destroyed it. But he quoted its final sentence in his reply: 'Sometimes I feel it would be simpler to give it all up.' He immediately telegraphed: '*Dernière lettre* *incompréhensible et inquiétante. Dois-je la prendre au sérieux? Réponds télégraphiquement oui ou non. Très anxieux.'* She replied the same day: *'Non. T'en demande pardon. N'en crois pas un mot.'* From that moment until her death fifty years later her love for him never wavered.*

It may seem strange that a single telegram could have made so much difference. She partly explained it in the letter which she wrote next day:

Mea culpa! Mea maxima culpa! My letter was just an ill-tempered storm from a wanderer who felt caged again after weeks of liberty, and was cross in consequence and rebellious of iron bars – and that is the person (you poor, rash, ill-advised Harold), that is the person you so lightly contemplate undertaking for life, someone you know nothing about. How much happier you would be with someone in the nature of Rosamund, not Rosamund herself, *mais dans ce genre là*, very gentle and dependent and clinging. Oh Harold darling, I am sorry. I didn't mean to upset you. I want you back frightfully. It was too awful you always being away, and eight months is a lifetime, and I don't know what I shall do if it has to happen again. I did write to you the very next day [after her 'simpler to give it up' letter], but I didn't dare send it, so I tore it up and waited to see what would happen. Now your telegram has happened, and I answered it. Harold darling, I do want you to forgive me.

But it was more than that. Her love for Rosamund was cooling, and Rosamund was half-engaged to a sailor named Raikes, whom she had met at Dartmouth while Vita was in Spain. Violet had not taken Rosamund's place. Vita was alone. She was genuinely anxious not to hurt Harold, for whom her feelings veered from tenderness to sudden

* His telegram: 'Your last letter incomprehensible and disturbing. Am I to take it seriously? Telegraph yes or no. Very anxious.' Her reply: 'No. Forgive me. Don't believe a word of it.' They telegraphed in French in order to conceal the sense of the messages from the post office in Sevenoaks.

spurts of genuine love. His letters affected her profoundly, his presence even more. Besides, she *must* make up her mind. Almost daily she heard from Lord Lascelles, who knew only of Granby as his rival, and there were others too who imagined that she could still be won. Her mother's anxious looks and none-too-discreet inquiries were becoming intolerable. She wanted a refuge, and Harold offered one. By her letter she had tested him. Had he faltered at that moment he would have lost her irretrievably, and this book would never have been written. His telegram was a cry of despair, but to her it was a lifebelt. The letter which he wrote before he received her answer confirmed everything: 'If you let me down, I feel I could kill you. I love you so much more than ever before, and the longing after you is like a stretched cord within me.' Here, at last, was the language that she could understand.

The effect of it is seen in her diary of 11 June: 'These days I think so much of Harold that I can't sleep. I so much want him to come home. I have an insane wish to see him again; and I cannot let him out of my life. I shall marry him.' She wrote to him frequently in the same strain, and when he returned from Constantinople on 3 July 1913, all that remained was to announce their engagement and fix the date of the wedding.

He travelled home through the Mediterranean, and the first European newspapers which he saw, at Marseilles, were full of the Scott case, which had just begun. In Paris, at Dover, he followed its progress, agonizingly, and at Victoria station the posters blazed with the latest news. He rushed to Hill Street, found Lady Sackville in tears, gathered Vita into his arms, and next morning went with Rosamund to the court to hear Vita give her evidence. When the Sackvilles won the case, they held a jubilant party in London, and then came an absurd anti-climax. The *Daily Sketch* identified Harold as 'Kidlet's constant companion at the court', and forecast that 'their engagement will be announced soon'. Lady Sackville, furious, issued a statement under her own name: 'The announcement of the forthcoming engagement of the Hon. Victoria Mary Sackville-West to Mr Harold Nicolson is entirely unauthorized', but not, it was noted, denied. Their tattered little secret was fluttering in the winds of publicity. Letters of congratulation began to arrive, and those from the three people who had most disturbed Vita's recent life were self-portraits of the writers. First, Lord Lascelles, gallantly lowering his flag:

> Dear Vita [until then she had been *Carissima mia*], It is not easy for me to sit down and congratulate you, although I hope you know that I do most really wish for your happiness. Nobody can say but yourself whether you have chosen right. I only know that H.N. seems very nice indeed, and I wish I knew him better. This is a sort of goodbye, but I hope that we may be good friends again after you are married.
>
> > Yours ever,
> > Harry

In 1922 he married Princess Mary, only daughter of King George V.

Secondly, Rosamund in despair:

> Don't ask me to visit you. I can't. I am so utterly miserable. I feel that you are going. I simply cannot begin to face it. I am ill with misery.

Thirdly, Violet, contemptuous:

> *Accepte mes félicitations les plus sincères à la nouvelle de tes fiançailles.* I never could write letters on this subject in any language, but somehow it seems less absurd in French. I wish you every possible happiness (et cetera) from the bottom of my heart (et cetera). Will you and Mr Nicholson [sic] come and have tea with me? ... I see in the evening papers that the rumour is contradicted, in which case this effusion would be (officially, at least) in vain. *Ma non importa.* You can keep it till the day when it ought publicly to be forthcoming. It will suit the same purpose at any age, with no matter whom.

Their engagement was officially announced on 5 August. Lady Sackville was generous to them. She gave Vita an allowance of £2,500 a year, of which the capital was to become hers on her mother's death.

The visit to Interlaken, between the announcement and the wedding, was farcical. The reason for it was not to give the couple a holiday together, but to provide Lady Sackville and William Waldorf Astor with chaperones. Astor suggested that they might meet 'by accident' in Switzerland, having failed to entice her to come 'veiled and unnoticed' to his office suite in London. Lady Sackville was prepared to come, provided that she might bring her daughter and her daughter's fiancé with her, and she enjoyed the escapade as much as Vita and Harold. The two pairs of chaperones left each other discreetly alone all day and reunited for dinner before withdrawing to their four strictly separated bedrooms.

As the wedding-day drew near, Vita felt no qualms, except about leaving Knole. She cried for a whole hour on her wedding-eve, comforted by Rosamund, who was struggling to suppress her own sobs:

> *To Knole. 1 October 1913*
> I left thee in the crowds and in the light,
> And if I laughed or sorrowed none could tell.
> They could not know our true and deep farewell
>
> Was spoken in the long preceding night . . .
> So in the night we parted, friend of years,
> I rose a stranger to thee on the morrow;
> Thy stateliness knows neither joy nor sorrow,
> I will not wound such dignity by tears
> (From *Poems of West and East*, 917)

The wedding was not like other weddings. Rosamund was a bridesmaid. It was very grand and hugely publicized, for Kidlet was news, but the chapel at Knole was so small that only twenty-six people could fit in. It was a lovely day, the sun streaming through the chapel windows. While they waited, the other guests, who included by Lady Sackville's special invitation all the jurymen from the Scott case, milled around the Great Hall examining an array of six hundred wedding-presents. The only absentee was Lady Sackville herself, who remained in bed all day. She was genuinely ill, but could have roused herself if she had felt able to bear the strain of parting, or, as people unkindly so said, if she had been the centre of attention. Vita was quite calm, dressed in a cloth of gold and veiled in Irish lace which her mother had worn at the Coronation of the Czar. That night she wrote in her diary, but not resignedly, '*Dunque si è culminato così!*' – 'So it has reached this conclusion!' Years later she told me that Harold had talked for so long about his uncle (Lord Dufferin), that she had to remind him that he also had a wife.

They spent a few days at Coker, a lovely Elizabethan house in Somerset, and then went to the cottage of the Villa Pestellini. To Vita's annoyance her mother had arranged that on their way to Constantinople they should spend a week with her friend Kitchener at Cairo. In *Passenger to Teheran* Vita recalled that visit, disguising that it was also her honeymoon:

> I had not wanted to stay with him; I had protested loudly . . . The recollection survives with horror, a sort of scar on the mind. I had arrived at the Residency suffering from sunstroke and a complete loss of voice – not an ideal condition in which to confront that formidable soldier. Craving only for bed and a dark room, I had gone down to dinner. Six or eight speechless and intimidated officers sat around the table. Kitchener's bleary eye roamed over them; my own hoarse whisper alone penetrated the silence. Egyptian art came up as a topic. 'I can't,' growled Kitchener, 'think much of a people who drew cats the same way for four thousand years.'

In Constantinople she was supremely happy and became reconciled even to diplomatic parties. She and Harold leased

a Turkish house at Cospoli, overlooking the Golden Horn,
and there she made her first garden:

> The gardens of her terraced hills
> Rose up above the port,
> And little houses half-concealed
> The presence of a light revealed,
> And here my journey's end was sealed.
> And I reached the home I sought.
>
> [*Poems of West and East*]

'Harold appears to me perfect', she wrote in her diary. 'So
gay, so amusing, so intelligent, so *young*. I feel that until now
I never really knew him.' Her father came to visit them; so
did Rosamund (now bored with Raikes, but Vita was
bored with Rosamund).* They went sailing on the Bos-
phorus and bought Persian pottery in the bazaars. Loaded
with oriental treasures, they returned to England in June
1914, and Ben was born at Knole two days after the outbreak of war. Believing that she might not survive his birth,
she wrote a letter to Harold to be opened if she died:

> If you marry again, which I expect you will, don't be
> just the same with her as you were with me; give her a
> place of her own, but don't let her take mine exactly.
> Don't teach her our family expressions. Darling, I hope I
> shan't die. I want years and years more with you as my
> play-fellow. I love you so, my own darling husband. We
> are so young, and we have such fun together always that
> I refuse to believe that it can be cut off. If you ever get
> this, we shall have had nearly a year of absolutely un-
> marred happiness together, and you will know that I have
> loved you as completely as one person has ever loved
> another.

She left him everything – except a diamond watch to Rosamund, and a sapphire and diamond ring to Violet.

I do not intend to describe the war years in any detail, for

* Rosamund married Jack Lynch, a soldier, in 1924, and was killed
by a German bomb in London, in 1940.

they add nothing to the theme of this narrative. Harold was exempt from military service (what would she have felt if he had been sent to the trenches, and how did she feel about his not going?), and gained in the Foreign Office a reputation which made him the pet of successive foreign secretaries. They bought a house in London, 182 Ebury Street, where I was born in January 1917, and a tumbledown cottage, Long Barn, two miles from Knole, which they restored and extended with the advice of Sir Edwin Lutyens, who had now replaced Seery as Lady Sackville's constant companion.

At Long Barn Vita became seriously interested in gardening, and Harold in garden design; and she was busy writing, poetry mostly, but also a vast history of the Italian Renaissance which she rightly decided not to publish. The event which brought them closest together (but then they were scarcely ever apart) was the death at birth of their second son on 3 November 1915, to which Vita refers in her autobiography, but attributes it to an unlikely cause, the accident to Rosamund which had taken place more than ten months earlier. In her diary it is simply recorded thus: '*La mattina alle dieci nacque il bambino, ma morto.*' She wrote to Harold a few days later a letter which illustrates what tenderness underlay her rebellious nature. She would, I suppose, have called it another example of her dual personality:

Harold, I am sad. I have been thinking of that white velvet coffin with that little still thing inside. He was going to be a birthday-present to you next Sunday. Oh darling, I feel it is too cruel. I can't help minding, and I always shall. I mind more when I see Ben, how sweet and sturdy he is, and the other would have been just the same. I mind his being dead because he is a person. It is silly to mind so much. I can't bear to hear of people with two children. Oh Harold darling, why did he die? Why, why, why did he? Oh I wish you were here. I am in bed, and haven't got any more paper. [But she tears out of her Bible a map of St Paul's journeys, and continues on the back]: I try and stave it off, not to think about it, but when I am alone, it rushes me. I am so frightened of being alone now. Harold, I want you so badly.

There was another event which must be mentioned at this point, for although it did not culminate until 1919, it had long been foreshadowed, and to give it its proper chronological place would only interrupt irrelevantly Vita's extraordinary story which follows. This was Lady Sackville's decision to leave her husband and Knole. In *Pepita* Vita gave a very guarded account of it, placing most of the blame on her mother for failing to understand that a man who had commanded troops at Gallipoli should wish, on coming home, to assert his authority in his own house. Lady Sackville, she says, 'suddenly lost her temper . . . and left the room never to return'.

Of course there was something in Vita's version of the story. Lady Sackville was a maddening person to live with, and she aggravated an already difficult situation by her tactlessness. Harold, who spent Christmas 1918 at Knole, gave Vita this example of it:

There was a terribly acrid row last night. It began this way. Just as B.M. ['Bonne Mama', the family name for Lady Sackville] was going to bed, she said suddenly to Dada, 'Did you tell your French officers about my passion for sitting out-of-doors?'. To which Dada rather crossly replied: 'Of course not. Why should I? I don't suppose that they knew I was married.'

Of course it was an idiotic question for B.M. to ask. I suppose she has some sentimental idea of stern-faced soldiers – *vaillants et alliés* – grouped round a camp-fire, with the silent sentry against the stars, and discussing their children and their homes in dear old England, and her own stern-faced warrior dwelling with silent emotion upon his dear one in the great ancestral home, and speaking lovingly and with gentle fancy of her qualities, the inflexions of her voice, and her dear personal idiosyncrasies.

And Dada, who is always irritated (like most men,

mark you, Vita) by the *eau sucrée* of schoolgirl romance, and who, after all, would be most unlikely, in the intervals of telephoning, to pour out his heart to a French colonel however *vaillant* and however *allié*, felt a fool at the mere suggestion and answered her roughly and in a greater hurry than he intended.

Any how, B.M. threw up her head with a hard little laugh and went out of the room humming a hard little tune. We were left behind with the odd sense of something rather silly and rather cruel having happened. I slipped away, and with commendable courage crept into her room where she was sobbing away: '*Enfin, mon petit Harold, je m'en vais demain – c'est décidé –* and after all that I've done for Knole, and of course I shall not make a scandal – *tu sais que je suis trop grande dame pour ça – je dirai que je veux voir l'entrée du Président Wilson.*'

I soothed her down as best I could. I really don't know whether she is more hurt than angry. Anyhow, she decided not to go after all. But isn't it hopeless? B.M. keeps on saying, '*Je compte pour rien maintenant. Je ne suis que son unpaid housekeeper.*' Poor B.M.! Poor Dada! How happy each could be without the other! I don't know what will happen. But I have the impression that Dada wants to make Knole more or less impossible for B.M. Perhaps I am wrong, but I feel that he has come to the conclusion that it is only by being rather cruel that he can beat her. I think he is right, of course, because if he is nice to her, she will take advantage of it.

But there was something else. Since about 1905, Lionel had found his wife useful but no longer desirable. There had been Lady Connie, and now there was Mrs Walter Rubens, whom, with Mr Rubens, he intended to install in an apartment at Knole itself. The final scene came in May 1919, and the immediate cause of the breach seemed trivial. Lionel said that the Rubens were coming to stay 'for a day or two'. Lady Sackville retorted that if they came, she would leave. They parted in anger. Vita, who was in the house at the time, went to her mother's room to make peace, but found that she had finally made up her mind. She packed up and left next day, with Lutyens, and went to Brighton, where she lived for the remainder of her life. Feminine jealousy was the reason for her leaving, dignified and complicated by her intense pride.

Part Three

BY V. SACKVILLE-WEST

In April [1918], when we were back in the country, Violet
wrote to ask whether she could come and stay with me for a
fortnight. I was bored by the idea, as I wanted to work, and
I did not know how to entertain her; but I could scarcely
refuse. So she came. We were both bored. My serenity got
on her nerves, and her restlessness got on mine. She went
up to London for the day as often as she could, but she came
back in the evenings because the air-raids frightened her.
She had been here [Long Barn] I think about a week when
everything changed suddenly – changed far more than I
foresaw at the time; changed my life. It was the 18th of
April. An absurd circumstance gave rise to the whole thing;
I had just got clothes like the women-on-the-land were
wearing, and in the unaccustomed freedom of breeches and
gaiters I went into wild spirits; I ran, I shouted, I jumped, I
climbed, I vaulted over gates, I felt like a schoolboy let out
on a holiday; and Violet followed me across fields and
woods with a new meekness, saying very little, but never
taking her eyes off me, and in the midst of my exuberance I
knew that all the old under-current had come back stronger
than ever, and that my old domination over her had never
been diminished. I remember that wild irresponsible day.
It was one of the most vibrant days of my life. As it happened,
Harold was not coming down that night. Violet and I dined
alone together, and then after dinner, we went into my
sitting-room, and for some time made conversation, but
that broke down, and from ten o'clock until two in the
morning – for four hours, or perhaps more – we talked.

Violet had struck the secret of my duality; she attacked
me about it, and I made no attempt to conceal it from her or
from myself. I talked myself out, until I could hear my own
voice getting hoarse, and the fire went out, and all the

servants had long since gone to bed, and there was not a soul in the house except Violet and me, and I talked out the whole of myself with absolute sincerity and pain, and Violet only listened – which was skilful of her. She made no comments and no suggestions until I had finished – until, that is, I had dug into every corner and brought its contents out to the light. I had been vouchsafed insight, as one sometimes is. Then, when I had finished, when I had told her how all the gentleness and all the femininity of me was called out by Harold alone, but how towards everyone else my attitude was completely otherwise – then, still with her infinite skill, she brought me round to my attitude towards herself, as it had always been ever since we were children, and then she told me how she had loved me always, and reminded me of incidents running through years, which I couldn't pretend to have forgotten. She was far more skilful than I. I might have been a boy of eighteen, and she a woman of thirty-five. She was infinitely clever – she didn't scare me, she didn't rush me, she didn't allow me to see where I was going; it was all conscious on her part, but on mine it was simply the drunkenness of liberation – the liberation of half my personality. She opened up to me a new sphere. And for her, of course, it meant the supreme effort to conquer the love of the person she had always wanted, who had always repulsed her (when things seemed to be going too far), out of a sort of fear, and of whom she was madly jealous – a fact I had not realized, so adept was she at concealment, and so obtuse was I at her psychology.

She lay on the sofa, I sat plunged in the armchair; she took my hands, and parted my fingers to count the points as she told me why she loved me. I hadn't dreamt of such an art of love. Such things had been *direct* for me always; I had known no love possessed of that Latin artistry (whether instinctive or acquired). I was infinitely troubled by the softness of her touch and the murmur of her lovely voice. She appealed to my unawakened senses; she wore, I remember, a dress of red velvet, that was exactly the colour of a red rose, and that made of her, with her white skin and the tawny hair, the most seductive being. She pulled me down until I kissed her – I had not done so for many years. Then she was wise enough to get up and go to bed; but I kissed her again in the dark after I had blown out our solitary lamp. She let herself go entirely limp and passive in my arms. (I shudder to think of the experience that lay behind her abandonment.) I can't think I slept all that night – not that much of the night was left.

I don't know how to go on; I keep thinking that Harold, if he ever reads this, will suffer so, but I ask him to remember that he is reading about a *different person* from the one he knew. Also I am not writing this for fun, but for several reasons which I will explain (1) As I started by saying, because I want to tell the *entire* truth. (2) Because I know of no truthful record of such a connection – one that is written, I mean, with no desire to appeal to a vicious taste in any possible readers; and (3) because I hold the conviction that as centuries go on, and the sexes become more nearly merged on account of their increasing resemblances, I hold the conviction that such connections will to a very large extent cease to be regarded as merely unnatural, and will be understood far better, at least in their *intellectual* if not in their physical aspect. (Such is already the case in Russia.) I believe that then the psychology of people like myself will be a matter of interest, and I believe it will be recognized that many more people of my type do exist than under the present-day system of hypocrisy is commonly admitted. I am not saying that such personalities, and the connections which result from them, will not be deplored as they are now; but I do believe that their greater prevalence, and the spirit of candour which one hopes will spread with the progress of the world, will lead to their recognition, if only as an inevitable evil. The first step in the direction of such candour must be taken by the general admission of normal but illicit relations and the facilitation of divorce, or possibly even the reconstruction of the system of marriage. Such advance must necessarily come from the more educated and liberal classes. Since 'unnatural' means 'removed from nature', only the most civilized, because the least natural, class of society can be expected to tolerate such a product of civilization.

I advance, therefore, the perfectly accepted theory that cases of dual personality do exist, in which the feminine and the masculine elements alternately preponderate. I advance this in an impersonal and scientific spirit, and claim that I am qualified to speak with the intimacy a professional scientist could acquire only after years of study and indirect information, because I have the object of study always to hand, in my own heart, and can gauge the exact truthfulness of what my own experience tells me. However frank, people would always keep back something. I can't keep back anything from myself.

29 SEPTEMBER [1920]

I think Violet stayed on for about five days after that. All the time I was in fantastic spirits; and, not realizing how different she was from me in many ways, I made her follow me on wild courses all over the country, and, because she knew she had me only lightly hooked, she obeyed without remonstrance. There was very little between us during those days, only an immense excitement and a growing wish to go away somewhere alone together. This wish was carried out, by arranging to go down to Cornwall for the inside of a week; it was the first time I had ever been away from Harold, and he obviously minded my going.

We went. We met again in London, lunched at a restaurant, and filled with a spirit of adventure took the train for Exeter. On the way there we decided to go on to Plymouth. We arrived at Plymouth to find our luggage had of course been put out at Exeter. We had only an assortment of French poetry with us. We didn't care. We went to the nearest hotel, exultant to feel that nobody in the world knew where we were; at the booking office we were told there was only one room. It seemed like fate. We engaged it. We went and had supper – cider and ham – over which we talked fast and tremulously; she was frightened of me by then.

The next day we went on to Cornwall, where we spent five blissful days; I felt like a person translated, or re-born; it was like beginning one's life again in a different capacity. We were very miserable to come away, but we were constantly together during the whole of the summer months following. Once we went down to Cornwall again for a fortnight. It was a lovely summer. She was radiant. But I never thought it would last; I thought of it as an adventure, an escapade. I kept telling myself she was fickle, that I was the latest toy; she used to assure me of the contrary. She did this with such gravity that sometimes I was almost convinced; but now the years have convinced me thoroughly.

She no longer flirted, and got rid of the last person she had been engaged to, when we went to Cornwall. But there was a man out in France, who used to write to her; she hardly knew him, and I wasn't jealous. He was called Denzil [Denys Trefusis]. She described him to me as fiery – hair like gold wire, blue eyes starting out of his head, and winged nostrils. I listened, not very much interested. I now hate him more than I have ever hated anyone in this life, or am likely to; and there is no injury I would not do him with the utmost pleasure.

Well, the whole of that summer she was mine – a mad and irresponsible summer of moonlight nights, and infinite escapades, and passionate letters, and music, and poetry. Things were not tragic for us then, because although we cared passionately we didn't care deeply – not like now, though it was deepening all the time; no, things weren't tragic, they were rapturous and new, and one side of my life was opened to me, and, to hide nothing, I found things out about my own temperament that I had never been sure of before. Of course I wish now that I had never made those discoveries. One doesn't miss what one doesn't know, and now life is made wretched for me by privations. I often long for ignorance and innocence. I think that if anything happened to bring my friendship with Violet to an end, I might have the strength of mind to blot all that entirely out of my life.

At the end of that summer Denys came home on leave, and I met him. He was very tall and slender, and had the winged look that she had described – I could compare him to many things, to a race-horse, to a Crusader, to a greyhound, to an ascetic in search of the Holy Grail. I liked him then (oh irony!), and he liked me. I could afford to like him, because I was accustomed to Violet's amusements. Even now I see his good points, and they are many; but I see them only by translating myself into an impersonal spectator, and I see them, above all, when Violet makes him suffer. I see that he is a rare, sensitive, proud idealist, and I recognize that through me he has undergone months of suffering, and that his profound love for Violet has been thwarted of its fulfilment. And I am sorry enough for him, at moments, just sorry enough to wish vaguely that he could have cared for someone other than Violet. I see his tragedy – for he is a tragic person. But none of this softens my hatred of him, which is certainly the most violent feeling I have ever experienced. I only hope he returns it in full measure; he has a hundred times more cause to hate me than I to hate him.

He was in London for about ten days. It was already arranged that Violet and I were to go abroad together that winter for a month. There were scenes connected with our going. Violet and I had a row over something; I refused to go abroad; she came round to my house and we made friends again; then I had a dreadful scene with Mother, who was furious at my going; however to make a long story short, we left for Paris at the end of November [1918]. I was to be away until Christmas!

5 OCTOBER [1920]

Paris . . . We were there for about a week, living in a flat that was lent us in the Palais Royal. Even now the intoxication of some of those hours in Paris makes me see confusedly; other hours were, I admit, wretched, because Denys came (the war being just over), and I wanted Violet to myself. But the evenings were ours. I have never told a soul of what I did. I hesitate to write it here, but I must; shirking the truth here would be like cheating oneself playing patience. I dressed as a boy. It was easy, because I could put a khaki bandage round my head, which in those days was so common that it attracted no attention at all. I browned my face and hands. It must have been successful, because no one looked at me at all curiously or suspiciously – never once, out of the many times I did it. My height of course was my great advantage. I looked like a rather untidy young man, a sort of undergraduate, of about nineteen. It was marvellous fun, all the more so because there was always the risk of being found out. Of course it was easy in the Palais Royal because I could let myself in and out by a latchkey; in hotels it was more difficult. I had done it once already in England; that was one of the boldest things I ever did. I will tell about it: I changed in my own house in London late one evening (the darkened streets made me bold), and drove with Violet in a taxi as far as Hyde Park Corner. There I got out. I never felt so free as when I stepped off the kerb, down Piccadilly, alone, and knowing that if I met my own mother face to face she would take no notice of me. I walked along, smoking a cigarette, buying a newspaper off a little boy who called me 'sir', and being accosted now and then by women. In this way I strolled from Hyde Park Corner to Bond Street, where I met Violet and took her in a taxi to Charing Cross. (The extraordinary thing was, how natural it all was for me.) Nobody, even in the glare of the station, glanced at me twice. I had wondered about my voice, but found I could sink it sufficiently. Well, I took Violet as far as Orpington by train, and there we found a lodging house where we could get a room. The landlady was very benevolent and I said Violet was my wife. Next day of course I had to put on the same clothes, although I was a little anxious about the daylight, but again nobody took the slightest notice. We went to Knole!, which was, I think, brave. Here I slipped into the stables, and emerged as myself.

Well, this discovery was too good to be wasted, and in Paris I practically lived in that role. Violet used to call me Julian. We dined together every evening in cafés and restaurants, and went to all the theatres. I shall never forget the evenings when we walked back slowly to our flat through the streets of Paris. I, personally, had never felt so free in¹ my life. Perhaps we have never been so happy since. When we got back to the flat, the windows all used to be open on to the courtyard of the Palais Royal, and the fountains splashed below. It was all incredible – like a fairy-tale.

It couldn't go on for ever, and at the end of the week we left for Monte Carlo, stopping on the way at St Raphael. The weather was perfect, Monte Carlo was perfect, Violet was perfect. Again as Julian, I took her to a dance there, and had a success with a French family, who asked me to come and play with them, and, I think, had an eye on me for their daughter, a plain girl whose head I tried to turn with compliments. They said '*On voit que monsieur est valseur*', and their son, a French officer, asked me about my '*blessure*', and we exchanged war reminiscences.

I didn't go back at Christmas. I didn't go back till nearly the end of March, and everybody was very angry with me, and I felt like suicide after those four wild and radiant months. The whole of that time is dreadful, a nightmare. Harold was in Paris, and I was alone with Mother and Dada, who were both very angry, and wanted me to give Violet up. (There had been a lot of scandal, by then.) On the other hand, Denys had been in England a month, and was agitating to announce his engagement to Violet. Violet was like a hunted creature. I could have prevented the engagement by very few words, but I thought that would be too outrageously selfish; there was Violet's mother, a demon of a woman, longing to get her safely married, and having told all London that she was going to marry Denys. She had already so bad a reputation for breaking engagements that this would have been the last straw. Besides, we both thought she would gain more liberty by marrying, and Denys was prepared to marry her on her own terms – that is, of merely brotherly relations.

I was absolutely miserable. I went to Brighton, alone, in a great empty dust-sheeted house, and all night I used to lie awake, and all day I used to wonder whether I wouldn't throw myself over the cliffs. Everyone questioned me as to why I looked so ill. On the fifth day Violet's engagement was announced in the papers; I bought the paper at Brighton station and nearly fainted as I read it, although I had expected to find it there. Not very long after that I went to Paris, to join Harold, who by that time knew the whole truth of the affair. I was terribly unhappy in Paris. When I came back to London, Violet began to declare that nothing would induce her to go through with the thing, and that I must save her from it by taking her away; in fact I believe she used Denys very largely as a lever to get me to do so. Living permanently with me had become an obsession in her mind. I don't absolutely remember the process in detail, but I know that I ended by consenting. After that we were both less unhappy; I could afford to see her ostensibly engaged to Denys when I knew that instead of marrying him she was coming away with me. I really intended to take her; we had every plan made. We were to go the day before her wedding – not sooner, because we thought we should be overtaken and brought back. It was of course only this looking-forward which enabled me to endure the period of her engagement.

Then about five days before her wedding I suddenly got by the same post three miserable letters from Harold, who had scented danger, because, in order to break it to him more or less gently (and also because I was in a dreadful state of mind myself during all that time), I had been writing him letters full of hints. When I read those letters something snapped in my mind. I saw Harold, all sweet and gentle and dependent upon me. Violet was there. She was terrified. I remember saying, 'It's no good, I can't take you away.' She implored me by everything she could think of, but I was obdurate. We went up to London together, Violet nearly off her head, and me repeating to myself phrases out of Harold's letters to give myself strength. I telegraphed to him to say I was coming to Paris; I had only one idea, to fly as quickly as I could and to put distance between me and temptation. I saw Violet twice more; once in my own house in London; she looked ill and changed; and once in the early morning at her mother's house, where I went to say goodbye to her on my way to the station. There was a dreary slut scrubbing the doorstep, for it was very early, and I stepped in over the soapy pail, and saw Violet in the morning-room. Then I went to Paris, alone. That is one of the worst days I remember. While I was in the train going to Folkestone I still felt I could change my mind and go back if I wanted to, for she had told me she would wait for me up to the very last minute, and would come straight away if I appeared, or telephoned for her. At Folkestone I felt it becoming more irrevocable, and tried to get off the boat again, but they were moving the gangway and pushed me back. I had Harold's letters with me, and kept reading them until they almost lost all sense. The journey had never seemed so slow; it remains with me simply as a nightmare. I couldn't eat, and tears kept running down my face. Harold met me at the Gare du Nord. I said I wanted to go straight back, but he said, 'No, no', and took me out to Versailles in a motor. The next day was Sunday, and he stayed with me all day. By then I had got such a reaction that I was feverishly cheerful, and he might have thought nothing was the matter. I gave him the book I was writing [*Challenge*], because I knew Violet would hate me to do that, as it was all about her. I was awake nearly all that night. Next day was Monday, 16 June [1919]; Harold had to go into Paris, and I sat quite dazed in my room holding my watch in my hand and watching the hands tick past the hour of Violet's wedding. All that time, I knew, she was expecting a pre-arranged message from me, which I never sent.

I was so stunned by all this at the time that I could not

even think; it is only since then that I have realized how every minute has burnt itself into me.

On Tuesday night Violet and Denys came to Paris. On Wednesday I went to see her, at the Ritz. She was wearing clothes I had never seen before, but no wedding ring. I can't describe how terrible it all was – that meeting, and everything. It makes me physically ill to write about it and think about it, and my cheeks are burning. It was dreadful, dreadful. By then I had left Versailles, and was living alone in a small hotel. I took her there, I treated her savagely, I made love to her, I had her, I didn't care, I only wanted to hurt Denys, even though he didn't know of it. I make no excuse, except that I had suffered too much during the past week and was really scarcely responsible. The next day I saw Denys at an awful interview. Violet told him she had meant to run away with me instead of marrying him; she told him she didn't care for him. He got very white, and I thought he was going to faint. I restrained myself from saying much more. I wanted to say, 'Don't you know, you stupid fool, that she is mine in every sense of the word?', but I was afraid that he would kill her if I did that. That night I dined at the Ritz, and from the open window of her room Violet watched me, and Denys sobbed in the room behind her. That day seems to have made a great impression upon him, as he constantly referred to it in his letters to her afterwards.

After that they went away to St Jean de Luz, and I went to Switzerland with Harold, and then back to England alone. After three weeks Violet came back. Things were not quite so bad then. She had a house in Sussex, and Denys only came there for the weekends, and I spent all the rest of the week there. He and I never met, because in Paris he had said to me it must be war or peace. We met once, when he arrived earlier than was expected; I was just leaving, and Violet threw some things into a bag and came with me. I never saw anyone look so angry as he did. He was dead white and his lips were shaking. I tried to make Violet go back, because I thought it was really humiliating the man too much, but she wouldn't. On the whole, however, she was on friendly terms with him, and I am bound to say that he was friendly as an angel to her, and above all he kept the promises he had made, which I think few men would have done. I think on the whole that that was the period when Violet liked him best.

21 OCTOBER [1920]

But she was incessantly trying to get me to come away with her. For a very long time I wouldn't, because I thought she had played me a mean trick over her marriage, and I wouldn't sacrifice Harold to someone whom I thought unworthy. I thought she had played Denys a worse than mean trick too, marrying him like that and accepting his devotion, and deceiving him all the time, and I held myself in almost equal contempt for being a party to the deception, and altogether I was pretty miserable and sickened of the whole thing. My only consolation was that Harold knew all about it; and so did Mother, for I had told her the whole truth about myself the evening I came back from Paris; and if Violet didn't choose to be as frank as I had been, it wasn't really my business. It wasn't my business to look after Denys and see that he wasn't deceived. So I tried to argue, but without bringing myself much satisfaction.

It was not till the end of August that I agreed to go away with Violet. Harold was still in Paris, and I could leave Ben and Nigel at Knole, so it was comparatively easy. We were to go to Greece, because my book was about Greece, and that provided a reason; and there wasn't much opposition except from Mother at the last minute, but I went in spite of that. We started in October – not a very propitious departure, because Violet was so ill that we had to spend the night at Folkestone. Once we got to Paris it was different, and we led the same life as the year before, of cafés, theatres, and 'Julian'. There was no abatement, rather the reverse, in our caring for one another; there was no abatement either in my passion for the freedom of that life. I used to stroll about the boulevards as I had strolled down Piccadilly,

Vita and her mother in 1900, in the first car to be added to the Knole stables.

Knole, near Sevenoaks, Kent, which the Sackvilles had owned since the mid-sixteenth century, and where Vita spent her childhood. Her room was the middle window of the bay on the right, next to the chapel.

Vita's mother, aged thirty-five.

Sir John Murray Scott ('Seery').

Left to right: Harold, Vita, Rosamund Grosvenor and Lord Sackville, on their way to the courts on 4 July 1913 to hear Vita give her evidence in the Scott case.

Violet Trefusis, a portrait by Jacques-Emile Blanche which she gave to Philippe Jullian.

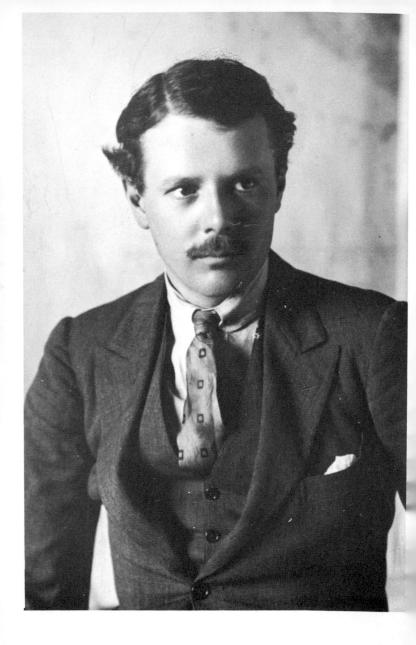

Harold and Vita in 1919.

Geoffrey Scott at the Villa Medici, Florence, in 1923.

Virginia Woolf at Knole in 1928, when she was writing ORLANDO.

Harold and Vita with Ben, left, and Nigel, at Long Barn in the summer of 1929, before Harold's resignation from the Foreign Office.

Sissinghurst from the air. The Priest's House, left, contained the kitchen and dining-room, and in the first floor of the tower was Vita's sitting room.

Vita in her sitting-room at Sissinghurst. The portraits on her writing table are of the Bronte sisters and Virginia Woolf.

I used to sit in cafés drinking coffee, and watching people go by; sometimes I saw people I knew, and wondered what they would think if they knew the truth about the slouching boy with the bandaged head and the rather *voyou* appearance, and if they would recognize the silent and rather scornful woman they had perhaps met at a dinner-party or a dance?

I never appreciated anything so much as living like that with my tongue perpetually in my cheek, and in defiance of every policeman I passed.

We didn't stay very long in Paris, but went on to Monte Carlo en route for Greece. It was divine, returning to Monte Carlo where we had been so happy, and we stood at the open window of our old rooms looking out over the lights and the night and the sea, and really it was one of those moments when one can hardly believe one is alive for sheer happiness. For complicated and merely practical reasons we never went to Greece after all, and although I was disappointed I wasn't heart-broken, because it was delicious at Monte Carlo and Violet so loved being there. A complication arose over Denys announcing his arrival at Cannes. Violet didn't want to go; she wanted to make off, but I thought that if he arrived at Cannes confidently expecting her and then found she had bolted, he might do anything in a fit of despair. So I took her to Cannes, and went on myself to Paris; she was to tell Denys and I Harold, we hated leaving one another, even for (as we thought) a few days. We had then been together two months. But when I got to Paris I found Harold with an abscess in the knee, and he had to be operated, and had a great deal of pain, so of course I dismissed every idea of letting him know anything was amiss. I stayed with him a fortnight (Mother was there too), and then went to England to see after Ben and Nigel. Violet came back to England a day or two later, and Harold was to follow. In the meantime Violet, Denys and I met at a grotesque interview in London, when he asked me how much money I should have to keep Violet and myself on if we went away, so that I felt like a young man wanting to marry Violet and being interviewed by her father. Denys, who had come to see me by his own request, was very quiet and business-like, and looked like death. We did not shake hands. He turned to Violet and asked her if she wished to renounce everything and live with me. She was frightened, and asked for a week. We both agreed to that, and to abide by her decision, and he went away.

On the day that Harold came home Violet tried to rush things. She telephoned to me and told me Denys had said we must be gone by the following evening or not at all. Like a fool I believed her. This entailed telling Harold the moment he arrived. I met him at Victoria; he was very lame and on two sticks; the recollection of him goes through me like a stab even now. We dined at his parents' house, and after dinner I went upstairs to his room and told him I was leaving England with Violet next day. He broke down and cried. Then his mother came in, and I told her what I was going to do, and why; and of course she implored me not to; she had taken off her false hair, and although she didn't realize it a bit, was one of the most pathetic and sincere figures at that moment I have ever beheld. I felt so alien from the whole kindly, law-abiding house; I felt like a pariah, and his mother's tolerance only increased my shame; she didn't push me away, but put both her arms round me and said that nothing I could do was wrong but only mistaken. I felt blackened, and I was so unhappy, and felt my alienation from them and my affinity with Violet so keenly that I only wanted to fly where I would not pollute their purity any longer. I went away to a little hotel, where I had got a bedroom already, and sat up half the night writing letters. The room was full of white lilac that Violet had sent me. Next day I went round to see Harold. He pleaded his illness, and asked me at least to spend the fortnight of his sick leave with him. In order to arrange that, I went to find Violet. I was harsh to her as I never have been to Harold; I absolutely refused to go with her that day. After luncheon I took Harold to see her. He told her that at the end of the fortnight he would let me go with her if I still wanted to. Then he and I went to Knole, and the subject was not renewed between us. I don't know what he thought about during all that fortnight – I don't even know whether he took the danger of my leaving him at all seriously. There were he and I, Ben, Nigel, and Dada; because I was so pre-occupied with my own affairs that I forgot to say that in the May of the previous year Mother had left Dada and Knole, and had never returned. So there were only us five, and to me at least it was pretty fantastic, and not the least fantastic part was the fact that Harold never made any allusion to my going.

On the very last day (it was January), I went up to London with him and still he wouldn't talk about it except when I forced him to. He went back to Paris, and I to Knole, wondering when, if ever, I should see him again. At Knole I made every arrangement, and next day went up to London with my luggage. Violet behaved in an extra-ordinary fashion, which I have never been able to explain. She said she must have that evening in which to talk business with Denys, but I then discovered that she had arranged to go to a play with him. However we agreed to go the next day. I would go back to Knole for the night. Violet came to the station with me, with her luggage, wanting to come away then and there; but she had given her word of honour to Denys that she would be at home that evening, and I said she must wait until next day. She implored me not to make her go back, and I almost had to push her out of my train, where she had forced her way into my carriage. As soon as I got to Knole she rang me up from a hotel in Trafalgar Square, saying that nothing would induce her to return to Denys, but as I couldn't bear to think of her alone in goodness knows what *bouge* of an hotel I persuaded her to go back. She wanted to come to the inn at Sevenoaks. I un-derstood nothing then, and understand no more of it now; but I ought in justice to her always to remember that she tried desperately to get to me that night, and that she had told me for days that she was terrified of Denys breaking his promise.

Next day I called for her in a taxi in London, and we left for Lincoln.

It was bitterly cold, but we were happy in Lincoln. I took her with me to the fen country, which I was writing a book about; that was the object of going to Lincoln. Then we came back to London to the Liverpool Street hotel, and she telephoned for Denys, who came, and she told him she was leaving England next day. I was not present, but I saw him. As we were waiting for a taxi with our luggage in the hall of the hotel next morning, he came in again. He asked her to go and speak to him, but I don't know what he said. He gave her a long letter he had written her, and she gave it to me to read in the taxi on the way to Victoria, and having read it did the only thing I am in the very least proud of: I said I would give her up if she would go back to him. She refused vehemently and said nothing would induce her to, not even my leaving her. I urged her – I really did urge her; he had written her a letter that really touched me. I travelled down to Dover with her, and all the way I tried to persuade her. But she was adamant. The only concession she would make was to start for France by herself, because she seemed to think he would mind that less. So I saw her off, absolutely firm in her resolution, but childishly terrified of the journey on the boat, and I was to join her at Amiens the next day.

I remained alone at Dover, watching her boat out of sight, and then I went to a lodging house and got myself a room for the night. I lunched, and feeling very disconsolate I walked down to the the station and stood staring out over the sea, when turning round I saw Denys coming towards me. He looked very anxious, and wore big motor gloves. He said, 'Where's Violet?', and I answered that she had gone. He wanted to follow her. I took him back to my lodging house, and he paced up and down my bedroom there for the rest of the afternoon. At first I would not tell him where she had gone, but as he threatened to stay with me until I left Dover, saying that he knew I was going to join her, I told him I was leaving next day. He promised not to steal a march on me, and we said we would go together and give her the choice between us. I did not hate him in the least then; I was only very sorry. We stalked out together to the post office, and sent telegrams to Violet's family and to mine, and then parted with extreme grimness. During the evening I got a panic-stricken telegram from Violet, which I telephoned through to Denys.

During the night a gale got up, and as I lay in bed I could feel the whole house – which was old and probably frail – shaking under me. I couldn't sleep. I lay in a sort of waking nightmare; at one moment I was convinced that the house would catch fire, that the wind would blow it instantly into a roar of flame, and that as my bedroom was at the top of the house I would stand no chance of escape. I got up, and went to peer over the well of the staircase; gas-jets burnt on every landing, flickering in the draught, and I thought nothing more likely than that the fire should be started by one of them. I took some aspirin, went back to bed, and presently slept; I dreamt horribly, and woke once with the tears running down my face. I woke constantly, until the dawn began to show behind the blinds, and I got up and dressed.

It poured with rain, and the wind seemed stronger than ever; I went out, and was blown clean across the road. The sea was mud-coloured, and very rough; even the ships in the harbour rocked violently, and outside the harbour the waves flung showers of spray over the piers. I never remember such a gale. I went to the boat to get a cabin, and there encountered Denys on the same errand. The sight of us both bribing for cabins in the purser's office was so comic that it made us less grim to one another. I don't know what Denys thought, but personally I was rather exhilarated at the prospect of steaming out into that storm and insecurity after the nervous and inactive hours I had lived through. Once out there, there could be no weakness or turning back; one might pray for a respite but one would pray in vain; one wouldn't be let off or eased for a minute; one would have to fight one's way to the other side before one could find peace. Very salutary to one who, like me, had been fighting with human affairs that could be shelved or postponed when one felt one's strength failing one! Out there one was given no time to breathe or recover; the ship ran again right down under the grey valleys of waves; water broke all over her, running blackly off her decks; everything was wet, uncomfortable, and quite remorseless; the wind buffeted one, shook and raged at one, noise and tumult bewildered one; one had to think primarily of keeping one's feet and fighting for one's balance; all the hair-splitting niceties that assailed one on dry land, were, thank heaven, in this good rough world of elements entirely out of the question.

Anyhow, that symbolic crossing beat cordiality into Denys and into me, and we joked about sea-sick remedies, and he dared me to smoke, and by the time we drew alongside at Calais he was asking me to lunch with him in the buffet. He then said he would look after my luggage if I would go on and get a table. I went into the buffet, and there Violet rushed up to me, white and shaking and nearly hysterical. I said, 'Good God, why aren't you at Amiens? Denys is with me,' and she said she must get away at once, but at that moment he came in. We realized at once that she was ill and starving (she had had nothing to eat since twenty-four hours or more), so we made her sit down and eat chicken and drink champagne. She said she had left all her possessions at Amiens, but there was no question of taking her there that day, or of anything except putting her to bed and getting a doctor. We all three trundled across Calais in a shut cab, found a hotel, and started putting her to bed; but it was so dirty that we took her to another one. She was completely docile in our hands, and we were too busy getting her hot-water bottles, sponges, soup, and a doctor, to realize the absurdity of the whole thing. What made it more ridiculous, was that Denys and I were given communicating rooms, while she was a little way off. When we had got her safely to bed, we both sat in her room and beamed at her with relief. She had recovered then, and amused us by telling us stories of her adventures on the way to Amiens. We had both been anxious about her, and were conscious of nothing but delight in merely having her safe; at least I know that was what I felt, and I am sure from Denys's manner that he felt the same. The immense problem that the three of us had got to solve, and all the agony and heartburning its solution must entail for one of us – all that was set aside by triple consent. We were all gay, we were even light-hearted, not negatively, but positively; it was as though time were suspended, and all human relations suspended too, except Denys's and my common love for Violet. We had no hostility, I think, towards one another. We were foes who, while our enmity was in abeyance, were prepared to like one another. Our enmity was an extrinsic, not an intrinsic thing. We argued and discussed upon all the detached topics that were as dear to Denys as they were to me; we discussed music, poetry and immortality, and all the while Violet lay like a princess propped up by a pillow in an enormous bed and listened to us with a *narquois* expression of amazed amusement, and frank relish at the farcical turn affairs had taken. This was after dinner. We had all three dined in her bedroom, and Denys and I had, in turn, waited upon her. She was altogether charming and amusing that evening. At the beginning of dinner our lips were twitching with the temptation to *fou rire*, and Violet alone saved the situation. After dinner, as I have said, it was Denys and I who talked. I saw that evening how intelligent he was, how absorbed in un-sordid things; I even saw with regret what good friends we might have been under other circumstances; and above all I was touched by his very naïve joy at having Violet safe, and present; I was touched by this, because I shared and could understand it.

Next morning Violet was better, and we three breakfasted together, and afterwards got a motor to go across to Boulogne. Still the essential subject has not been raised, except as a joke on the previous evening by Denys, who suggested that we should go to Jamaica and grow sugar. We were both grimmer again now, realizing that the discussion could not much longer be put off. The motor drive was a dreary business. It was a black day, and the road lay across bleak country, hedgeless, monotonous country, and once we nearly got smashed up, and Denys said to me, 'Perhaps

that would be the best solution after all.' We lunched at
Boulogne, then took the train to Amiens. We had agreed to
discuss it at Amiens, but in the train in the midst of writing
limericks and jokes, Denys wrote on a piece of paper that he
knew Violet's mind was made up, and that he would leave
us at Amiens and go on himself to Paris, never to see Violet
again. Everything was tragic again in an instant. I was
tongue-tied, and could say nothing. We were then about two
hours' distant from Amiens, and feeling that the journey
would really be too painful, I went away and sat in the
compartment next door. Denys cried the whole way to
Amiens, and at Amiens Violet and I got out, and so did he,
as he had to get into another train; he looked awful as he
went away, and Violet and I were alone.

That was a bad two hours.

We went to the Hôtel du Rhin, where Violet's things already were. I think I was more sorry for Denys than she was.
If he had not made up his mind like that in the train I had
meant to urge her again to go with him, although I knew it
would be quite useless. I could not understand her indifference towards him, for even I was oppressed by the thought
of what he must be suffering, and of what he would suffer
next day on his way through from Paris to London, when
he passed through Amiens knowing that Violet was still
there with me. I was so much disturbed by all this, that I
telephoned myself to Paris to find out if he was all right, and
was told that he had already left for London.

We spent that day looking at the devastations of Amiens
and at the very lovely cathedral. I telegraphed to Harold
where I was in case he should be anxious. (I did not know
that he had had no letters or telegrams from me at all, as he
was by then looking for me in England, having crossed in
the same gale, only in the opposite direction.) Violet and I
meant to motor past Paris (I couldn't bear to go actually
into Paris where I thought Harold was), and then to get a
train and go to Sicily. If she had been well we should probably have done this the same day, but she was still ill from
the effects of her fright and starvation, so we stayed in

Amiens. After dinner that night her father [Colonel George Keppel] arrived at our hotel. He was pompous, theatrical, and unimpressive. He stormed at us, and it was all we could do to keep from laughing. The tiresome part was, that he had wired for Denys, and refused to leave us lest we should slip away.

Now comes the worst part. Denys and Harold arrived together by acroplane early in the morning [14 February 1920]. I was very much astonished, because of course I had thought Harold was in Paris all this time, getting letters more or less all the time from me. He came up to my room, hard on Violet's heels, and told me to pack. Then there was an unpleasant scene. I sat on the windowsill, and Violet stood near me, and we defied first Harold and then Denys, and then both together. This sounds absurd and childish, and so I dare say it was. Denys was the most silent of all; he just looked at Violet while she abused him. The upshot of it was that we refused to leave each other, and Harold said we should be starved out by having someone always with us till we gave way – it was all undignified and noisy to a degree, and I hated it, and was rude to Harold, and he said a lot of silly things that showed him in a wrong light to Violet, and I was sorry about that too. Then Violet and I went together and met Denys in a passage, and he leaned against the wall looking like a stained-glass window saint, very pale and frail, and quite golden-haired, while she said she loathed him, and never to my dying day shall I forget the look on his face. He said nothing at all, but again only stared at her, and if he had slipped down and died at our feet I should scarcely have been surprised.

Then I went upstairs again, to where Harold was sitting in my room, and he tried to talk to me sensibly, and I was less rude, but firm. Then he said a thing which made all the room spin round my head. He said, 'Are you sure Violet is as faithful to you as she makes you believe? Because Denys has told your mother quite a different story.' I thought I should go mad when he said that. I rushed downstairs, and at the foot of the stairs I met Denys. I stopped him and said,

'I am sorry, but I must ask you the most terribly indiscreet question: have you ever been really married to Violet?' He answered, 'I refuse to tell you; that is a matter which lies entirely between Violet and myself.' (I can remember every single one of the words we all spoke at that time.) I caught his sleeve; I kept him; I insisted. I said, 'If you tell me you have, I swear to you I will never set eyes on Violet again.' He hesitated a little at that, and then said again, 'I can't answer'.

I let him go; I went into the restaurant where Violet was sitting at a little table waiting for her breakfast. I went straight up to her and said (as though the words were being put into my lips), 'Why have you not told me you have deceived me with Denys?' I never saw such absolute terror leap into anyone's face. She stammered something. I don't know what. I said, 'You have belonged to him.' She said 'Yes.' I said 'When?', and she said, 'The night before we went to Lincoln.' Yet I knew she was a virgin.

I don't know what I said then; I only know that I broke away from her as she tried to hold me, and said quite wildly that I was going away from her. She followed me, and we got into the sitting-room; somehow the doors and woodwork of the sitting-room were pocked with bullet marks. Denys was there too, and she kept saying all kinds of wild things, like, 'Let me explain', or, 'Tell her it isn't true', and I kept saying only that I wanted to go. I was half mad with pain and not understanding. She was crying, and held me so strongly that I couldn't get away till Denys helped me. Then I rushed upstairs while he held her in the sitting-room, and I packed my things, blind with passion and pain, not able to think or speak, but only thinking that I must get away at all costs. I went downstairs, and found that Harold was with her. Denys was guarding the door. I had just enough sense left to beg him not to leave her for a moment. When Harold came out I went in, although they tried to prevent me. I kissed Violet. Then I went away as quickly as I could, in a motor, with Harold. We had to get his bag out of the aeroplane, and we waited a long time on the aerodrome. That was awful, as Amiens was so near, and we had to drive through Amiens again to get to the station, but I heard Harold tell the chauffeur to avoid the street where the hotel was, and we went by slums. There was no train for Paris for about an hour.

22 OCTOBER [1920]

Harold had lunch in the buffet, but I couldn't eat anything. I saw Violet's father also going to Paris by the same train, so I knew she was alone with Denys, and I hated him then as I never had before. But I couldn't think of anything clearly at all. Harold took me to his hotel in Paris; I didn't care where I went or what became of me. I couldn't cry. I don't remember when we got to Paris, or what I did until it was time for dinner. I had not swallowed a mouthful of food all day, and I was beginning to feel slightly light-headed, so I went down to the restaurant and had some soup. I began to get the usual reaction after one has gone through too much strain, and in consequence I started talking to Harold and making jokes, and all the time a hammer in my head went 'Violet! Violet!', and it was rather like the day before her wedding, when I was at Versailles with Harold.

We hadn't been in the restaurant long when I saw Violet come in. I dropped my knife and fork, and went to her; it was like warmth rushing back when one has been deadly cold, because for the first second I forgot that something much worse than mere distance had parted us. Harold told me to take her upstairs, and I was shut into the sitting-room alone with her. I got behind a chair so that she shouldn't come near me; I was shivering all over. I don't remember our conversation very distinctly; I remember saying over and over again, 'You mustn't ask me to think; I've been stunned and I haven't recovered.' She was very urgent and desperate, and said that if I cast her off altogether she would throw herself into the river, and I am sure this was true. She also said that things had not been quite as I had first believed. She had never belonged to Denys, although

137

matters had gone halfway in that direction. I still kept shivering and saying that I couldn't think. At that moment Harold and Denys came in. She asked Harold to go out, and asked Denys to corroborate what she had just told me. He walked up and down the room and seemed to be struggling with himself. Then he said, 'This must never go further than this room: I promise you that there has never been anything of that kind between Violet and me.' I could have cried with relief, but still it was bad enough that she should have deceived me even to a certain extent – especially on the very night when I was innocently making every disposition to give up everything in the world for her next day. That was what hurt me most bitterly. When I was again alone with her I said I could not bear to see her for at least two months.

Next day she left Paris for the south of France, and every day she used to telephone to me from the various provincial towns where they stopped for the night; and every day her voice was fainter as the distances increased. It must have been a nightmare journey – Denys collapsed and fell ill, but she urged on the motor as though she had been driven by a demon, and it was on that journey, I think, that Denys finally lost what slight hope he still had that she might come to care for him.

I won't say what I went through during the six weeks that passed before I saw her again. I seemed to know every variety of torment – that of longing and aching miserably for someone in whom I had lost faith, that of loving to desperation someone in whose worth I no longer believed. Before, I had always buoyed myself with the thought that although she might hold no other moral precept, at least she was whole-hearted and true where she did love. To this day I don't understand what prompted her to give in, even so little. I think it was a mixture of pity and remorse because she knew she was intending to leave him for good the next day, and she had certainly told me for weeks that he was increasingly importunate. Anyhow I don't want to speculate, it's too painful.

I stayed in Paris for some time, then came back to England. Violet was at Bordighera, living in a villa, while he lived in an hotel. In March I went out to join her at Avignon. I hadn't seen her for six weeks, and I travelled straight through. It ought to have been a good meeting, but it wasn't. Three hours after my arrival we were already quarrelling because she had apparently thought she could persuade me to stay with her for good, and was angry when she found she couldn't. We motored from Avignon to Bordighera, and quarrelled the whole time, and I was acutely wretched. Then at San Remo I lost my head and said I would stay, and for a few days we were happy. We went on to Venice, but I don't really look back on that journey with much pleasure. She was ill, with a touch of jaundice, a most unromantic complaint, and I could do nothing with her, especially after I had gone back on what I had said at San Remo. I admit that I behaved badly over that. One ought not to allow oneself the luxury of losing one's head.

26 OCTOBER [1920]

She wanted to remain abroad by herself, but I couldn't allow that – she is as helpless as a child, and would happily have entrusted her passport, her ticket, her jewels, and her money to the first person who offered to relieve her of the responsibility of looking after them, and anyway I saw the sort of life she would lead, ranging from hotel to hotel, quite irresponsible, and horribly lonely, so I dragged her reluctant person back to England with me.

Then began a very unsatisfactory summer; we each bitterly resented the other living officially with someone else, and our brief and comparatively infrequent meetings were stormy with quarrels, and the additional worry of having no place where we could spend a little time peacefully together got upon our nerves, and that added to the ever-renewed wound of parting, made us the more irritable to one another. I have a confused recollection of hours spent in the writing-rooms of various London hotels, where we would order coffee to enable us to remain there for a little; lingering over lunches in restaurants, because a restaurant, too, was a place where one could sit and talk; going to plays, for that, also, provided chairs and a roof over our heads. All this contributed to our discomfort and dissatisfaction. Sometimes we met in the National Gallery, sometimes in the flat of a friend; but wherever it was, we felt the sordidness and the humiliation of the whole thing, for we cared far too deeply to derive the slightest amusement out of any excitement of danger or difficulty. We wanted far too thirstily to be uninterruptedly together. She very rarely came to stay with me. Whenever she did come, the antagonism between her and the house was ludicrous and painful. The country would seem deliberately to drape itself in tenderness and content, and she, feeling the place to be an enemy, would turn yet more fierce, yet more restless, while I stood bewildered and uncertain between the personification of my two lives. When I passed from one to the other, keeping them separate and apart, I could just keep the thing within my control; but when they met, coincided, and were simultaneous, I found them impossible to reconcile. My house, my garden, my fields, and Harold, those were the silent ones, that pleaded only by their own merits of purity, simplicity, and faith; and on the other hand stood Violet, fighting wildly for me, seeming sometimes harsh and scornful, and riding roughshod over those gentle defenceless things, but sometimes piteous and tragic, reduced to utter dependence upon me, and instantly defeated by any rough word of mine, until I really knew not where the truth lay. No sooner did I hit her where alone she was vulnerable – in her caring for me – than her harshness and pitilessness vanished, leaving her at my mercy. No plea, no exhortation could touch her; I had only one weapon that she understood.

Those were very cruel weeks, when our only preoccupation seemed to be the desire to score off one another, or to catch one another out. The Amiens incident had (not unnaturally) destroyed all trust on my part, and the temporary death of the possibility of our living together drove her into the usual embittering despair. She tried again to get me to go away, by making me believe that Denys threatened to break his promises to her; but I was more wary now, and before making any promise I made her write to Denys, a letter whose reply showed quite clearly that he had not attempted to break his promises nor had any intention of doing so.

There was a strange period when Denys went away by himself to Devonshire, and wrote her daily letters from there telling her that he no longer cared for her. In fact when he returned to London he refused for a long time to set eyes on her, and she spent that time with me, chiefly at Hindhead (Harold was in Paris), but of course when Denys saw her, everything began again. He cared for her too fatally for it to die like that. There was one evening when she was staying with me, and he telephoned to her to come at once; it was after dinner; I got out my car and drove her to the station, but the last train had gone, so I drove her on to London, to the hotel where Denys was waiting for her, and went myself to lodgings I knew of, where I had to have the room of someone who was away; I had nothing whatever with me, and it took me ages to find anywhere to sleep. Of course I dared not go to Mother's house [Hill Street], as it was after midnight.

The whole summer was made up of episodes like that. We weren't happy – how could we be? We were happy once for five days when we went motoring; we went from Hindhead to Rye, and it was a great success, but it didn't make up for all the wretchedness and jealousy and turmoil we went through at other times. Other people were wretched too; I mean Denys, who actually fell into consumption, and had to go and do a cure in Holland, where Violet's mother had a house, and Violet of course had to go too, for five weeks. During the whole of those five weeks we didn't quarrel by letter, and when she came back it was like two flames leaping together. She arrived from Holland at one station, and drove straight across London to another station where I was waiting for her, and we went down to her house in the country where we spent four absolutely unclouded days.

28 MARCH [1921]

I am writing now in the light of later events, and writing in the midst of great unhappiness which I try to conceal from poor Harold, who is an angel upon earth. It is possible that I may never see Violet again, or that I may see her once again before we are parted, or that we may meet in future years as strangers; it is also possible that she may not choose to live; in any case it has come about indirectly owing to me, while I remain safe, secure and undamaged save in my heart. The injustice and misfortune of the whole thing oppresses me hourly; it gives me an awful sense of doom – Violet's doom, which she herself has consistently predicted.

Chronology

1918 18 APRIL: Vita and Violet at Long Barn:
    beginning of their love affair

    28 APRIL: Vita and Violet in Polperro, Cornwall
    till 10 May

    14 MAY: Vita begins writing *Challenge*

    4–23 JULY: Second visit to Polperro

    OCTOBER: 'Julian' in London

    11 NOVEMBER: The Armistice

    26 NOVEMBER: Vita and Violet go to Paris

    6 DECEMBER: Vita and Violet go to Monte Carlo,
    and remain there till mid-March

    CHRISTMAS: Harold at Knole, without Vita

1919 JANUARY: Harold on British staff,
    Paris Peace Conference, till June

    15 MARCH: Vita leaves Monte Carlo, rejoins Harold
    in Paris

    19 MARCH: Vita returns to England

    26 MARCH: Violet's engagement to
    Denys Trefusis announced

    19 MAY: Lady Sackville leaves her husband
    and Knole for ever

    16 JUNE: Violet marries Denys; Vita with Harold
    at Versailles

    19 OCTOBER: Vita and Violet return to Monte Carlo

    18 DECEMBER: Vita joins Harold in Paris:
    operation on his knee

1920 2 JANUARY: Vita returns to Knole

    17 JANUARY: Harold returns on leave; Vita tells him
    she intends to elope with Violet

    18–31 JANUARY: Vita and Harold at Knole

    1 FEBRUARY: Harold returns to Paris, now on
    League of Nations staff

3–8 FEBRUARY : Vita and Violet in Lincoln

9 FEBRUARY : Violet crosses to France, leaving
Vita at Dover

10 FEBRUARY : Vita, with Denys, joins Violet at Calais

11–13 FEBRUARY : Vita and Violet in Amiens

14 FEBRUARY : Crisis day: Harold and Denys fly to
Amiens, and take their wives separately to Paris

16–20 FEBRUARY : Violet and Denys motor to Toulon

28 FEBRUARY : Vita returns to London

20 MARCH : Vita joins Violet in Avignon;
they go to San Remo and Venice

10 APRIL : Vita and Violet return to England

23 JULY : Vita starts writing her autobiography

1921 JANUARY–MARCH : Vita and Violet at Hyères

SUMMER : Gradual end of their love-affair

AUTUMN : Violet returns to Denys

Part Four

BY NIGEL NICOLSON

There is one essential matter which must be explained, and I prefer to do it at the outset. Vita has described her nature quite frankly: she was physically attracted by women more than by men, and remained so all her life. She was by no means frigid, but she came to look upon the 'normal' act of love as bestial and repulsive. In one of her novels, *Grand Canyon* (1942), she gives expression to this feeling: 'One wonders how they ever brought themselves to commit the grotesque act necessary to beget children.' Once, when she was a child, a gamekeeper's son at Sluie had initiated her, by demonstration, into the physical difference between boys and girls, and she had run away, dreadfully shocked. Her mother's fastidiousness and her father's reluctance to discuss any intimate subject with her deepened her sexual isolation. With Rosamund she tumbled into love, and bed, with a sort of innocence. At first it meant little more to her than cuddling a favourite dog or rabbit, and later she regarded the affair as more naughty than perverted, and took great pains to conceal it from her parents and Harold, fearing that exposure would mean the banishment of Rosamund. It was little more than that. She had no concept of any moral distinction between homosexual and heterosexual love, thinking of them both as 'love' without qualification. When she married Harold, she assumed that marriage was love by other means, and for a time it worked.

The very existence of myself and my brother is proof of it, and there is ample evidence in the letters and diaries that for the first few years of their marriage they were sexually compatible. After 1917 it gradually became clear that their mutual enjoyment was on the wane. Lady Sackville refers in her diaries to frank conversations with Vita on the subject ('She remarks about H. being so physically cold').

When I myself married, my father solemnly cautioned me that the physical side of marriage could not be expected to last more than a year or two, and once, in a broadcast, he said, 'Being "in love" lasts but a short time – from three weeks to three years. It has little or nothing to do with the felicity of marriage.' Simultaneously, therefore, and without placing any great strain upon their love for each other, they began to seek their pleasure with people of their own sex, and to Vita at least it seemed quite natural, for she was simply reverting to her other form of 'love'. Marriage and sex could be quite separate things. In a letter which she wrote to Harold in 1960, two years before she died, she said:

When we married, you were older than I was, and far better informed. I was very young, and very innocent, I knew nothing about homosexuality. I didn't even know that such a thing existed, either between men or between women. You should have told me. You should have warned me. You should have told me about yourself, and warned me that the same sort of thing was likely to happen to myself. It would have saved us a lot of trouble and misunderstanding. But I simply didn't know.

When she said 'I simply didn't know', she must have meant that she didn't know how strong and dangerous such passion could be, until Violet replaced Rosamund. Of course she knew that 'such a thing existed', but she did not give it a name, and felt no guilt about it. At the time of her marriage she may have been ignorant that men could feel for other men as she had felt for Rosamund, but when she made this discovery in Harold himself, it did not come as a great shock to her, for she had the romantic notion that it was natural and salutary for 'people' to love each other, and the desire to kiss and touch was simply the physical expression of affection, and it made no difference whether it was affection between people of the same sex or the opposite.

It was fortunate that both were made that way. If only one of them had been, their marriage would probably have collapsed. Violet did not destroy their physical union; she

148

simply provided the alternative for which Vita was unconsciously seeking at the moment when her physical passion for Harold, and his for her, had begun to cool. In Harold's life at that time there was no male Violet, luckily for him, since his love for Vita might not have survived two rivals simultaneously. Before he met Vita he had been half-engaged to another girl, Eileen Wellesley. He was not driven to homosexuality by Vita's temporary desertion of him, because it had always been latent, but his loneliness may have encouraged this tendency to develop, since with his strong sense of duty (much stronger than Vita's) he felt it to be less treacherous to sleep with men in her absence than with other women. When he was left stranded in Paris, he once confessed to Vita that he was 'spending his time with rather low people, the *demi-monde*', and this could have meant young men. When she returned to him, it certainly did. Lady Sackville noted in her diary, 'V. intends to be very platonic with H., who accepts it like a lamb.' They never shared a bedroom after that.

Harold had a series of relationships with men who were his intellectual equals, but the physical element in them was very secondary. He was never a passionate lover. To him sex was as incidental, and about as pleasurable, as a quick visit to a picture-gallery between trains. His a-sexual love for Vita in later life was balanced by affection for his men friends, by some of whom he was temporarily, but never hopelessly, attracted. There was no moment in his life when love for a young man became such an obsession to him that it interfered with his work, and he had no affairs faintly comparable to Vita's. Their behaviour in this respect was a reflection of their very different personalities. His life was too well regulated to be affected by affairs of the heart, while she always allowed herself to be swept away.

He saw Vita as the companion of a lifetime. Each brought as a dowry to the other new interests (he French literature, she English domestic architecture), and others, like gardening, they discovered together. Her rapid output of novels and poetry encouraged him to write too, but never in rivalry, for the style and subjects of their books were quite different, and jealousy was a handicap he never knew. When her first novel *Heritage* was published in 1919 and met with unusual acclaim, he wrote to her:

> Darling, that's done it. The Secretary of the Marlborough Club, otherwise an intelligent and quite polite man, has just said to me: 'By the way, are you any relation to the Nicolson whose wife wrote *Heritage*?' Now look here: I don't mind being Hadji [her use of that name dates from about this time]; or you being Vita; or my being your husband. I might even put up, from foolish people, with being called 'Vita's husband' or 'V. Sackville-West's husband'. I might (though I'm not sure) put up with being 'that fellow Nicolson whose wife wrote *Heritage*'. But I *will not be asked* if I am 'by any chance' (by *any* chance mark you) 'a *relation* of *the*' (just think, *the*) 'Nicolson whose wife etc. . . .'

That's as far as it went. His pleasure at her literary success was unforced. So was his sympathy with the romantic side of her nature. He loved the countryside of England as much as she did, and shared her yearning for places abroad where they might live in solitude and discomfort, on holiday, or even permanently. They discussed seriously buying a ruined castle in the Abruzzi, another on a tiny island called Giglio in the Tyrrhenian Sea, or the island of Herm in the Channel Islands, and at one moment during the height of Vita's affair with Violet all was temporarily forgotten in their excitement at discovering that Bodiam Castle, the shell of which rises so unexpectedly from the hop gardens of the Sussex Weald, was for sale. But for the moment they remained content with Long Barn, the calm centre of their harassed lives, the symbol of their marriage.

Harold soon abandoned any expectation that Vita would take an interest in his career. She was pleased, vaguely, that he was doing well in it, and would pass on to him any compliments which she heard, but scarcely noticed the award to him of the CMG at the early age of thirty-four. Her ignorance of foreign policy was profound, and she made no effort to acquire even a headline-reader's familiarity with the crises that absorbed Harold's every working day, and they would never discuss such things on his return home. To her a new crisis meant simply that he would be kept late at the Foreign Office, or be sent to Lausanne or Prague. The middle stages of the Violet affair coincided with the Paris Peace Conference, when Harold was in almost daily consultation with world-leaders like Lloyd George, Clemenceau, President Wilson and A. J. Balfour, and his narrative of those days in *Peacemaking* makes poignant reading when one knows the concurrent drama of his private life. In his letters to Vita he rarely referred to political events, knowing that they would bore her, but one obtains an occasional glimpse:

> There is such a thunderstorm brewing here against the P.M. [Lloyd George]. It is all about this Asia Minor business, and it is difficult for me to guide my row-boat safely in and out of these fierce Dreadnoughts. Even A.J.B. is angry: 'Those three all-powerful, all-ignorant, men sitting there and partitioning continents with only a child to take notes for them.' I have an uneasy suspicion that by the 'child' he means me. [*17 May 1919*]

> I really feel that this bloody bullying peace is the last flicker of the old tradition, and that we young people will build again. I hope so. [*1 June 1919*]

To these remarks she never responded. When, after the signing of the Treaty of Versailles, Harold was appointed to Sir Eric Drummond's staff on the nascent League of Nations, Vita did not even know what the League of Nations was.

My father's was a gentle nature. If he had fought in the First World War, he might have returned a slightly different man, like Lord Sackville, but his character remained as rounded and supple as a rubber ball. He was in no sense indecisive or frivolous. He took his professions, diplomatic and literary, very seriously, and throughout his life worked extremely hard, but his resilience had a puppyish quality, an innocence and playfulness, and he tended to avoid direct confrontation with unpleasant truths. Just as in his two earliest biographies he toned down the homosexuality of Verlaine and the masochism of Swinburne, so in the crisis of his own life, he hoped that by joking about it he could make it go away. His sense of fun, his literary arabesques, his capacity always to see the other person's point of view, softened his indignation, weakened its impact. A letter of mild reproach to Vita would immediately be followed by another, or by a telegram, telling her to ignore it. He suggested that she might buy Violet as a Christmas present 'a copy of Sappho's poems – I believe you can get one quite cheaply in Tauchnitz'. He invited Violet to stay at his flat when she came to Paris. His distress at Vita's behaviour alternated with disconcerting tolerance; 'come back at once' with 'enjoy yourselves'; hatred of Violet with sympathy for her predicament. He could write to Vita. 'I really don't feel that anything so deep or so compelling as her love for you can be called unnatural or debasing.' So Vita never knew how much he minded, and guessed, correctly, that no matter what she did, she would always be forgiven. She thought his melancholy partly unreal, or at least fitful, knowing that he knew that she would always come back to him in the end. Here is one of his crosser letters:

I have never loved you so much as during the last few months, when you have been slipping away from me. Violet in her clever way has made you think I'm unromantic. Oh dear, how can a middle-aged civil servant [he was only thirty-one!] deal with so subtle an accusation? You see, if I were rich, I could have a valet and an aeroplane and a gardenia tree, and it would all be very Byronic; but not being rich or successful, it is just Poor little Hadji. I wish Violet was dead. She has poisoned one of the most sunny things that ever happened. She is like some fierce orchid – glimmering and stinking in the recesses of life, and throwing cadaverous sweetness on the morning's breeze. Darling, she is evil, and I am not evil.

Oh my darling, what is it that makes you put her above me? We seemed, you and I, to be running hand-in-hand on the Downs, and now I am wandering about alone and rather frightened in the fog. What is it? It may be your bloody Sackville looniness, or it may be a sort of George Sand stunt, or it may be that I am just a bad, futile, unconvincing, unromantic husband. Is it that I am not amorous enough? How can I even think such things! And against me I have that little tortuous, erotic, irresponsible, irremediable and unlimited person. I don't hate her. No more than I should hate opium if you took it. [*10 September 1918*]

He followed this letter by two others written on the same day, telling her to pay no attention to the first, 'as I was writing in a depressed mood. I get cold panics in the rain. I am not in the least depressed really.'

He was nervous lest she should think that he was too safe for her, too domesticated; that she should feel 'your glowing youth is being wasted on a curate'. He realized that she needed a 'safety-valve for your gipsy instincts', the chance to escape occasionally from the 'yoke 'of marriage. This was true. Vita had Wanderlust. The desire to be free from interruption, free from being available, was as real and painful to her as love or jealousy. She longed to be in new places where nobody would ask her to order luncheon or pay house-bills or come to her with a grievance against someone else. In a sense she had at Long Barn everything which her romantic heart desired:

> My Saxon Weald! My cool and candid Weald!
> Dear God! the heart, the very heart, of me
> That plays and strays a truant in strange lands,
> Always returns and finds its inward peace,
> Its swing of truth, its measure of restraint,
> Here among meadows, orchards, lanes and shaws.
>
> [*Orchard and Vineyard* 1921]

But she could rebel against the tameness of the English land-
scape, where the hills are small hills, the lakes small lakes,
and at night the stars are small stars. At these moments the
whole countryside appeared to her a horrible compromise,
like its smug society, and she longed for a crueller climate, a
more tempestuous people, and to shake the mud of 'this
beastly grey place' off her shoes.

In *Heritage* she wrote: 'Serenity of spirit and turbulence
of action should make up the sum of man's life'; and in the
character of the Romany-Kentish Ruth, the heroine of her
novel, she drew her self-portrait. Ruth's lover says: 'What
am I to believe – that she is cursed with a dual nature, the
one coarse and unbridled, the other delicate, conventional,
practical, motherly, refined? Can it be the result of the
separate, antagonistic strains in her blood, the southern and
northern legacy?' Vita believed that the Spanish blood ran
even more strongly in herself than in her mother. She felt it
to be the more vehement strain, the source of her creative
talent; but she also acknowledged that it was wild and irresponsible, and conflicted with the stability which she also
coveted. Violet was the Mediterranean in her; Harold was
Kent. She felt for his patience a mixture of admiration and
pity. She would have liked him to pull her back by the hair,
as a Spaniard would have done, but loved him because he
would not do so. She found in Violet a fascinating and passionate girl who awoke all the adventurousness of her spirit,
her hatred of the *Gemütlichkeit* of domestic life, her fear that
her youth would pass before she had lived it, and lived it
recklessly. 'Women', she wrote to Harold,

> . . . ought to have freedom the same as men when they
> are young. It is a rotten and ridiculous system at present;
> it's simply cheating one of one's youth. It was alright for
> Victorians. But this generation is discarding, and the next
> will have discarded, the chrysalis. Women, like men,
> ought to have their youth so glutted with freedom that
> they hate the very idea of freedom. [*1 June 1919*]

Periodically she felt ashamed of these ideas. When Harold

asked her, 'What has happened to you?', she couldn't honestly answer, or couldn't answer honestly.

Towards us, her children, she felt distant affection. Babies were an interruption, a reminder of duty, of her place in the home, a reminder of their innocence compared to her guilt, a reminder, even, of maternity, which by then, under Violet's influence, she found distasteful. But Violet never shook her love for Harold:

> Oh Hadji, I couldn't ever hurt someone so tender and sensitive and angelic and loving as you are – at least, I know that I have hurt you, but I couldn't do anything to hurt you dreadfully and irrevocably. What a hold you have on my heart; nobody else would ever have such a hold. I love you more than myself, more than life, more than the things I love. I give you everything – like a sacrifice. I love you so much that I don't even resent it. [8 June 1919]

> You have met and understood me on every point. It is this which binds me to you through every storm, and makes you so unalterably the one person whom I trust and love. Oh Hadji, what more can I say? Appearance and facts are so hopelessly at variance, I know. But when I say I love you, it is true, true, true. You are the best and most sacred and the most tender thing in my life. [1 November 1919]

I hear her unmistakable voice across more than fifty years. Before she steeled herself to tell him the whole truth about Violet, the deceit was agony to her. She wrote this scrap of a poem on her return from their first visit to Cornwall:

> I wish you thought me faithless, whilst within
> My heart I knew my innocence from sin.
> This I could bear; I cannot bear that you
> Should think me faithful, when I am untrue.

When she did tell him, she looked to him for strength. The victim of her love-affair must rescue her from it:

Hadji, my darling, there is only one thing left in which I unshakeably believe, and that is your essential goodness. I don't know what is going to happen or become of me, and I simply cling and cling to the thought of you. You are my only anchor. I hate myself. Oh, I do crave to be with you. I feel like a person drowning who knows there is an absolutely safe boat somewhere on the sea, and if they can only keep up their strength long enough, they will reach it. Hadji, I am so frightened sometimes. [*25 May 1919*]

At first she thought the division within herself 'so neat'. She could love Harold, she thought, and be 'in love' with Violet. Then she realized that it was not neat at all, for she was swept away by the current while he remained lonely and miserable on the shore. Such was her shame that she gave up writing to him, telling him in response to his heartbroken reproaches that she felt it 'indecent' to write to him while she was with Violet: a sort of *pudeur* prevented her from mingling her two lives. Harold saved her from isolation by writing every day even when he received no answer, keeping himself and his love for her constantly in her mind, cherishing her when he thought her brutal, trusting her when he knew that she was not to be trusted. It was not 'his' struggle, but 'their' struggle. He never thought of leaving her, only of showing her the way back. Slowly she responded, but the ordeal lasted three whole years.

Violet Keppel suffered from no such conflicts of loyalty. Vita and Harold had five years of married happiness behind them when the affair began. Violet had no equivalent, and when she married it was on the impossible condition that the affair must be allowed to continue. Her marriage was a spur to infidelity; to Vita marriage was its only rein. Acknowledging no responsibilities, Violet was the more reckless of the two, the leader of their truancy, the more insistent that they break all their ties. Hers was the stronger character, and she used her strength not to dominate, but to seduce. She converted Vita's surrender to her into her surrender to

Vita. She was attractive in its most liberal sense: she drew people after her, men and women. Brilliantly gifted, richly subtle, loving everything that was beautiful, she had all the qualities which Vita most admired, and many of which she shared. Violet taunted her, dared her to practise the excesses of their joint imaginations, while remaining submissive to her in love. She was a true rebel, conscious from an early age of the hypocrisy of the society in which she had been brought up, and wished to shock it by openly violating the code which society violated in secret. She would show the world what love really meant, what sacrifice meant, what moral courage meant, and how shallow were the conventions that ruled the boring lives of the great majority. She would break open the cast of respectability which imprisoned her lover. Vita called her Lushka; she called Vita Mitya; their very names must be changed to something more suited to their rebellion:

The fact remains, my beautiful romantic Mitya, our scruples are not worthy of our temperaments. Think of the life we could have together, exclusively devoted to the pursuit of beauty. What have we to do with the vulgar, prattling, sordid life of today? What care we for the practical little *soignées* occupations of our contemporaries? You know we're different – gipsies in a world of landed gentry. They've taken and burnt your caravan, they've thrown away your pots and pans and your half-mended wicker chairs. They've pulled down your sleeves and buttoned up your collar. They've forced you to sleep beneath a self-respecting roof with no chinks to let the stars through. But they haven't caught me yet! Come! Come away! I'll await you at the crossroads. [*15 September 1918*]

Once again you have gone and left me – left me for Brighton, hard, mechanical, vulgar Brighton, and the joys of domesticity, *la rentrée au bercail*, correct comfortable *Familienleben*. My wildlife, devil-may-care Mitya is no longer, Mitya is ousted by Vita, someone gentle, affectionate, considerate, nice, someone inordinately fond of her husband, her mother and her children . . . It is the incongruity of the whole thing that I mind so much. It's like playing the *Walkürenritt* on a piccolo and a penny trumpet; it's like hanging the *Nachtwacht* in a house-keeper's room; it's like a panorama of the Dolomites painted on the back of a menu. And then there's my jealousy. All the time I see how different it might be – the wild hawk and the windswept sky. I can see you splendid and dauntless, a wanderer in strange lands, in the inviolable chastity of inspiration. [*22 October 1918*]

For sixteen nights I have listened expectantly for the opening of my door, for the whispered 'Lushka!' as you entered my room, and tonight I am alone. How can I sleep? This can't go on. We must once and for all take our courage in both hands and go away together. What sort of life *can* we lead now? Yours an infamous and degrading lie to the world, officially bound to someone you don't care for [Harold!], perpetually with that someone. And I, who don't care a damn for anyone but you, am condemned to lead a futile existence. [*22 July 1918*]

Mitya, do you think I am going to waste any more of my precious youth waiting for you to screw up sufficient courage to make a bolt? Not I. Damn the world, and damn the consequences. [*24 August 1918*]

Heaven preserve me from littleness and pleasantness and smoothness. Give me great glaring vices, and great glaring virtues, but preserve me from the neat little neutral ambiguities. Be wicked, be brave, be drunk, be reckless, be dissolute, be despotic, be an anarchist, be a suffragette, be anything you like, but for pity's sake be it to the top of your bent. Live fully, live passionately, live disastrously. Let's live, you and I, as none have ever lived before. [*25 October 1918*]

Her daily letters, unpremeditated, uncorrected, scrawled in pencil with no address and no date (but Vita fortunately kept them in their postmarked envelopes), no beginning (like two intimates telephoning) and no ending except occasionally a huge L splashed across half a page, intoxicated both the writer and the troubled woman to whom they were written. Vita's replies do not survive: they were destroyed by Denys. But one can imagine her response to this insistent drum-beat, for her actions prove it.

The best evidence of Vita's feelings for Violet is contained in her novel *Challenge*, which is dedicated to Violet and is about her. She began it in May 1918 within a few days of their return from Cornwall, and finished it in Monte Carlo in November 1919. It was never published in England. Both Vita's and Violet's parents insisted that it be suppressed (much to Violet's fury), since the portrait of her was too easily recognizable and they feared a scandal. But it was published in the United States in 1924, and I have the manuscript at Sissinghurst. While Vita was writing it, she was living her life on two levels, the actual and the fictional, and as her love for Violet intensified, so did that between Julian and Eve in the novel, with incidents, conversations and letters lifted into the book from reality. Every evening Vita would read to Eve's model the pages which she had written during the day, and Violet loved the game, glorying in the splendidly romantic situations in which she found her fictional self, suggesting extra touches to the drama and her own portrait, and adding from time to time huge chunks of her own invention.

It is the story of Julian, a rich young Englishman living in a small republic on the Greek coast, who incites the offshore islanders of Aphros to revolt, and becomes their illegal president. Eve, his cousin, lovely, wayward, contemptuous of all other suitors, joins him there, and they become happy lovers, until jealousy of Julian's commitment to Aphros leads Eve to betray him. Eve wants Julian absolutely, and to hell with convention and his political beliefs:

I understand love in no other way. I am single-hearted. It is a selfish love. I would die for you gladly, without a thought, but I would sacrifice my claim on you to no one and to nothing. It is all-exorbitant. I make enormous demands. . . . Freedom, Julian, romance! The world before us to roam at will! . . . Tweak the nose of propriety, snatch away the chair on which she would sit down!

Julian is Vita; Aphros stands for Harold, the rival for Eve's love; Eve is Violet to the very inflexions of her voice, the tossing of her dark hair, 'turbulent, defiant, courting danger, and then childishly frightened when danger overtook her, deliciously forthcoming, inventive, enthusiastic, but always at heart withdrawn . . . She lives constantly, from choice, in a storm of trouble and excitement.' 'She was spoilt, exquisite, witty, mettlesome, elusive, tantalizing, a creature that from the age of three has exacted homage and protection.' 'Was Eve to blame for her cruelty, her selfishness, her disregard for truth? Was she, not evil, but only alien, to be forgiven all for the sake of the rarer, more distant, flame? Was the standard of cardinal virtues set by the world the true, the ultimate, standard?'

Julian sprang up. He caught Eve by the wrist.
'Gipsy!'
'Come with me gipsy', she whispered.
Her scented hair blew near him, and her face was upturned, with its soft sweet mouth.
'Away from Aphros?', he said, losing his head.
'All over the world!'
He was suddenly swept away by the full force of her wild irresponsible seduction.
'Anywhere you choose, Eve.'
She triumphed, close to him and wanton.
'You'd sacrifice Aphros to me?'
'Anything you asked for', he said desperately.
She laughed and danced away, stretching out her hands towards him.
'Join in the saraband, Julian?'

'Vagabond', says Julian in another passage: 'Is life to be one long carnival?' 'And one long honesty', Eve replies. 'I'll own you before the world and court its disapproval.'

Challenge is Vita's defence of Violet, and of herself. Vita was twenty-six in 1918, Violet twenty-four. When together their feet barely touched the earth. They were carried on the breezes towards the sun, exalted and ecstatic, breathing the thin air of the empyrean. Violet seemed to her a creature lifted from legend, deriving from no parentage, unprecedented, unmatched, pagan. Their bond of flesh was so compelling that it became almost a spiritual, not a bodily, necessity, exacting so close and tremulous an intimacy that nothing existed for them outside. It swept away their careful training, individual and hereditary, replacing pride by another pride. They loved intensively, with a flame that purged all from their love but the essential, the ideal, passion. Marriage was nothing to this: marriage was only for husbands and wives. When Eve betrays Julian, his final insult is to offer her marriage. And she, proud to the end, drowns herself. It is very reminiscent of *Behind the Mask*, which Vita had written as a child.

Let me retrace the story of the second part of Vita's autobiography, and add some of the detail which she omits.

Her rediscovery of Violet at Long Barn on 18 April 1918 is simply recorded in her diary as 'How eventful a day!', and her account of their subsequent holidays together at Polperro in Cornwall is equally reticent. They went there twice, and the cottage where they stayed belonged to Hugh Walpole, the novelist. One can recover the picture from one of Violet's later letters, when she remembered with anguish how happy they had been:

> That little room of Hugh Walpole, with the sea almost dashing against its walls, the tireless cry of the seagulls, the friendly books, the friendlier atmosphere, the complete liberty of it all. And I was yours, yours to bend over and kiss as the fancy seized you. And sometimes we loved

each other so much that we became inarticulate, content only to probe each other's eyes for the secret that was a secret no longer. [*10 July 1919*]

Lady Sackville was quite without suspicion ('they have gone to see the spring flowers'), and Harold wrote Vita six letters on the day of her departure, the very number suggesting his light-heartedness (at his office, before dinner in his club, during dinner, after dinner and so on), and in one of them he drew caricatures of Violet enjoying the simple life, paddling, shrimping, cooking, hiking, her Mayfair dresses tucked up to her knees. But that both Vita and Harold acknowledged that there was something a little more serious behind it is shown by the letter which she wrote him just before she left:

> Yes, I have got Wanderlust, and got it badly. I want to go away with you, where no one knows where we are, where no letters can follow. It's absurd. I have everything I want – you, two little boys, a cottage, money, flowers, a farm. Of course I know you will trace it to Violet, but you're wrong. I want to be free with you, a thing I can't have until the war is over. In the meantime I feel that people like Violet can save me from a sort of intellectual stagnation, a bovine complacency. So don't be jealous of Violet, darling silly. [*27 April 1918*]

It was on her return that William Strang painted the portrait of Vita which forms the frontispiece of this book, while Violet sat in his studio, never taking her eyes off her. How different it is from the Laszlo! Here no longer is Vita the dusky beauty, but Vita an Elizabethan youth, straight and arrogant, hand on hip, resting a moment, one could imagine, before leaping on to horse or pinnace. 'Julian' began that autumn, in London, Julian the bandaged subaltern, escorting his girl from Ebury Street to Piccadilly and down to Knole, Julian who was living another life of parallel adventure in *Challenge*. 'Julian!' Vita wrote in her diary. 'Oh the wet dark evening at Hyde Park Corner! This is the *best* adventure!' But the risk they took! For though Vita thought her disguise impenetrable, Violet was herself, a fashionable society girl, a little scatter-brained, it was generally considered, but not vicious, and here she was in company with this disreputable boy in public places where at any moment she, or both, might be recognized. On the day when her acknowledged suitor, Denys Trefusis, went back to the front, Violet wrote to Vita:

> You could do anything with me – or rather Julian could. I love Julian overwhelmingly, possessively, exorbitantly. For me he stands for all emancipation, for all liberty, for youth, for ambition, for attainment. He is my ideal. There is nothing he can't do. I am his slave, body and soul. Horrible thought what friends Denys and Julian would be! They would be in open competition for Lushka. [*14 October 1918*]

In fact, they already were. Both were desperately in love with Violet. In character Denys and Vita were not unalike. 'It was impossible to look better bred, more audacious', wrote Violet in *Don't Look Round*. 'Slim and elegant, he could not help dramatizing his appearance. Intrepid, rebellious, he had led an adventurous exciting life, having run away to Russia when he was little more than a schoolboy.' Thence he had returned on the outbreak of war, and was now commanding a company on the western front. Almost contemptuously he won the Military Cross, and when on leave in London disdained the amusements of other men. When Sonia, Violet's sister, first met him, 'He had a Crusader's flare to his nostrils and a cold bright eye which I felt would unhurriedly size up an enemy.' (*Edwardian Daughter*, 1958.) Vita, on the other hand, took to him immediately. 'I can't tell you how much I like him', she wrote to Harold. 'I really, really do. He is very intelligent.' Violet set her cap at him, as she confesses in her book: 'Never did I work so hard. At long last he began to respond, taking care to explain that, like Julian [but this was Julian Grenfell, killed in the war, who had also been in love with her] he was anti-matrimony.' This was the wayward side of Violet's nature: some would call it by a harsher name. She could set out to capture the devotion of a proud man, while her own was utterly committed elsewhere. Denys for her was chiefly important as a baited hook, a rival with whom to tease Vita.

In the autumn of 1918, two weeks after the Armistice, Vita and Violet carried their love to Monte Carlo. It was not easy to obtain permits, and incongruously it was Harold who did so, with his special influence in the Foreign Office. He thought that Vita needed a holiday, and 'it would be nice for you to have Violet as a companion'. He cannot have been ignorant of what was going on, for by this time Lady Sackville was feeding him with her fears, but he thought that their holiday was intended to last no more than a fortnight. It lasted four months. As soon as they reached Paris, Violet began to extract promises from Vita that she would stay with her indefinitely, threatening to kill herself if she did not agree, and these scenes were repeated whenever Vita tried to escape. But Vita did not try very hard. She experienced in Monte Carlo during 'those wild and radiant months' a repetition of the delirious happiness she had enjoyed with Rosamund in Florence, with the added pleasure that their absence was now illicit, and they must fight for their freedom. Very quickly they ran out of money. They moved from the Hôtel Bristol to the less expensive Hôtel Windsor, but found themselves by mid-December quite penniless ('We have fifty centimes between us', says Vita's diary), and they were obliged to pawn their jewels to pay the hotel bill and raise enough money to gamble, successfully, at the Casino. Harold then cabled them £130. They spent their days reading, writing Challenge, playing tennis, walking in the hills and the garden of Château Malet, and their evenings at the tables.

Christmas came, which Harold spent miserably at Knole attempting to reconcile the quarrelling Sackvilles. It was in the New Year that he began to grow really anxious and, for the first time, angry, particularly when Vita's letters almost ceased.

... but I know how extremely busy you are and how much of your time is taken up by playing tennis and talking to your dirty little friend. At times I get racked with longing for you, and the slightest thing gives me a *crise de jalousie*, not jealous of you loving other people (you know I am calm about that), but jealous simply of your *being* with other people *dont je ne connais pas la puissance sur ton coeur*. [*8 January 1919*]

Vita replied with her 'indecent' argument, which was quite hollow, for if it was indecent to write to Harold when she was with Violet, was it not even more indecent to write to Violet when she was with Harold?

It is dreadful of me not to write to you. I know. Don't think it is indifference or forgetfulness – it is not. But as I have so often said to you in talking, it's so difficult for me to write to you when I'm staying with Violet. It seems so *indecent*. Oh do, do, do, try to see it. [*11 January 1919*]

Still she would not come home. It was the moment of her greatest cruelty: it was worse than Amiens, for at Amiens at least she made no attempt to conceal the truth. Harold rented a flat in Paris to entice her back, brought over their silver and a few of her very personal possessions from Long Barn, hired two servants, and told her that all was ready. He expected her on 1 February, for she had given him a promise to come. At the last moment she chucked, pleading that Violet was too ill and miserable to be left alone. He wrote to her what seems to me the most heartrending letter in their entire correspondence – heartrending because it was so generous:

I woke up so happy this morning, thinking you were perhaps at that very moment getting into the train to come to me. And I got out my box and began packing to go round to *our* flat, where we should be together again and sit over the fire. Oh God, how it hurts me to think of it! And then they brought me your two letters – with Violet's. Poor Vita. Poor Hadji. Poor *poor* Violet. After all, what does our pain mean in comparison with hers? It isn't fair that people should be made to suffer so. My disappointment is terrible. I feel quite ill with it. But our love is an eternal thing, like the sea and the wind, and what is time, a few days, a few weeks, to that? And what does all the gossip matter compared to Violet's suffering? I have destroyed her letter. How sad it was. I shall write to her. How I like her to love you like that, darling – it is the best thing she has ever done.

He added a postscript:

Being a woman, you will say when you put this letter down, 'Well, he can't love me very much, as he would have made more fuss'. Good God! More fuss! When my heart feels like a *pêche Melba*. [*1 February 1919*]

Two days later he wrote:

Don't think I shall be permanently miserable. I am only feeling crushed and sore and sad today. But it is childish of course; disappointment is after all a very transitory thing, and nothing compared to poor Violet's tragic and hopeless position. But all the sun has gone out of Paris, which has become a cold grey meaningless city, where there is a Conference going on somewhere. I feel you are slipping away, you who are my anchor, my hope and all my peace. Dearest, you don't know my devotion to you. What you do, can never be wrong. I love you, in a mad way, *because* of it all. [*3 February 1919*]

He should, of course, have taken the night-train to Monte Carlo, if only to quell the mounting gossip. All London, all Paris, hummed with it. Nothing appeared in the news-papers, but both Vita and Violet were well known, and this was something entirely new: the unmentionable had become mentionable. Lady Sackville took perverse pleasure in de-fending her daughter against 'that viper', 'that sexual pervert', writing to all her friends that Vita was bewitched, thus spreading still more widely the news which she was anxious to suppress.

To her the most distressing aspect of the affair was Vita's unnatural neglect of her children. Ben was four and I was two, far too young to know what was happening, and already accustomed to spending most of our time in nurseries. We did not feel neglected. I should like to be able to inject a note of pathos at this point, telling how childish letters brought our mother home, but no such letters were written, because neither of us could write. We stayed at Knole; and when Lady Sackville dismissed our nanny and simultaneously the pipes froze, we were sent to a hotel in Eastbourne, which we enjoyed enormously (so her diary says), then to the Carnocks, Harold's parents, in Cadogan Gardens, and finally to her own house in Brighton, which Lutyens was converting in his lavish style. She now began sending angry telegrams to Monte Carlo: 'Come back immediately; Katie Carnock and I cannot accept any more responsibility for the boys' [26 February 1919]. Vita replied that it was quite impossible for her to return before 15 March, as she couldn't get seats on the train. This did not ring true. But on 15 March she did return, and described to Harold our touching reunion at Brighton:

> Ben plays in the bathroom, and every now and then I hear him say, 'Tell Mummy to come'; and then there is a scuffle and a shuffle, and I hear something come trotting along very busily, like the White Rabbits in *Alice*, muttering to itself, 'Tell Mummy ... Tell Mummy ...', and sticky fingers tug at me to come and see the miraculous Ben. I can't see in Nigel the faintest resemblance to anyone. He calls me 'darling' in an absent-minded way when I ask him if he loves me. He is extremely polite, even to Ben and inanimate objects like wooden ducks and cows, to whom he says, 'Please'. Ben is not the criminal we were led to expect; he is just as sweet as ever. They are both absolute darlings. [*22 March 1919*]

The purpose of this quotation is to show, not what darlings we were, because we were almost certainly not, but how fond, basically, she was of us.

Vita was forgiven by Harold, scolded by her mother, incessantly pursued by Violet. A new twist to their story was now given by Violet's engagement to Denys Trefusis. It was announced on 26 March 1919, and the Keppels and the Sackvilles sighed with relief, brightly telling everyone that there had never been anything to worry about, for Violet was as deeply in love with Denys as Vita was with Harold. If only they could have read Violet's panic-stricken letters:

It is so awful, Mitya, being constantly with someone whom one doesn't care two rows of pins about, a someone incredibly grim and silent, and who I obscurely feel only wants to marry me out of revenge. We are not even on friendly terms. I feel there is something implacable about him. We don't talk to each other, and all the time I think tortured thoughts of you. I ache for you, Mitya. What is going to happen? Are you going to stand by and watch me marry this man? It's unheard of, inconceivable. You are my whole existence. How am I to get out of it? What is this hideous farce I am playing? If we could go away, even for a few months, I could get out of it. It would be so infinitely cleaner if we were to run away openly together. [*21 March 1919*]

I don't care if you were married six times over, or if you had fourteen children. In my desperate plight I have more right to you than anyone on this earth. Last night on the telephone you murmured something about a month. What are you made of, that for a whole month you want me to undergo this hell – this hell of having to endure the caresses of someone I don't love? He is adamant; nothing in this world will move him. He has got the will of a thousand fiends. [*24 March 1919*]

How could Violet, how could Denys, have involved themselves open-eyed in this grotesque engagement? It became all the stranger when Denys agreed that their marriage would be one in name only: they were to have no sexual relations whatever. Here were an intelligent proud man, an intelligent proud woman, binding themselves to a marriage which was nonsensical and humiliating from the start. One must allow for Violet's exaggeration in her letters to Vita: she was, as usual, dramatizing her dilemma. People who saw Violet and Denys together were unanimous in saying that they behaved towards each other with an affection that could not have been simulated. There was also family pressure. Alice Keppel insisted on the marriage taking place, and Violet adored her mother. Denys was genuinely in love with his fiancée: she was the only woman whom he ever loved deeply, and he was prepared to let her have her way. He knew all about Vita, of course, but thought that such an affair could be no more than transient, and that his pledge of continence would sooner or later be broken by Violet herself. There was another possible reason, of which a hint is contained in a letter from Violet to Vita written in 1920. Denys may have been at least partially impotent. Violet had been to see his doctor, and the doctor had told her certain things about him, which, when she repeated them to Denys, drove him to an outburst of anger and despair. It is therefore conceivable, though by no means proved, that at the time of their marriage Denys was not too anxious to have his virility put to the test. But when all these reasons have been given, it remains the most inexplicable part of the whole story:

Denys said that he would marry me on any terms I chose to make, that he would consent to anything rather than that I should leave him. He said that if I left him he would kill himself. He gave me his word of honour as a gentleman that he would never do anything that would displease me – you know in what sense I mean. What am I to do? What can I say? There is only one thing to be done – that is to run away, without saying anything to anyone. Wretched man. He cares for me drivellingly. His one *chic* was that I thought he didn't. [*30 March 1919*]

By running away she meant elopement with Vita:

I want you more than ever for my very, very own, for always. It is quite beyond my control. Mitya, fly, fly, fly – fly with me now, before it is too late. Why don't you assert your claim on me before all the world? You know that you have only to say the word. Away we'd go, away from the pretty countryside with its neat hedges and decent revelry. Away! Away! [*14 April 1919*]

'We were to go the day before her wedding', Vita says in her autobiography. Harold was now too experienced to overlook the danger-signals, but he did not know the worst. Vita had told him jocularly that she would go to the wedding, and when the vicar put the question, 'If any man can show just cause or impediment why these two may not be joined together, let him now speak', she would rise to her feet and say, 'Yes I can.' But it was not quite a joke, as he well knew. He told her that he did not expect her to break entirely with Violet, but he would not allow them to go away together for a long period. She must cease sacrificing her reputation and happiness to a hopeless passion, this 'scarlet adventure'. He understood what a terrible thing it was for Violet to marry a man she didn't love, but Denys might in the end be her salvation, and Vita's, if Violet could grow fond of him. Of the intended elopement Harold had no idea. He was far away, in Vienna, Budapest and Prague, attempting with Smuts to sort out the political confusion of Central Europe, while Violet spent much of her time alone with Vita at Long Barn.

In May *Heritage* was published; and Lady Sackville left Knole. Harold returned to England for a week's leave, and Violet was enraged by his very presence, 'with its Hadji this, and Hadji that, and you and he strolling about arm in arm (God I shall go mad!). And I, who love you, fifty times more than life, am temporarily forgotten, set aside.' She began to load on Denys new conditions, hoping that they would break him, but he agreed to everything, even to Vita sharing their honeymoon, even to the two women remaining abroad together when he returned. Violet felt trapped and desperate.

Reproached by Vita for telling people that she and Denys were in love, she replied: 'Of course I told them that. But why? To camouflage our going away. . . . I hate men. They fill me with revulsion, even quite small boys. Marriage is an institution that ought to be confined to temperamental old maids, weary prostitutes, and royalty.' When she thought that Vita was weakening in her resolution to elope, she wrote: 'They have taken you from me, Mitya. They have taken you back to your old life; you are so prone to take fakes for the genuine article. Julian is dead.'

It was a measure of Vita's fidelity to Harold that Violet became so hysterical with jealousy. But Vita knew that she could only save herself from total surrender by escaping to Paris before the wedding, which was now fixed for 16 June. Her decision to 'betray' Violet was reached quite suddenly. She says that it was due to three letters which she received from Harold at that time. She had written to him:

I can't believe that the wedding will come to pass. A great solemn social set-out wedding – it seems too grotesque. And I know that I could prevent it even now. I can't be in England, *or it will never take place*. I AM ABSOLUTELY TERRIFIED. I tell you about it in order to protect myself from myself. I shall do something quite irretrievable and mad if I stay in England. You are my only anchor, as I told you. If it wasn't for you, I'd give London something to talk about' [*1 June 1919*]

Here is one of his replies:

I know that we will win through this terrible struggle one day – both of us – but I don't want you to come out of it changed and broken, like France out of the war. Darling, when you are in London, you write so cynically, but the babies and the cottage seem to touch the ice to tears, and you write in a way that wrings my heart but doesn't break it. You say it is only for my sake that you are making this sacrifice, and it frightens me that you should say that. Why do you imagine that there is nothing

171

between eloping with Violet and cooking my dinner? Oh what am I to do to win you back to calm and sanity? My love for you is certain; but yours for me sometimes seems so frail that it could snap. [*9 June 1919*]

Vita, rushing to Paris as if to an asylum, sent this reassurance ahead:

Oh my Hadji, of course I love you. I love you unalterably. You don't know how I respond to any letter of yours, *Je m'humilie devant toi*. I have no words for my contempt for myself. Oh Hadji, you will never know. No one on this earth has the power to touch me as you have. One word from you moves me instantly, more than the tears or lamentations of anyone else. You don't know your power over me; you don't know it. [*13 June 1919*]

Violet Keppel and Denys Trefusis were married in London on 16 June 1919, while Vita was at Versailles. Violet wrote her a single line before she left her mother's house for the church: 'You have broken my heart. Goodbye.'

Never can such letters have been written during a honeymoon as those which Violet wrote to Vita:

Oh give me back my freedom! I was so happy once, so irresponsible and free. What am I now? A heartbroken nonentity, a lark with clipped wings. I feel desperate. The rows have begun worse than ever; we have been odious to each other. I can't help it. I don't care. [*23 June 1919*]

And constant telegrams from Saint Jean de Luz: 'Tell Julian Lushka loves him as much as ever.' This was dated 28 June 1919, the day when the Germans signed the Peace Treaty at Versailles.

When they returned to England, Violet and Denys lived at Possingworth Manor, near Uckfield in Sussex, and Violet renewed her efforts to persuade Vita to go away with her. She drew heartbreaking comparisons between Vita's marriage and her own, the one affectionate, intimate, secure, the other stony and sterile. Already she was talking of a legal separation from Denys, who had told her that he no longer cared for her. She gave him all Vita's letters to read so that he should have no illusions left, and then he burnt them. Vita eventually agreed to go abroad with her, and Harold, astonishingly, consented. The excuse was that *Challenge* was about Greece as well as about Violet, and Vita had never seen Greece except from the rail of the steamer when she returned from Constantinople in 1914:

> I suppose that you will want to take Violet with you, so as to get both your copies at the same time? Anyhow, you can't go alone, and Violet is the obvious person, and I trust you, dearest, not to let her make you hate me. You said in the car, 'I shall be beastly to Violet after seeing you', and I feel you are cold to me after seeing Violet. You know that you can rely on my love for you, on my understanding everything. I get an odd vicarious pleasure from feeling that you will be in lovely places. Think of me as someone who enjoys you enjoying yourself. [*9 August 1919*]

They did not leave till 19 October, and travelled slowly, by Paris, Carcassonne and Saint-Raphael, to Monte Carlo. Harold immediately began to regret his tolerance. All his anguish of ten months before revived, particularly when he heard that they were not going to Greece after all, because there was rioting there, and Vita explained that since the Mediterranean was much the same everywhere, she could draw her local colour as easily from one part of it as from another. Fireworks at Monaco one day became fireworks on Aphros the next. They resumed their old life: the Casino, tennis, and (once in Vita's diary) *Thé dansant: Julian.* The same reproaches began to flow to the Hôtel Windsor from Knole and Paris – scandal, neglect of children, cruelty to husbands (now two of them), refusal to answer letters. Vita was at last driven to jolt Harold into accepting the fact that her conduct was more fundamental than mere naughtiness:

> I don't think you realize, except in a very tiny degree, what's going on. I don't think you have taken the thing

seriously. You have looked on it as more or less transitory and 'wild oats' – your own expression. But surely, darling, you can't think that I've gone away from you and risked all that I have risked – your love, Mama's love, Dada's love and my own reputation – for a whim? (I really don't care a damn about the reputation, but I do care about the rest.) Don't you realize that only a very great force could have brought me to risk these things? Many little things have shown me that you don't realize it: 'wild oats'; you talk about my being away as a 'holiday'; you write of V. as 'Mrs Denys Trefusis' – don't you realize that that name is a stab to me every time I hear it, every time I see it on an envelope? Please never refer to it again.

Then, oh Hadji, my darling, darling, Hadji (you *are* my darling Hadji, because if it wasn't for you, I would go off with Violet), there is another thing. You say you want to make love to me again. But that is impossible, darling; there can't be anything of that now – just now, I mean. Oh Hadji, can't you realize a little? I can't put it into words. It isn't that I don't love you. I do. I do.

The whole thing is the most awful tragedy, and I see only too clearly that I was never fit to marry someone so sane, so good, so sweet, so limpid as yourself. I wasn't fair on you. But at least I love you with a love so profound that it can't be uprooted by another love, more tempestuous and altogether on a different plane. [*5 December 1919*]

She rejoined Harold in Paris, alone, on 18 December, to find him laid up with an abscess on his knee, and Lady Sackville spoiled their reunion by her tactless solicitude towards both.

Things then built up quickly towards the climax. Vita was infatuated by Violet. Her audacity gave an impression of strength which she did not really possess. As Harold wrote to her, 'When you fall into Violet's hands, you become like a jellyfish addicted to cocaine.' She succumbed to an overwhelming temptation. She was angelic to Harold during his pain and sickness, but as soon as she and Violet were reunited in London in early January 1920, they began to plot their elopement, this time for good. She told Harold of their intention as soon as he arrived. Her diary adds a few details to her autobiographical account:

17 Jan. 1920. A perfectly awful day. Go round early to Cadogan Gardens and stay until midday talking to H., who refuses to agree to my going off today. Go round to see L. [Lushka]. Lunch with Harold and take him to Grosvenor Street [the Keppels' house] afterwards. L. agrees to wait a fortnight, and then, when H. has gone, she says she won't. Come back to Knole in a state of collapse.

The next fortnight was spent at Knole, and Harold avoided any reference to the crisis, returning to Paris on the first day of February without any idea whether he would ever see his wife again, consoling himself with the thought (as he wrote to her in the London–Dover train), 'I do feel that we are really closer than any two people have ever been, and that whatever happens we shall come together in the end.' At the same moment Vita was writing to him from Knole:

Hadji, Hadji, I feel lonely and frightened. There is so much in my heart, but I don't want to write it, for *à quoi bon*? Only if I were you, and you were me, I would battle so hard to keep you – partly, I dare say, because I would not have the courage and the reserve to do like you and say nothing. Oh Hadji, the reason why I sometimes get you to say things, to say that you would miss me, is that I long for weapons with which to fortify myself; and when you do say things, I treasure them up, and in moments of temptation I say them over to myself, and I think 'Then he *does* mind, he *would* mind, you *are* essential to him. It *is* worth while making yourself unhappy to keep him happy', and so on. But when you say things like you don't miss me in Paris, and that scandal matters, I think, 'Well, if it is only on account of scandal and convenience and above all *because I am his wife* and permanent and legitimate – if it isn't more personal than that, is it worth while my breaking my heart to give him, not positive happiness, but mere negative contentment?'

So I fish and fish, and sometimes I catch a lovely little silver trout, but never the great salmon that lashes and fights and *convinces* me that it is fighting for its life. You just say, 'Darling Vita', and leave me to invent my own conviction out of your silence.

But I *have* struggled. I tore myself away and came to Paris in June last year. And it was only, only, out of love for you; nothing else would have weighed for me the weight of a hair, so you can see how strong a temptation it must have been to sweep everything aside, and you must see also how strongly my love for you must be. My darling, I shall love you till I die; you know I shall. [*1 February 1920*]

It is important to give Harold's reply, lest it be thought that he had grown indifferent.

When did I say that I didn't miss you in Paris? Darling, I miss you all the time. I suppose I said I didn't miss you in Paris as much as in England. If I said that, I meant that it was rather as if I was a soldier and said I didn't miss you in the trenches. It would be quite true – but it wouldn't mean that I didn't *want* you. I want you all the time, wherever I may be – and if I were not to see you again, I cannot contemplate what my attitude would be. It would be despair like one can't imagine – a sort of winter night (Sunday) at Aberdeen, and me in the streets alone with only a temperance hotel to sleep in.

Then about my general attitude. You see, what appeal can I make except that of love? I can't appeal to your pity and it would be doing that if I let you see what I feared and suffered. It would be ridiculous to appeal to your sense of duty – that's all rubbish. So what is there left except to appeal to love – my love for you, and yours for me? How can that appeal be anything but inarticulate?

If you left me, I should never love anyone else. I see that quite clearly. I should be so lonely, so terribly lonely; it would be worse than that, for even my memories would be painful.

And you are all wrong to think that I look on you as my *légitime*. You are not a person with whom one can associate law, order, duty – or any of the conventional ties of life. I never think of you that way – not even from the babies' point of view. I just look on you as the person whom I love best in the world, and without whom life would lose all its light and meaning. [*4 February 1920*]

Then came Lincoln: and after Lincoln, Amiens.

The excuse for Lincoln was Vita's new novel, *The Dragon in Shallow Waters*, which was set in the Fen district, but she also told her mother that she was taking Violet to the country to escape Denys, who was threatening to shoot her. People were now telling each other so many lies to protect themselves that it is difficult to know where the truth lay. Lady Sackville recorded in her diary this account of a conversation with Denys:

5 *Feb. 1920.* I had an extraordinary interview with Denys Trefusis. He hates Vita – that's obvious. He said that he wished he could confront people who gossiped about his marital relations with Violet. He was her husband absolutely. It was a pity she didn't want a child – she hated children – but she was very fond of him physically, and they were very happy together. It was Vita who had taken Violet away from him. He said they were very bad for one another, and that this friendship and their 'jaunts' together ought to be stopped; and that if Violet went away with Vita, she would get bored in three days and would return to him. Violet had been telephoning to him to say how bored she was in Lincoln. What *am* I to believe!

The truth was that Vita and Violet were very happy in Lincoln, staying at the Saracen's Head Hotel. There they made their plan to fly the country together. It was a hot-blooded plot, and Vita was a willing partner to it. Harold was in Paris, busy with the Adriatic question and the fate of war-criminals, quite unconscious, in spite of all Vita's warnings, that the climacteric moment had arrived. He knew that she was in Lincoln, but he did not know that Violet was with her. He thought that Vita was collecting local colour for *Dragon*.

Vita and Violet returned to London, saw Denys, spurned his pitiful entreaties, and travelled together to Dover. Violet crossed that night to France, leaving Vita in Dover to follow next day (an odd concession to respectability), when they were to meet at Amiens, never to return.

Vita has described what happened next. Denys confronted her on the Dover quayside, and she told him what was afoot. She spent that night in the King's Head Hotel, most of it writing letters. First to her mother:

I daren't think what you must imagine now after my telegram. Briefly, I got back from Lincoln late last night, and Violet saw Denys and told him that she wanted to leave him. I travelled with her as far as Dover and honestly did my utmost to persuade her to go back to him, but she wouldn't listen to a word of it. I honestly, honestly tried, though it was torture for me to do so, as you will appreciate better than anybody, knowing as you do all the true facts. Anyway, she left Dover by the afternoon's boat and promised to wire to me. This afternoon, Denys arrived, and he and I are going out to France tomorrow (what a ridiculous journey! I can't help seeing that, even at this moment), and he will ask her to return to him, and I alas! shall again do all I can to make her, but whether I shall succeed, I very much doubt. If she does go with him, I think I shall go to Paris for a few days with Harold. But if she refuses, God alone knows what is going to happen. I have never been in such an extraordinary situation in my life, and the *décor* is all so much in keeping – a howling gale, and my awful little lodging-house room with a single

178

gas-jet – it seems very unreal, and the only real thing is the anguish which he [Denys] and I both endure.

Oh Mama, don't think I am not taking it seriously. I know only too well that somebody's heart will be broken tomorrow night, probably mine – I *hope* mine – and I think of you. [*9 February 1920*]

To Harold she wrote:

Perhaps I shall try to find V. Nothing will induce her to remain with Denys, even if I never saw her again. In the most absolute and sacred confidence, I will tell you why: he is no longer willing to keep his original promises to her. If she goes back to him, I will come to you. I am trying to be good, Hadji, but I want so dreadfully to be with her. Oh, darling, it's awfully lonely here. [*9 February 1920*]

She never said what she would do if Violet refused to go back to Denys. But she hinted at it in another letter to Harold written from Dover early next morning. It was a sort of Will, and she sent it to Paris registered:

I am leaving in an hour's time. It is terribly rough, but the ships are going, so I must go, and if it were not for the ignominy of being seasick, I would not be sorry to have the battle with the sea and wind; it would be rather a relief. Look here, darling, I am sending you a few facts, in case I get drowned or anything.

(1) I send you a blank cheque by which you will be able to get all the money at present in my Sevenoaks bank.

(2) The rates and taxes on Edbury Street are paid up to date.

(3) Then the gardeners' wages at Long Barn are paid, and

(4) The interest on the money which Dada lent us to buy Long Barn has been paid.

I leave you everything: and will you be my literary executor?

I suppose this is sufficiently legal. Perhaps I'd better sign it.

She signed it 'Victoria Nicolson' over a 1½d stamp.

'In case I get drowned or anything.' In case I never come back.

Vita has described in her autobiography what happened on the Channel crossing, and when she and Denys reached Calais. Nothing is suppressed. No doubt is left that at this moment she and Violet had decided to live together for the rest of their lives. They took money with them to buy a house, perhaps in Paris, as she says in her diary, perhaps in Sicily, as she says in her autobiography. Her promise to persuade Violet to return to Denys was qualified by her hope, the virtual certainty, that Violet would refuse. What sort of life did they imagine ahead of them? Was everything to be abandoned – children, homes, husbands? Apparently, yes. They were utterly defiant. By chance the poem which Vita scribbled on the train between Boulogne and Amiens has survived:

> We have cleared the Northern seas
> While you thought we took our ease,
> But you won't be mistaken very long.
> And you think that you will win,
> But that's just where you are wrong, wrong,
>   wrong.
> Here we come swinging along;
> We will lead you such a dance
> If in Belgium or in France,
> But we aren't going to trifle very long.

On arrival at Amiens Denys left them, giving up hope, and the sentry-duty was taken over by George Keppel, Violet's father, with whom the two runaways had a ridiculous and abusive scene. As soon as he had heard of their elopement, he had gone to Scotland Yard and 'had the ports watched to prevent them leaving the country' (Lady Sackville's diary), but his precautions had been singularly ineffective. Now he was in Amiens, totally unable to cope with a situation beyond his comprehension, and he hung around the Hôtel du Rhin for the next two days, while Vita and Violet went sightseeing.

Vita's mother now took the leading role in organizing the salvage operation from Knole and Hill Street. In a perverse way she was enjoying herself: her daughter was proving herself worthy of Pepita.

13 Feb. 1920. Harold has just arrived from Paris. He told me that he had no idea where Vita was. I persuaded him to see Denys, which he agreed willingly to do. He is in a most pitiful state. After he had left me to go to his conference [League of Nations], I went straight to Grosvenor Street and interviewed Denys . . . He is going to fly to Amiens tomorrow morning at 7, and I asked him to take Harold, as he had a two-seater aeroplane, and he most readily said he would. I took him to Cadogan Gardens where he saw Harold and arranged everything with him. Denys was very cool and collected, and fully determined either to bring Violet back or have done with her.

I wish I knew more about that flight. How did Denys happen to have a two-seater aeroplane? From which airfield did they take off? When had he learnt to fly? What plan did they concoct? Lady Sackville's diary, the only source, is silent on these matters:

14 Feb. 1920. No news from Vita. I have been thinking all day of those two husbands flying to Amiens to try and each get his wife back; quite like a sensational novel.

About the events in Amiens itself I should know little but for Vita's full autobiographical record. In her diary for that culminating day, she wrote simply this, enigmatically:

14 Feb. 1920. Denys and Harold arrive together by aeroplane from London, landing at Amiens. Return to Paris with H. In the middle of dinner L. [Lushka] comes in, and I feel restored to life to a certain extent. My God, what a day! I am broken with misery, and if things were as bad as I had at first thought, I should have put an end

to myself. I *had* to go. I should have killed her if I had
stayed an instant longer. I have told her I cannot even see
her for two months. She calls it banishment – it is *not*.
It is simply the impossibility of bringing myself to see her
for the moment.

Let it not be supposed that Violet's infidelity (the infidelity
of sleeping with her husband) had destroyed Vita's love for
her. They felt themselves defeated, not by each other, but by
convention, by 'them', by what today would be called the
Establishment, the Establishment of two such totally un-
Establishment figures as Harold and Denys. In 1921 Vita
published in *Orchard and Vineyard* this remarkable poem,
which must have been written in Paris at that time, for her
fury could not have lasted much longer at that pitch. The
simple change of pronoun does nothing to disguise her
anguish. The poem's very title is *Bitterness*:

Yes, they were kind exceedingly: most mild
Even in indignation, taking by the hand
One that obeyed them mutely, as a child
Submissive to a law he does not understand.
They would not blame the sins his passion wrought.
No, they were tolerant and Christian, saying, 'We
Only deplore . . .', saying they only sought
To help him, strengthen him, to show him love; but he
Following them with unrecalcitrant tread,
Quiet, towards their town of kind captivities,
Having slain rebellion, ever turned his head
Over his shoulder, seeking still with his poor eyes
Her motionless figure on the road. The song
Rang still between them, vibrant bell to answering bell,
Full of young glory as a bugle; strong;
Still brave; now breaking like a seabird's cry 'Farewell!'
And they, they whispered kindly to him, 'Come,
Now we have rescued you. Let your heart heal. Forget!
She was your danger and your evil spirit.' Dumb
He listened, and they thought him acquiescent. Yet
(Knowing the while that they were very kind)

Remembrance clamoured in him: 'She was wild and free,
Magnificent in giving; she was blind
To gain or loss, and loving, loved but me – but me!'

I did not know Violet. I met her only twice, and by then
she had become a galleon, no longer the pinnace of her
youth, and I did not recognize in her sails the high wind
which had swept my mother away, because I did not know
that she had been swept away. I did not know that Vita
could love like this, had loved like this, because she would
not speak of it to her son. Now that I know everything, I love
her more, as my father did, *because* she was tempted, *because*
she was weak. She was a rebel, she was Julian, and though
she did not know it, she fought for more than Violet. She
fought for the right to love, men and women, rejecting the
conventions that marriage demands exclusive love, and that
women should love only men, and men only women. For
this she was prepared to give up everything. Yes, she may
have been mad, as she later said, but it was a magnificent
folly. She may have been cruel, but it was cruelty on a
heroic scale. How can I despise the violence of such passion?
How could she regret that the knowledge of it should now
reach the ears of a new generation, one so infinitely more
compassionate than her own?

So they came from Amiens to Paris – Vita and Harold
to the Alexandre III, Violet and Denys to the Ritz. By
letter and telephone between the two hotels, Violet tried
desperately to correct the misunderstanding which had
lost her Vita, to retrieve her fatal admission, to persuade
her that nothing conclusive had happened the night before
Lincoln:

I am absolutely dazed and sodden with pain. How can
I bear it? My God, and happiness was so near, Mitya.
We'd gone, we'd gone, we'd got away! What is so perfectly awful to me is the feeling that our separation is due
to a misunderstanding. There has never, never, never in
my life been any attempt at what you thought from that

183

person – *never*. Oh Mitya, why didn't you give me time to explain? [*14 February 1920*, Paris]

Next day Denys supported Violet's version of what had occurred. But later he told Harold that he had 'perjured himself' (Lady Sackville's diary), 'which Harold thought meant that he had told some big lie to Vita, such as he was not really married to Violet', to save Violet from suicide. We shall never know the truth – and what does it matter now?

Violet and Denys began their nightmare journey by road from Paris to Toulon, scarcely speaking to each other except to sob out some extra insult, some additional reproach, and at every town Violet stopped the car to telephone or wire to Vita. A shabby packet of French telegram-forms preserves her anguish: '*Viens! Viens!*' 'Oh Julian! Julian!' And each night she wrote agonizing appeals:

> I am going mad with longing for you. Half my day has been spent in a dead stupor, the rest in tears. I have hardly eaten and hardly slept since I left Amiens. . . . I have still got the money, *our* money, that was to have been for our house. [*17 February 1920*]

> He is abhorrent to me with his tears and his servility. I told him that I looked upon him merely as my jailor, and that my one ambition was to get away from him. I hate him. I *hate* him. I have never belonged to him in any sort of way. I look on men as animals. [*18 February 1920*]

At Toulon they met Mrs Keppel, who treated her daughter with great consideration. She did not insist that Violet should remain with Denys, nor that she should break completely with Vita, who could, if she wished, stay with them in England from time to time: and she offered her an allowance of £600 a year. But Violet was untouched by her generosity and soft persuasion. She wrote to Vita, 'I shall bolt from Bordighera at the first opportunity. You must meet me in a town in the south of France.' Vita calmly returned to England, even agreeing, as an act of renunciation more than of contrition, to abandon the publication of *Challenge*, now in proof. She appeared with Harold at the theatre, at lunch parties, without betraying by a word or look what they had both been through, and they were almost the only people not to speak about it.

In March she joined Violet at Avignon. Harold encouraged her to do so, sensing that the crisis was past. But it was not, as her diary shows:

> *San Remo. 23 March 1920.* L. horrible to me all day, and makes me very miserable and exasperated. After dinner I lose my head and say I will stay with her. Paradise restored.

> *Venice. 28 March 1920.* Everything is black again. I have had to tell L. that I should only be followed and brought back. It is horrible. She is in the depths. So am I. I feel the Grand Canal, in spite of slime and floating onions, would be preferable.

On Vita's return in April, the spring held no pleasure for her. 'Beastly grey country', she wrote again. When she tried to pick up the threads of *Dragon*:

> Oh my good Lord, I can't write nowadays. It drives me mad to remember my fluency once upon a time – ten or twelve sheets a day! And as for poetry, it's gone, gone, gone from me. How I envy Harold his clear-cut intellect. I must shake myself out of this inertia. I wish I was poor, dirt-poor, miserably poor, and obliged to work for my daily bread or go without. I need a spur. I am a rotten creature.

She sought distraction and a temporary escape from Violet's incessant letters ('We shall have to fight tooth and nail for each other') by sailing in the Channel on her father's yacht *Sumerun*. The day after her return to Long Barn, she sat down in the corner of a field, opened a notebook, and began writing: '*23 July 1920.* Of course I have no right whatsoever to write down the truth about my life . . .'

The end of the story can be told quite quickly. As Vita was writing her autobiography, the last scenes were being enacted, so that it became in its final stages a running commentary. At the end of 1920 Violet's passionate love for Vita was unabated; Vita's was cooling off, as the opening paragraph of her autobiography shows. Apart from flares and flickers, it never survived the shock of Amiens.

> Oh Mitya [wrote Violet reproachfully], you don't know how unhappy I am. It seems to me that we are completely severed from one another. You do not know what the human heart can suffer. You were so stiff on the telephone: it was the last straw. I mind so much. Think how much happier your life is than mine. If you let me down, what will there be left for me? Do try to love me. This time last year it wasn't necessary for me to say this. It breaks my heart to have to say it now. [*31 December 1920*]

'Think how much happier your life is than mine.' That was the rub. They had been accomplices, yet one returned to warmth and love and freedom, while the other was imprisoned and despised. There was nothing in Violet's life comparable to Harold's love, to Lady Sackville's love. She had no children. She had no other close friends. Denys would have nothing more to do with her; nor, temporarily, would her mother. Every post brought Vita new evidence of her isolation. Let us compare two letters written within less than a week of each other. The first, from Denys to Violet, was forwarded by Violet to Vita, in order, one can only suppose, to arouse her pity:

> It is nothing short of monstrous to start reproaching me with coldness after the absolutely inhuman and abominable way in which you have treated me. You think the hardness and coldness of a few days comparable with the absolute cruelty of a year! I will endure it no longer. *Voici la vraie vérité – je ne t'aime plus.* [*21 July 1920*]

The second was from Vita to Harold:

I have been gardening and writing a lot. I've been alone on purpose. I do love you so – it's like a well, so deep that if you went to the very bottom, you would see stars. [*26 July 1920*]

Harold had won, though he never thought of it as winning. He had been winning not only during the past few months, but during the last ten years.

Of course so great a furnace could not die down at once. In January 1921 Vita yielded to Violet's entreaties sufficiently to go with her to Hyères for six weeks, and on her return she wrote the last paragraph of her autobiography, dated 28 March 1921. She was trying desperately to make the final break.

I am dead with grief [wrote Violet]. I am utterly alone. You cannot want me to suffer so. You had to choose between me and your family and you have chosen them. I do not blame you. But you must not blame me if one day soon I seek for what escape I can find. [*26 March 1921*]

By that she meant suicide. Vita was seriously worried. She felt her responsibility dreadfully, and this was the hold that Violet had on her during the whole of that year. I don't quite know how it ended. Violet's letters tail off in misery and sad recollection. By the end of the following year, 1922, Vita was sure enough of Violet's resilience to be cruel. She wrote to Harold:

Not for a million pounds would I have anything to do with Violet again, even if you didn't exist, you whom I love fundamentally, deeply and incurably. Oh yes, I know you will say, 'But you loved me then, and yet you went off with her'. It's quite true, I did love you, and I always loved you, all through those wretched years, but you know what infatuation is, and I was mad. [*8 December 1922*]

Four years later, she wondered, not for the first time, whether Harold had been too gentle with her:

You have never understood about Violet: a) that it was a madness of which I should never again be capable: a thing like that happens only once, and burns out the capacity for such a feeling: b) that you could at any moment have reclaimed me, but for some extraordinary reason you wouldn't. I used to beg you to: I *wanted* to be rescued, and you wouldn't hold out a hand. I think it was a mixture of pride and mistaken wisdom on your part. I know you thought that if you tried to hold me, I should go altogether. But in this you were wrong, because I never lost sight of how you were the person I loved in the sense of loving for life. Only I suppose you either didn't believe this, or else you wouldn't take the risk. [*17 August 1926*]

'You wouldn't hold out a hand.' Oh, but he did, over and over again. It should be rephrased: 'You wouldn't *seize* my hand'. There she was right. It was pride and mistaken wisdom; and one should add his respect for her, his courtesy towards her. He had given her all his love, and if that was not enough, it would be selfish to hold her back by force.

It may be wondered what Violet had to say about the affair, for several times I have quoted from her autobiography *Don't Look Round*. Simply this:

Marriage can be divided into two categories: those that begin well and end badly, those that begin badly and end well. Mine came (roughly) under the latter heading. It was not until a full year had elapsed that we were able to establish a *modus vivendi*. I hasten to add that the fault was entirely mine. I was spoilt, egocentric, insensitive, odious.

Denys and she came back to each other. 'We both loved poetry, France, travel. We were both Europeans in the fullest sense of the term. The same things made us laugh. We quarrelled a lot, loved not a little. We were more to be envied than pitied.' They had no children, but they lived together in Paris until Denys's early death, from consumption, in 1929. Violet's life was a full one. She became a distinguished novelist, a focus of Parisian intellectual society. She was well known for her wit and verve, retaining until the end of her life something of the grand manner of the Edwardian age. She was always a bird-of-paradise, different, electric, a brilliant, exciting woman, whose character is summed up by her two houses, St Loup near Paris, strong and Gothic, and the Villa Ombrellino outside Florence, dreamy, sunlit, scented and seductive. I remember her springing gait when she visited Sissinghurst, her elegant French clothes, her power. She looked at us with curiosity, which I did not then understand.

She and my mother did not meet or correspond for eighteen years. Then in 1940 another war brought them together again. Violet fled from France to England, and telephoned to Vita. Vita's terror is a measure of how much Violet still meant to her:

> Lushka, what a dangerous person you are. I think we had better not see too much of each other. We loved each other too deeply for too many years, and we must not play with fire again. We both upset the other's life; we mustn't do it again. The very sound of your voice on the telephone upsets me. I loved you and I think you loved me. Quite apart from those three years of our passionate love-affair, we had years and years of childhood love and friendship behind us. This counts. It makes you dear to me. It makes me dear to you. [*31 August 1940*]

Violet came to Sissinghurst. Vita wrote afterwards:

> It is as though great wings are beating round me – the wings of the past. Am I at Carcassonne? At Avignon? In Venice? (How I wish we had been more enterprising, instead of always ending up at Monte Carlo!) Yes, it was good to see you ... The past does not worry me ... I told you I was frightened of you. That's true, I don't want to fall in love with you all over again ... My quiet life is dear to me ... But if you really want me, I will come to you always, anywhere.

Ten years later, in 1950:

The time when we were in love has gone by, leaving us with this queer deep love, that seems to have lasted from the time we were at Duntreath. There is a very odd thing between you and me, Lushka. There always was.

How ignorant we were in our childhood of these events, seeing in our parents' marriage unruffled conjugal bliss. Surely, we thought (if we thought of it at all), it must always have been so. Then one day Lady Sackville told my brother, inexcusably, all about it. I have asked him, as his contribution to this book, to describe what happened. Let Ben take over, and end, the story:

'On leaving Eton and before going up to Oxford, I started a diary. I was eighteen. Out of a back shelf I have pulled my first dusty volume bound in *carta Varese*. I can hardly bear to repeat the flat, childish words I found. We were still children at eighteen in those days, not really interested in the ways of the adult world:

Tuesday, 9 May 1933. Went alone to see G. [Lady Sackville] at White Lodge [Roedean, Brighton]. She was not in a bad temper but merely tired. She spent the whole time saying things about M. and D. [Vita and Harold] to put me against them – stories about M. getting hold of women and D. of men – about Violet Keppel, Virginia Woolf, etc. All quite without foundation. I should have prevented her, but meekly listened. When she had finished, she made me promise not to tell M. and D. Stopped at Hawkhurst golf-club on my way back and saw the pro. Of course told M. and D. all about it. D. said she was like Iago, and that nobody would ever believe that such a person could exist. M. said she was a genius gone wrong. I don't think I understand.

Wednesday, 10 May. After I wrote yesterday's account, M. came to my room at midnight and said that what G. had said was true. My bookshelves have come . . .

and so it continues about my golf-lesson that afternoon, quite unconcerned.

'That was all I felt fit to record. And yet that day forty years ago, at Brighton, and its aftermath over the dinner-table at Sissinghurst, are engraved more sharply on my mind than the events of last week. Nigel had gone back to Eton, and that is why I motored to Brighton alone. I was proud of my first two-seater. My grandmother was then living in a windswept house on the cliffs near Roedean School. She was bedridden and going blind. Every two months or so Nigel (when he was at home) and I would spend the day with her, never knowing what to expect when we drove up: abuse, wild generosity, lunch cooked by the gardener at her bed-side or on an icy terrace at half-past three, a cheque for £10, or dismissal after a five minutes' stormy interview. This day her exhaustion provoked the wicked revelations. Either my mother had "stolen all her jewels" or had not written for six months (she wrote every day): I seek some explana-tion for her outburst. There might easily not have been a cause, real or imaginary, of any kind; she may just have wished to give vent to her misery and loneliness – this blind old woman with a gardener on a cliff, with nothing to keep her alive but dreams of Washington, Knole and her lost beauty – by poisoning an innocent grandson's mind: so she hoped.

'"How ignorant we were in our childhood of these events", my brother has written above. I never thought much about my parents because they were grown-up, but if I thought at all, I had no reason to suspect that their con-jugal bliss had ever been interrupted. Then for hours on end my grandmother disillusioned me by unfolding the whole Violet story; explaining how my mother had been determined to desert her husband and two little boys for a "Circe"; how she would have succeeded, had she (my grandmother) not taken resolute steps at the last moment to prevent it; how a few years later a second woman entered my mother's life and again almost wrecked the marriage. ("That Mrs Woolf, who described in that book [*Orlando*] how your mother *changed her sex!*") Then she turned on her angelic son-in-law, describing the boys he had had in Persia and in all the capitals of Europe. And – shame upon me – I was too indifferent to protest or to leave the house in a huff. After tea she must have thought she had gone too far, because she made me promise not to repeat it. I left unruffled, partly because I did not believe a word of it, partly because I was more worried about next day's mashie shots than about my parents' peccadilloes. I would have made a puzzling patient on the psychiatrist's couch.

'Anyhow, the impulse to repeat it all was stronger than my pledge of secrecy. There were only the three of us at dinner at Sissinghurst that night, my parents and myself. They listened in silence to my adventure, and occasionally cast inquiring glances at each other as the cruel words poured out. It was they who were deeply embarrassed, not I. I took their embarrassment to mean that they were shocked that Lady Sackville should do anything so monstrous. It never occurred to me that they were also distressed that the central drama of their lives was being played back to them by their own adolescent son.

'I can imagine the conversation that took place as they left the dining-room. The truth was out, but which of them was to confirm it? The argument cannot have gone on very long: for my father with his fastidiousness could never have brought himself to enlighten me; by letter, perhaps, but not face to face. It was my mother who sat on my bed at midnight and into the small hours, and I suppose it was the first intimate talk we had ever had. She told me that everything was true except the part about Virginia endangering their marriage, but none of it mattered a hoot because the love they bore each other was so powerful that it could withstand anything.

'My diary entry for Sunday, 28 May, three weeks later, reads:

> Virginia and Leonard came to lunch. Virginia looking well and happy after her Italian trip. She listened to the whole story of my visit to Brighton with her head bowed. Then she said: "The old woman ought to be shot".'

Part Five

BY NIGEL NICOLSON

Vita's elopement with Violet Trefusis was the only crisis of her marriage. Having survived it, she and Harold were able to confront with equanimity many later incidents so menacing that each separately would have broken up most homes. After Amiens there was six foot of water under their keel, and their rowboat, which had nearly foundered on the rocks, slid easily away from the shoals which it touched offshore. Violet had shown them that nothing could destroy their love, which was actually enhanced by the complete freedom they allowed each other. Both were completely frank about it, in speech and letters. It no longer required argument: simply a statement of fact and current emotion. Harold would refer to Vita's affairs as 'your muddles'; she to his as 'your fun'. No jealousy ever arose because of them. On his side there was only a concern that she might break the heart of someone else, a rival or the woman's husband, while she was more amused than worried by what was happening to him, knowing that he had these things under greater control. To scandal, or, in his case, to the law, they seem never to have given a thought, for their intellectual friends were infinitely tolerant, and they did not mind what was said by outsiders.

I suppose [wrote Vita], that ninety-nine people out of a hundred, if they knew all about us, would call us wicked and degenerate. And yet I know with absolute certainty that there are not ninety-nine people out of a hundred less wicked and degenerate than we are. I don't want to boast, but we *are* alive, aren't we? And our two lives, outside and inside, are rich lives – not little meagre repetitions of meagre cerebral habits.

So carefree were they that quite often at Long Barn

Harold's friend and Vita's would join the same weekend party, and the four of them would refer to the situation quite openly. Lady Sackville gives in her diary this instance of their attitude, her embarrassment leading her to an unfortunate choice of phrase:

23 Sept. 1923. Vita is absolutely devoted to Harold, but there is nothing whatever sexual between them, which is strange in such a young and good-looking couple. She is not in the least jealous of him, and willingly allows him to relieve himself with anyone. They both openly said so when I was staying at Long Barn, and Reggie Cooper [who had been at Wellington and in Constantinople with Harold] was there too. It shocked me extremely . . .

To this easy relationship they gave a moral base, both having analytical minds, and they evolved a 'formula' for their marriage, 'a firm, elastic formula', said Harold, 'which makes it so easy for us both to duplicate the joys of love and life, and to halve their miseries'; or, as she put it to him, 'We are sure of each other, in this odd, strange, detached, intimate, mystical relationship which we could never explain to any outside person.' The formula ran something like this: what mattered most was that each should trust the other absolutely. 'Trust', in most marriages, means fidelity. In theirs it meant that they would always tell each other of their infidelities, give warning of approaching emotional crises and, whatever happened, return to their common centre in the end. Vita once put her 'little creed' for Harold in these words: 'To love me whatever I do. To believe my motives are not mean. Not to credit tales without hearing my own version. To give up everything and everybody for me in the last resort.'

The basis of their marriage was mutual respect, enduring love and 'a common sense of values'. There were certain things which were wrong absolutely, and so long as they agreed on what those things were, it did not matter much if in other ways they behaved differently or even (in the eyes of the world) outrageously. When we were children, they divided misdemeanours into 'crimes' and 'sins', and applied the same rule to themselves. Crimes were naughtinesses, for which we were punished. (My mother was not very good at that. When I broke the greenhouse windows, she decided to spank me on the bottom with her hairbrush, but never having done such a thing before, she used the brush bristle side downwards, and the bristles were very soft.) Sins were so dreadful that for them we were never punished at all: their very exposure was enough. There were only three sins: cruelty, dishonesty and indolence. Vita herself had been guilty of the first in 1919–20; never again. Harold was innocent of them all. Their morality can be summed up as consideration for other people, particularly for each other, and the development of their natural talents to the full. It was an amalgam of the Christian virtues and the eighteenth-century concept of the civilized life.

In 1929 they debated on BBC radio their ideas about marriage, and this was their conclusion:

Harold: You agree that a successful marriage is the greatest of human benefits?
Vita: Yes.
Harold: And that it must be based on love guided by intelligence?
Vita: Yes.
Harold: That an essential condition is a common sense of values?
Vita: Yes.
Harold: That the only things that will stave off marital nerves are modesty, good humour and, above all, occupation?
Vita: Yes.
Harold: And give and take?
Vita: And give and take.
Harold: And mutual esteem. I do not believe in the permanence of any love which is based on pity, or the protective or maternal instincts. It must be based on respect.

Vita: Yes, I agree. The caveman plus sweet-little-thing theory is long past. It was a theory insulting to the best qualities of both.

Marriage, they thought (but not for a BBC audience in 1929), was 'unnatural'. Marriage was only tolerable for people of strong character and independent minds if it were regarded as a lifetime association between intimate friends. It was a bond which should last only as long as both wanted it to. (Both, for this reason, were strongly in favour of easier divorce.) But as a happy marriage is 'the greatest of human benefits', husband and wife must strive hard for its success. Each must be subtle enough to mould their characters and behaviour to fit the other's, facet to facet, convex to concave. The husband must develop the feminine side of his nature, the wife her masculine side. He must cultivate the qualities of sympathy and intuition; she those of detachment, reason and decision. He must respond to tears; she must not miss trains.

As it happened, mutual adjustment was particularly easy for them, because they already possessed these qualities. Vita since her childhood had never ceased to regret that she was not born a boy. Once she quoted to Violet Queen Elizabeth's magnificent phrase: 'Had I been crested not cloven, my Lords, you had not treated me thus.' She had inherited from her mother the aristocratic gift of command, and in most things was very competent. Harold had certain feminine attributes, his emotionalism and his clemency. Vita could be intimidating. Harold rarely was, though in social and diplomatic London he was a young lion. If they witnessed together an act of cruelty, such as a Greek peasant beating his donkey, he would express his horror; she would furiously intervene. He obeyed regulations with the instinct of a trained civil servant; she would protest, sometimes refuse. Harold had a sentimental side to his nature which she did not. He could be moved to tears by a film or play in which virtue was triumphant or innocence abused; she took both in her stride. She was the calculated-risk-taker in their marriage, sometimes to the peril of them both. The risks which he took were more spontaneous, motivated by a sudden surge of emotion, personal or political. But because they knew each other so intimately, and loved each other so deeply, neither was in the least irritated by these opposites. Vita would sometimes reproach him for being too mild, 'put upon' she said (for instance by the low fees he accepted from editors), and he would tease her about the odd gaps in her knowledge of the world, like her total inability to understand an Income Tax form or add up a simple column of figures, or her ineradicable belief that rivers like the Nile which flow northwards must run uphill. Never, never did I see them lose their tempers with each other, and my mother told me that it happened only once. The incident was typical. She came into his room one evening and he shouted, 'Go away!' Hurt and angry, she flung at him the lilies which she was carrying, and slammed the door. He rushed after her to explain that his birthday-present – a bust of Hermes – which he was to give her as a surprise next morning was sitting unwrapped on his table.

No reader could fail to be convinced of their love for each other if I were to give constant quotations from their letters spread over fifty years, but such an anthology would become tedious and cloying in the mass. In most marriages love after a time becomes inarticulate, or is expressed in bed. In their marriage there was no bed, but both, being writers, found infinite pleasure in analysing their emotions. As they were so often apart, they wrote to each other thousands of letters, and these formed the warp and woof of their marriage, which was thus continuously enriched and rewoven. She spoke of 'the great triumph of being loved by you', and both were perpetually amazed at their good fortune. Each loved most in the other the qualities which she or he did not possess, Vita his leniency, Harold her wildfire romanticism, and it amused them to identify the differences between them in order to highlight the qualities they shared. They had many common interests: literature and travel and gardening; their children; their cottages; their possessions; their tastes; their plans, past and present; memories of joy and near-disaster. All these things formed a rich *pot-pourri* which never staled. Separation sharpened its tang. Painful as it was, absence often seemed to them like an illusion: the other might be in the next room. 'Your letter', he once wrote to her from Persia, 'makes me feel that distance does not matter, and that loneliness is only a physical, not a spiritual, displacement.' They could reach out over continents to feel the other's pulse and measure it exactly. They could be together at Long Barn for hours, reading in silence, and then both speak suddenly at the same moment. This communion of feeling was as expressive as a touch or glance. If one were ill or in imagined danger (and to Vita every taxi seemed like a threat to him, every aeroplane certain murder), they would undergo tortures of anxiety. Harold would cable across half the world for the latest news of her mild attack of sciatica. A hostile paragraph about him in a newspaper would drive her to despair, while he would worry agonizingly about one of her lectures or broadcasts which alarmed her. It was their constant involvement in each other's lives and feelings, caring without interfering, which was both the expression of their love and its strength. In the middle of the Second War, Vita wrote for Harold a poem which was read by the Poet Laureate, Cecil Day-Lewis, at their joint memorial service in 1968:

> I must not tell how dear you are to me.
> It is unknown, a secret from myself
> Who should know best. I would not if I could
> Expose the meaning of such mystery.

> I loved you then, when love was Spring, and May.
> Eternity is here and now, I thought;
> The pure and perfect moment briefly caught
> As in your arms, but still a child, I lay.

> Loved you when summer deepened into June
> And those fair, wild, ideal dreams of youth
> Were true yet dangerous and half unreal
> As when Endymion kissed the mateless moon.

But now when autumn yellows all the leaves
And thirty seasons mellow our long love,
How rooted, how secure, how strong, how rich,
How full the barn that holds our garnered sheaves!

That poem was written at Sissinghurst; but for fifteen years, until 1930, their home was Long Barn, which lies at the edge of a village known after its district as Sevenoaks Weald, halfway down a slope which overlooks a quilted pattern of fields and small woods. When they first found it in 1915, it was a battered cottage in which Caxton, it was said, had been born, and a coin of 1360 found behind the plaster was evidence of its antiquity. So was its condition. The floors sloped crazily, so that every piece of furniture appeared crippled, and the roof was held together less by construction than by natural angles of repose. In place of a garden there was a chute of rubble and a tangle of briars and nettles. They restored the cottage, transformed it into a house by adding a new wing at a right angle (the timbers coming from an old barn which lay askew at the foot of the hill), and made a garden in a series of lawns and walled terraces, leading by gradual descent from formality to the artlessness of the surrounding copses. Long Barn was not simple. There were seven main bedrooms, four bathrooms and a sitting-room fifty feet long. There were always at least three domestic servants, and two gardeners. It could put up three or four guests at a time, and was sunny, pretty, romantic and comfortable. But it retained an atmosphere of fourteenth-century rusticated innocence. Vita's writing-room was low, timbered and nooked, and her bedroom above it seemed always on the point of collapse, though it still stands. Harold built his own study at the far end of the new wing; and we, the children, were set firmly apart in a cottage higher up the hill. This physical separation of the family was symptomatic of our relationship. Each person must have a room of his own, but there must be, and was, a common room where we could periodically unite.

Ours was a strange childhood, though we did not think it strange. Our parents were remote, and therefore admirable. Every day until we went to school was spent under a nanny's eye. Meals, lessons, walks, the nursery routines of bedding and awakening shaped our lives. The highpoint of each day was our descent to the house at 6 pm, when we would find our mother bent over her current book, patient of our interruption, uncertain how to amuse us. Only now, when I read the manuscript of *The Land*, can I understand what these daily incursions must have cost her in concentration. But she was pleased to see us; we to see her. My father was different. He showed more demonstratively his affection for us, took us for walks, drew funny pictures, read us Conan Doyle, studied us (though we did not notice it), wondering how he could help. Vaguely we realized that we could claim but a small share of their attention; dimly we acknowledged that the part of their lives that we saw was not the whole. What was the whole?

Vita was always in love. I do not know of any moment in her life when she was not longing to see or hear from the only person who could satisfy that longing. One of the first, after Violet, was a man, Geoffrey Scott. He had known Vita since her childhood, and was linked in her mind with its happiest period, for they first met in Italy in 1911. He had a part-time job at the British Embassy in Rome, but was primarily a writer. His first book, *The Architecture of Humanism* (1914), was perhaps the most important contribution to the history of aesthetics since Ruskin. His second, *Portrait of Zélide* (1924), is still regarded as one of the most charming biographies in the language. He was a tall, black-haired, short-sighted, sallow man, rather saturnine in expression and with a strong streak of melancholy, but he was humorous and witty, polished and profound, learned and inspired, critical and affectionate – the finished product of a high civilization. In 1923 he was forty. He was married to Lady Sybil Scott, and they lived in the Villa Medici, at Fiesole, overlooking Florence.

It was there that Vita went to stay in October 1923. Harold, who had been in Greece writing his book on Byron, joined them for a few days, but neither his presence nor Lady Sybil's did anything to deflect Vita's passionate response to Geoffrey's sudden declaration of love. On a hillside, one lovely evening, when the moon rose above a sea of olives, he took her into his arms. I cannot begin to explain (unless it was Florence and the moon) what reawoke her acceptance of a man's physical love which had lain dormant in her for five years, but there is no doubt that for a few weeks at least it was absolute. She returned to England dazed, telling Geoffrey, 'My love and tenderness is a bank on which you can draw unlimited cheques', and her mother that

> . . . she missed Geoffrey atrociously . . . She says he is very passionate. She is sure Harold does not mind, and Sybil says that if it had to be anyone, she's glad it's Vita. Geoffrey has had many affairs, but naturally she and he think that this is *the* one. He knows all about Violet, and says his love will redeem Vita's reputation. [Lady Sackville's diary, *3 November 1923*]

It was true about Sybil. Her marriage had not been going well. She wrote to Vita pathetically, 'You are in love with each other, and he is not in love with me. He must feel free, and I don't ever want to come between you.' She gave Geoffrey an 'unwedding' ring to symbolize her renunciation. Lady Sackville was also right about Harold. He knew about the affair from the start, and in a curious way was rather pleased. He had an inner conviction that this was not a serious threat. He admired Geoffrey, liked him, and found him refreshingly different from Violet. If Violet was clever, Geoffrey was intelligent; in place of Violet's hypnotic influence, here was Geoffrey's candid adoration. He enriched Vita's mind instead of confusing it. His letters were like an invigorating shower after a torrid breeze. He discovered quickly the importance to her of Harold and Long Barn, and never challenged it. He touched her most sensitive chords, echoing her love of Italy, honouring her writing by his gentle criticism:

> You are a poet, not a poetess. An unforgivable word always, but applied to you, odious. My dear, keep your *apartness*. There is real aloofness in your best work, the inward and solitary-minded quality which at all costs you mustn't smear. I'm terribly ambitious for you. Oh the joy of talking the same language as you, of being made the same way! [*23 November 1923*]

Vita was beginning to write *The Land*; Geoffrey was writing *Zélide*. Each was writing for the other, and as they completed key passages, they paid each other the supreme compliment of sending their manuscripts for the other's comment. He nursed her poem with vicarious pride as carefully as he cherished her:

> I feel the Georgics is our poem [the title *The Land* was chosen only at the last moment], just as *Zélide* is our book. 'The little sullen moons of mistletoe' and 'Clean as a cat in pattens, smelling good' – oh Vita I could hug you! Bless you for having it in you to write like that, for being so stored with memories, older than any personal memories ... Be very shy of moralizing your subject. Agriculture and husbandry ought to be sparingly moralized; it tends to weaken the impression. What you must never do is to pat your peasantry approvingly on the back. The bumpkin gesture – each muddy foot – must be placed inevitably and precisely right. No matter how heavy, how slow, how 'dull', one must never feel that you have relaxed one inch of your severity ... I worry about your work as if I had your gifts and the problem was my own. [*10 November 1924*]

What excellent advice, how tenderly conveyed! But behind it was a love which was strengthening in Geoffrey, as it weakened in Vita. Some months after her return to England she appeared aghast at the salmon she had hooked. In absence she could not match his mood, needing always

(except with Harold and Virginia) the presence of the be-
loved to evoke her response. While Geoffrey wrote to her
that their love was eternal, she in her replies became disconcertingly restrained. He could not fail to notice it. It was
only when he returned to England early in 1924 that he was
able to reassure himself temporarily that nothing had
changed. They met constantly, stayed some weekends at
Knole, others, with Harold, at Long Barn, and they shared
a room at Hill Street. Lady Sackville watched them with
protective eyes: '22 Jan. 1924. V. went again to Knole with
G.S. I am so afraid of gossip.' '24 Jan. Went to Hill Street,
and found V. and G.S. together. She looked very shy. I am
shocked that he shows so much proprietorship over her.'
'4 Feb. Went to Long Barn. I fear it is much more than a
flirtation. People are talking unkindly.' '16 Feb. Everybody
calls him a bounder.' Nobody was less of a bounder than
Geoffrey Scott. He felt for Vita something greater than
infatuation but never nurtured the hope that he might wrest
her from Harold. His love was doomed, because of Harold,
because of her restraint, because of his own chivalry. It was
a proposition more than a proposal. When he returned to
Florence in mid-Feburary, he found a loving letter from her,
written while he was still at her side. Then again her letters
began to cool, and one can sense his anxiety in his attempts
to fan her love into a fiercer flame:

> Now that we have found each other, for God's sake let
> us keep it and make it a kind of dazzling light ahead. Our
> love has to be 'domesticated' and made reasonable and
> commonsensical – against its very nature – and yet I
> don't have the reward of a shared life, as the dear reason-
> able Harold gets. You will help, won't you? It is going to
> be difficult to keep the edge of it firm, with blunting time
> and absence rusting it. Keep the feeling, the knowledge,
> that I would at any moment chuck everything else in my
> life for you, if that would help. [11 March 1924]

> You won't let difficulties come between us, will you?
> They do so easily, and love gets cold-shouldered by

degrees by the presence of other people who are *always* against it. You see, you are very conciliatory by nature. I think of you always as you were the first time you said ... [the rest of the sentence is heavily scored out by Vita]. So long as you really, unalterably, unhesitatingly feel that, I'm ready to be as good as a lamb. But remember the pressure to divide will be steady and persistent. However 'good' I am, I shall never be allowed to share your life in any real sense, like Harold ... You and I mean the same thing by love, something absolute and final, and if needs be, merciless. You know you want it that way; you want me to love you like that. [*16 March 1924*]

The trouble was that she didn't. Her affair with Geoffrey Scott lasted for a few days, followed by another period of a few weeks. It spurted, but never flowed. Her moderate love was killed by his greater love. It became for her something too demanding, too disruptive, and once she had begun to feel like that, her distaste gathered into disgust. If only he would stick to literature!

They met several times again, in England and in Italy, and she tried to calm his ardour by degrees, using Harold (who was half-amused) as her lightning-conductor. Long Barn was the scene of Geoffrey's final despair. He would look across the angle formed by the two wings and see the neighbouring lights of her bedroom and Harold's, symbols of their intimacy and his exclusion. I just remember him. I was seven. I thought him rather fierce, but this must be because I once burst into his bedroom by mistake when he was changing for dinner, and he was naked. He was very angry. How little did I realize that my trivial existence was a reminder of his hopelessness. He slowly gave up. In 1927 he and Sybil were divorced, and, loveless, he spent the last years of his life in New York, where he edited Boswell's papers. There he died in 1929, aged forty-six.

Vita had not been kind to Geoffrey – she had smashed his life and finally wrecked his marriage – but what part does kindness play in love? For him their pledge had been cut in granite; for her it had been written in chalk on slate. Her love for Geoffrey had been an experiment in love, an experiment which failed. It failed because he was a man, because he was an impossible rival to Harold, and because he was replaced by someone to whom he could not hold a candle, a woman, a genius, Virginia Woolf.

Virginia was the most remarkably human being I have ever known. She could attract, yet she could also remove to a distance. She did neither deliberately, for she was without conceit, being on the contrary anxious to please, anxious to discover (she was very inquisitive) and touchingly sensitive to praise or reproach, but one was aware of her occasional withdrawal, and never quite knew how deep to penetrate, how shallow should be one's own response. We were children then, and the uncomprehending casualness of childhood soon mellowed our relationship with her. To us she was not Virginia who had been mad and could go mad again, nor Virginia Woolf who had uncovered a whole new seam of literary perception. She was Virginia. Virginia who was fun, Virginia who was easy, who asked us questions about school and holidays (gathering copy, though we did not know it), and who floated in and out of our lives like a godmother. 'Virginia's coming to stay.' 'Oh good!' We knew that she would notice us, that there would come a moment when she would pay no attention to my mother ('Vita, go away! Can't you see I'm talking to Ben and Nigel'), and then she spoke to us about our simple lives, handing back to us as diamonds what we had given her as lumps of coal. I think of her as delicate, but in the cobweb sense, not the medical. I think of her as an autumn, indoor, person, though she loved the summer and the Downs, stretching tapered fingers towards the fire, elaborating her fantasies, provocative, delicious, matching gestures to her words, drawing back her long hair from her forehead as a new fantasy occurred to her, smiling often, laughing seldom, and with never a giggle in her laugh. I think of her at Knole, leaning S-curved against a doorway, finger to her chin, contemplative, amused. She instinctively assumed attitudes expressive of her moods.

Vita first met Virginia on 14 December 1922, with Clive Bell; and four days later she invited her to dine at Ebury Street, with Clive and Desmond MacCarthy. She wrote to Harold (who was with Curzon at Lausanne):

> I simply adore Virginia Woolf, and so would you. You would fall quite flat before her charm and personality. It was a good party. They asked a lot about your *Tennyson*. Mrs Woolf is so simple; she does give the impression of something big. She is utterly unaffected: there are no outward adornments – she dresses quite atrociously. At first you think she is plain; then a sort of spiritual beauty imposes itself on you, and you find a fascination in watching her. She was smarter last night; that is to say, the woollen orange stockings were replaced by yellow silk ones, but she still wore the pumps. She is both detached and human, silent till she wants to say something, and then says it supremely well. She is quite old [forty]. I've rarely taken such a fancy to anyone, and I think she likes me. At least, she's asked me to Richmond where she lives. Darling, I have quite lost my heart. [*19 December 1922*]

The growth of their intimacy is recorded in Vita's diary:

> *22 Feb. 1923.* Dined with Virginia at Richmond. She is as delicious as ever. How right she is when she says that love makes everyone a bore, but the excitement of life lies in 'the little moves' nearer to people. But perhaps she feels this because she is an experimentalist in humanity, and has had no *grande passion* in her life.

> *19 March 1923.* Lunched with Virginia in Tavistock Square, where she has just arrived. The first time that I have been alone with her for long. Went on to see Mama, my head swimming with Virginia.

Then there was a pause. They wrote to each other a lot, saw each other quite often, but Virginia grew alarmed to think where all this was leading. As Quentin Bell puts it from Virginia's corner: 'She probably became aware of Vita's feelings and perhaps acquired an inkling of her own at that first encounter: she felt shy, almost virginal, in Vita's company, and she was, I suspect, roused to a sense of danger.' There was also Harold, and Leonard, and from October 1923, Geoffrey Scott. Vita was too well aware of the delicacy of Virginia's mind and body to press her strongly, and their friendship developed affectionately, starting with small tendernesses by the fireside (Vita liked to sit on the floor by Virginia's chair) which gradually, so gradually, led to something a little more.

Virginia's influence on her is shown best, I think, in Vita's short novel *Seducers in Ecuador*, which she wrote for the Hogarth Press in 1924, for it is the most imaginative of all her fiction, as if she had wanted to write something 'worthy' of Virginia, in Virginia's allusive style, tuned to a new vibrancy by the thought of so critical an editor whom she was meeting almost every day. The effect of Vita on Virginia is all contained in *Orlando*, the longest and most charming love-letter in literature, in which she explores Vita, weaves her in and out of the centuries, tosses her from one sex to the other, plays with her, dresses her in furs, lace and emeralds, teases her, flirts with her, drops a veil of mist around her, and ends by photographing her in the mud at Long Barn, with dogs, awaiting Virginia's arrival next day.

Her friendship was the most important fact in Vita's life, except Harold, just as Vita's was the most important in Virginia's, except Leonard, and perhaps her sister Vanessa. If one seeks a parallel to Vita–Harold one can find it only in Virginia–Leonard, although one must admit differences, for Virginia was sexually frigid and Leonard was not homosexual. Their marriages were alike in the freedom they allowed each other, in the invincibility of their love, in its intellectual, spiritual and non-physical base, in the eagerness of all four of them to savour life, challenge convention, work hard, play dangerously with the emotions – and in their solicitude for each other. How well do I recall Leonard's look as he watched Virginia across a sitting-room to see that she did not grow tired or over-excited, caring for her much as Joseph must have cared for Mary, for their relationship was biblical. There was no jealousy between the Woolfs and the Nicolsons, because they had arrived independently at the same definition of 'trust'. Leonard, perhaps, was a little less tolerant than Harold, fearing not that Virginia might cease to love him, but that the strain on her emotions might again unsettle her mind. Harold feared this too.

But let them speak for themselves. First, Virginia in her diary, still slightly defensive:

Vita for three days at Long Barn : : : I like her and being with her and the splendour – she shines in the grocer's shop at Sevenoaks with a candle-lit radiance, stalking on legs like beech-trees, pink glowing, grape clustered, pearl hung. . . . What is the effect of all this on me? Very mixed. There is her maturity and full-breastedness; her being so much in full sail on the high tides, where I am coasting down backwards; her capacity I mean to take the floor in any company, to represent her country, to visit Chatsworth, to control silver, servants, chow dogs; her motherhood (but she is a little cold and off-hand with her boys), her being in short (what I have never been) a real woman. Then there is some voluptuousness about her; the grapes are ripe; and not reflective. No. In brain and inside she is not as highly organised as I am. But then she is aware of this and so lavishes on me the maternal protection which, for some reason, is what I have always most wished from everyone . . . [Quentin Bell. *Virginia Woolf*. Vol. II. pp. 117–18]

Professor Bell speculates on how things may have developed from there: 'There may have been – on balance I think there probably was – some caressing, some bedding together.' I can add a little to that from Harold's and Vita's letters. Harold was then in Teheran. 'V.' had become another V.

Vita to Harold: I fetched V. and brought her down here [Long Barn]. She is an exquisite companion, and I love her dearly. Leonard is coming on Saturday. Please don't think

a) I shall fall in love with Virginia
b) Virginia will „ „ me
c) Leonard „ „ „ „
d) I shall „ „ „ Leonard

because it is not so. Only I know my silly Hadji will say to himself *ça y est*, and so on. I am missing you dreadfully. I am missing you specially because V. was so very sweet about you, and so understanding. [*17 December 1925*]

Vita to Harold: Virginia read the Georgics [*The Land*]. I won't tell you what she said. She insisted on reading them. She read them straight through. She likes you. She likes me. She says she depends on me. She is so vulnerable under all her brilliance. I do love her, but not b.s.ly.* [*18 December 1925*]

Vita to Harold: I think she is one of the most mentally exciting people I know. She hates the wishy-washiness of Bloomsbury young men. We have made friends by leaps and bounds in these two days. I love her, but couldn't fall 'in love' with her, so don't be nervous! [*19 December 1925*]

Harold to Vita: I am not really bothered about Virginia, and I think you are probably very good for each other. I only feel that you have not got *la main heureuse* in dealing with married couples. [*8 January 1926*]

Harold to Vita: Oh my dear, I do hope that Virginia is not going to be a muddle! It is like smoking over a petrol tank. [*7 July 1926*]

Vita to Harold: Darling, there is no muddle anywhere. I keep on telling you so. You mention Virginia: it is simply

* The initials 'b.s.' stood for 'back-stairs'. But the expression changed its original meaning of 'gossipy', 'giggly' in Sackville shorthand to mean 'homosexual attitudes or behaviour'.

laughable. I love Virginia – as who wouldn't? But really, my sweet, one's love for Virginia is a very different thing: a mental thing; a spiritual thing, if you like, an intellectual thing, and she inspires a feeling of tenderness, which is, I suppose, owing to her funny mixture of hardness and softness – the hardness of her mind, and her terror of going mad again. She makes me feel protective. Also she loves me, which flatters and pleases me. Also – since I have embarked on telling you about Virginia – I am scared to death of arousing physical feelings in her, because of the madness. I don't know what effect it would have, you see: it is a fire with which I have no wish to play. I have too much real affection and respect for her. Also she has never lived with anyone except Leonard, which was a terrible failure, and was abandoned quite soon. So all that remains an unknown quantity; and I have got too many dogs not to let them lie when they *are* asleep. Besides *ça ne me dit rien*; and *ça lui dit trop*, where I am concerned. I don't want to get landed in an affair which might get beyond my control before I knew where I was.

Besides, Virginia is not the sort of person one thinks of in that way. There is something incongruous and almost indecent in the idea. I *have* gone to bed with her (twice), but that's all. Now you know all about it, and I hope I haven't shocked you. My darling, you are the one and only person for me in the world; do take that in once and for all, you little dunderhead. [*17 August 1926*]

Harold to Vita: Thank you for telling me so frankly about Virginia. It's a relief to feel that you realize the danger and will be wise. You see, it's not merely playing with fire; it's playing with gelignite. Don't let's worry about these things. I know that your love for me is central, as is my love for you, and it's quite unaffected by what happens at the outer edge. [*2 September 1926*]

Vita to Harold: I know that Virginia will die, and it will be too awful. I went to Tavistock Square yesterday, and she sat in the dusk in the light of the fire, and I sat on the floor as I always do, and she rumpled my hair as she always does, and she talked about literature and Mrs Dalloway and Sir Henry Taylor, and she said that you would resent her next summer. But I said, No you wouldn't. Oh Hadji, she *is* such an angel. I really adore her. Not 'in love' – just love – devotion. Her friendship has enriched me so. I don't think I have ever loved any-body so much, in the way of friendship; in fact, of course, I know I haven't. She knows that you and I adore each other. I have told her so. [*30 November 1926*]

Harold to Vita: I am far more worried for Virginia's and Leonard's sake than for ours. I know that for each of us the other is the magnetic north, and that though the needle may flicker and even get stuck at the other points, it will come back to the pole sooner or later. But what dangers for them! You see, I have every confidence in your wisdom except where this sort of thing is concerned, when you wrap your wisdom in a hood of optimism and only take it off when things have gone too far for mend-ing. [*3 December 1926*]

He need not have worried. These letters tell all there is to tell. Vita and Virginia did no damage to each other, and Harold was grateful to her for opening up in Vita 'a rich new vein of ore'. The physical element in their friendship was tentative and not very successful, lasting only a few months, a year perhaps. It is a travesty of their relationship to call it an affair. When they went to Burgundy together two years later:

Virginia is very sweet, and I feel extraordinarily pro-tective towards her. The combination of that brilliant brain and fragile body is very lovable. She has a sweet and childlike nature, from which her intellect is com-pletely separate. I have never known anyone who was so profoundly sensitive, and who makes less of a business of that sensitiveness. [*27 September 1928*]

Virginia did not admire Vita as a writer, and said so in a way which Vita would not mind. By *The Land*,

> . . . she was disappointed, but very sweet about it. She says it is a contribution to English literature, and is a solid fact against which one can lean up without fear of its giving way. She also says it is one of the few *interesting* poems – I mean the information part. [*26 January 1926*]

But *Orlando!* Imagine those two, seeing each other at least once a week, one writing a book about the other, swooping on Knole to squeeze from it another paragraph, on Long Barn to trap Vita into a new admission about her past (Violet, whom Virginia met once, comes into the book as Sasha, a Russian princess, 'like a fox, or an olive tree'), dragging Vita to a London studio to have her photographed as a Lely, tantalizing her, hinting at the fantasy but never lifting more than a corner of it – until on the day before publication, *Orlando* arrived in a brown-paper parcel from the Hogarth Press, followed a few days later by the author with the manuscript as a present. Vita wrote to Harold: 'I am in the middle of reading *Orlando*, in such a turmoil of excitement and confusion that I scarcely know where (or who) I am!' She loved it. Naturally she was flattered, but more than that, the novel identified her with Knole for ever. Virginia by her genius had provided Vita with a unique consolation for having been born a girl, for her exclusion from her inheritance, for her father's death earlier that year. The book, for her, was not simply a brilliant masque or pageant. It was a memorial mass.

By scattered references I have already landed Harold in Persia. He was sent to Teheran in October 1925 as Counsellor at the British Legation, and remained there for the next one and a half years. At first he seems to have hoped that Vita would go with him, as Persia was one of the few places in the world where she would find the diplomatic life tolerable, for it was 'unsmart' (Lady Sackville's phrase) and there were the compensations of a beautiful country and a proud romantic people. But she preferred not to. She would visit him there, but she would not be lodged in a Legation compound as his *légitime*, and be made to sit at dinner-parties in her correct order of precedence with a white card beside her plate proclaiming her 'The Hon. Mrs Harold Nicolson', when she could be V. Sackville-West at Long Barn, with her writing, her garden and Virginia. This sounds selfish, but neither of them thought it so. She cared so deeply for her independence that for both of them it out-weighed everything else, even their agony at being parted for months on end. There is no suggestion in their hundreds of letters that their misery could be ended at any moment by her joining him permanently in Teheran. Instead they ex-changed commiserations about his 'bloody profession' which forced them apart, and he began to consider seriously throwing it up for something less divisive. He went so far as to apply for a job in the Anglo-Persian Oil Company – the London end – but it came to nothing.

Lest it be thought that I exaggerate their unhappiness when separated, I will cite one incident – their parting at Rasht – which they saw afterwards as a watershed in their marriage, because it convinced them that never again must they expose each other to such pain. Vita went to Persia (the journey which she described in *Passenger to Teheran*) in March 1926, driving across the desert from Baghdad to meet Harold in a snowbound village on the Persian frontier late one night, the headlights of the car lighting up his figure on the road, suddenly. She much enjoyed her visit, and attended the coronation of the Shah ('a Cossack trooper' she described him in the book, which appalled Harold, for this was the sovereign to whom he was accredited), but in May came the dreadful moment when they must part. They had arranged that she would return home via Russia, cross-ing the Caspian from a northern Persian port near Rasht to Baku. Harold drove with her from Teheran to Rasht, and Raymond Mortimer went with them. They spent the night there, and early next morning Harold and Raymond left her to return to Teheran. Here is Harold's account in his letter written next day:

When I closed your bedroom door at Rasht, I stood for a moment on the landing with a giddy agony, which made the whole house swing and wobble. With a great effort I stopped myself bursting into your room again – where I should have found your dear head bowed in tears, and your green pyjamas still wet from them. I went down the stairs into the garden and looked back at your window. I longed to call, 'Vita, Vita, I can't bear it!'. I got into the motor with Raymond, and gradually I found my voice again. We talked of indifferent things . . . We stopped for lunch by the roadside, and put the water-bottle to cool under a spring. I went to wash a fork. Raymond said, 'Here's a tin of Ovaltine'. I said 'Yes, there are some little cakes in it.' I had put those cakes in before leaving, and you had had one of them. I crouched there, holding the fork in the stream – tears pouring down my face. I went up behind the rock and leant against it and shook and shook with sobs. Raymond was infinitely tactful . . .

Late that night they arrived back in Teheran:

I found your fur cap in my cupboard. I flung myself on the bed in an agony of suffering such as I have never known. I walked up and down in the dark saying, 'Vita, Vita, Vita, Vita, Vita!', with the tears splashing on the dark floor. I felt that this is not to be borne. One can't be as unhappy as this. This morning I broke down completely. I leant against the window with my back to Raymond. He said, 'I would give my head to have in my life a love such as you and Vita have.' That comforted me. Oh my dear, we can't go through this again. It is mad to inflict such suffering on each other. [7 *May 1926*]

From Rasht Vita wrote to him before the boat sailed:

I heard the motor start after what seemed an endless interval, and then I heard it hooting a long time through the streets. Oh my dear, God keep you safe. Life is empty and silent. I feel lightheaded with pain. Never, never, never again. I cannot bear it, and if Providence forgives me for having tempted it and allows me to be with you again, we will not leave each other any more. There is no one in the world who counts for me but you, and never will be. I simply can't live without you. [6 May 1926]

The strange fact is that there was nothing imperative to take her home. We, her children, were well cared for; Lady Sackville's selfish insistence that Vita must remain near her could have been ignored; Vita had enjoyed the easy intelligent company of Raymond and Gladwyn Jebb, who was Third Secretary at the Legation; she had even been able to write in Persia the concluding lines of *The Land*, invoking her Kentish Weald and the ghost of Virgil. I find it difficult to explain. Virginia was not the draw: Virginia could come alive in letters. But absence is something more endurable than separation. When Vita arrived back in England, she took up her old occupations, and the wound healed. The sense of unbroken communion with Harold was renewed by correspondence. Her letters to Persia were the best she ever wrote to him, perhaps because the long time-lag between posting and delivery (two weeks, at least, sometimes four) gave them a perspective and a rhythm, like a slow procession of waves advancing to a distant shore. She was able to be franker – a blush cannot last three weeks – and she became more contemplative:

I got a letter from Virginia, which contains one of her devilish, shrewd, psychological pounces. She asks if there is something in me which does not vibrate, a 'something reserved, muted ... The thing I call "central transparency" sometimes fails you in your writing'. Damn the woman, she has put her finger on it. There *is* something muted. What is it, Hadji? Something that doesn't come alive. I brood and brood, feel I am groping in a dark tunnel. It makes everything I write a little unreal; gives the effect of having been done from outside.

There is no doubt about it, as one grows older, one thinks more. Virginia worries, you worry, I worry. Yet I would rather do this and become introspective than rattle about London, where people's voices become more and more devoid of meaning. [*20 November 1926*]

Harold gained much from Persia. He loved the country, learnt the language, and professionally his grasp became more incisive – too much so for the taste of some of his superiors in the Foreign Office, for he could never bring himself to write his dispatches in the approved guarded manner. He also wrote *Some People*, his most original book, in the same months as Vita was putting the finishing touches to *The Land*, her most distinguished. *Some People* was autobiographical to the extent that he traced his intellectual development by placing himself in a series of confrontations, some real, some imaginary, with his nanny, a schoolboy hero, a French intellectual, a diplomatic pundit, Lord Curzon and so on – from all of which encounters he emerged slightly on top. In style the book owed something to Lytton Strachey, something to Max Beerbohm, but its amused detached analysis of the nudging and jostling of people in their relations with each other was wholly his own. He always regarded *Some People* as a lightweight book, and groaned inwardly whenever some acquaintance began, 'Now let me see, I read something of yours the other day – something about Lord Curzon's valet and a pair of trousers, was it?', but on the day when he finished writing it in Teheran, he obviously thought it contained a little more than mere entertainment:

This evening I wrote the last words of *Some People*. I then walked across to see Gladwyn, wishing to clear my mind. He was tired by his day's shooting and had a cold, and didn't in the least want to talk about the soul. But I made him. I said that the intellect was the only thing which made man a higher animal, and therefore virtue should simply mean the development of the intellect. He said I was leaving out the emotions. 'You know, Harold, you'd be an awful cad if it weren't for your emotions.' I said, 'No, you're completely wrong.' So then I came back and sat in my bath and realized that he was completely right. I mean, I *like* Gladwyn because he is intelligent; but I am *fond* of Gladwyn because he is sensitive and shy and reserved and distinguished. So my theory has broken down. [*20 December 1926*]

In February 1927 Vita returned to Persia by the Russian route, and their reunion at Rasht almost (but never quite) effaced in family legend their parting at the same place nine months before. This time they arranged things better. After a month in Teheran they went south to Isfahan, and thence, on foot, with Gladwyn, they crossed the Bakhtiari Mountains to the oil-fields, in hail and rain, pushing against sheep and tribesmen, for they had chosen the season of the annual migration. When they reached the plains of Abadan, the bungalows, Fords and telephones of the Oil Company were to Harold 'the joys of civilization', to Vita 'the horrible resources of modern ingenuity'. She wrote in her second book of Persian travels, *Twelve Days*: 'A wave of regret swept over me. I forgot the exhaustion of our toiling days. I would have turned back then and there into the mountains and be lost for ever.' Instead, Harold took her home to Long Barn. In his diary on the day of their arrival he wrote:

4 May 1927. It is a different place: wide lawns and tidy edges; tulips and aubretia, phlox, lilac, irises – a sea of colour. It is so exciting that I am violently sick and have to be given brandy. I have never felt so happy in my life. All the weary months of exile are wiped away as if by a sponge.

Odd things coincided during that summer and autumn. Maurice Couve de Murville, the future Prime Minister of France, came to Long Barn for six weeks, a shy youth brittle as a biscuit, dressed in midsummer tweeds, to teach us French. Vita was awarded the Hawthornden Prize for *The Land*. Virginia started to write *Orlando*. Roy Campbell, the poet, and his wife Mary, were lent the gardener's cottage, and Vita fell in love with Mary, to the fury of Roy, who wrote *The Georgiad*, a highly uncomplimentary portrait of Long Barn and the Nicolsons, in revenge. And Harold advanced another step towards his decision to leave the diplomatic service:

> *24 Aug. 1927.* I can now envisage the prospect of resignation without a pang. I have Vita and the boys. I have my home and my love of nature. I have my friends. I have my energy and my talent for writing. I shall be free. I can tell the truth. There is no truth now which I cannot tell.

Instead, when he was asked in October to go as First Secretary to Berlin, 'I accept, gloomily.'

The importance of Berlin in their personal lives was to confirm Harold's growing conviction that for Vita's sake he must abandon his diplomatic career at mid-point for another which would allow him to live in England. Berlin was nearer home than Teheran, near enough to send tulips from Long Barn with a chance that they would revive in water, but it was uglier and smarter. Vita went there several times and loathed it. Harold did not loathe it quite so much, because he found the work interesting (he was soon promoted to Counsellor), and he made many new friends among the Germans and visiting English, but 'I am far more homesick than I was in Persia, for Persia did appeal to my nature-love, but here there are no works of God at all'. Once again it was taken for granted between them that while he was in Berlin she would stay most of the time at Long Barn, writing him letters of mounting indignation against those who kept him there:

> Oh God, how I hate the Foreign Office! How I hate it, with a personal hatred for all that it makes me suffer! Damn it, damn it, damn it – that vile impersonal juggernaut that sweeps you away from me. [*15 November 1928*]

More profoundly:

> I am not a good person for you to be married to. Men
> and women who marry ought to be positive and negative
> respectively – complementary elements. But when two
> positive people like us marry, it resolves itself into a
> compromise which is truly satisfactory to neither. You
> love foreign politics; and I love literature and peace and
> a secluded life. Oh my dear, my infinitely dear Hadji, you
> ought never to have married me. I feel my inadequacy
> most bitterly. What good am I to you? [*13 December
> 1928*]

And he replied, What good was he to her? She should have
married Lord Lascelles.

He heard that it was likely that after two years in Berlin
he would be sent as Minister to Washington. The prospect
made less appeal to Vita than it had to her mother fifty
years before. She could not, she *would* not, do it. While
Harold had been able to explain her long absences when he
held more junior posts ('It rather amuses me that people
think we don't get on'), as he rose to be in charge of Legations and then Embassies, her refusal to join him as his
hostess (the word made her shiver) might be awkward for
him. It would be an overstatement to say that Vita wrecked
Harold's career, because he himself, on additional grounds,
had for some years been thinking of chucking it. *Some People*
had sown distrust in his 'soundness', and his 'too clever' dispatches from Teheran had ruffled feelings in Downing
Street. He felt himself to be under a slight cloud. He disliked exile as much as she did, and was not at ease on formal
diplomatic occasions, which would grow more formal as he
became more important. He loved his work, and in a non-
pushing way was ambitious. This was one of Vita's griev-
ances: 'How I wish you weren't ambitious; how I wish you
preferred books to politics, me to Hindenburg!' Literature
was his second string (while he was in Berlin he wrote the
life of his father, Lord Carnock, who died in 1928), but there
was something feeble, he thought, in the idea of 'lotus-eating

at Long Barn, writing books, at the age of forty-three', and even Vita might come to despise him for it. Not at all, replied Vita: 'I am all for some people doing public duty, but I think it ought to be reserved for those who can't do anything else, and people like you who can write marvellously should not waste themselves in a lot of humbug and fubsiness', by which she meant the preliminaries to the Second World War. The importance of his work made no greater impression on her when he was appointed to take charge of the Berlin Embassy between two Ambassadors.

Again and again they returned to the central problem of their separation, although they met far more frequently than during the Persian years. Harold often came home on leave, and we spent several of our school holidays in Germany, skating in the Tiergarten, sailing on the Heiligesee and playing badminton in the Embassy ballroom, while Vita managed to avoid most diplomatic parties and was able to work on her books: she began the first chapter of *The Edwardians* in the restaurant of Cologne railway-station. But more meetings meant more separations:

> I spent most of the evening in tears. It is sheer misery for me, these perpetual departures ... I simply feel that you are me and I am you – exactly what you meant by saying that you became 'the lonely me' whenever we parted.

This could have been written by either of them. In fact, it was written by Vita, in the spring of 1929.

When in June of that year Bruce Lockhart asked Harold out of the blue whether he would care to join the staff of the *Evening Standard*, he accepted, not impetuously, not very happily (for he thought journalism sordid), but gratefully. The salary which Lord Beaverbrook offered him, £3,000 a year, would make them independent of Lady Sackville, who was turning nasty about the allowance which she owed them as a legal right. He could come home, for good. He could write books as well as paragraphs for the Londoner's Diary. He asked Leonard Woolf's advice, and Leonard agreed.

Vita, who was walking in the Val d'Isère with Hilda Matheson (Talks Director at the BBC) when she heard the news, was delighted, feeling in an obscure way that his resignation was a snub to the Foreign Office. As the time drew near for his departure, he felt no regrets. He referred to it as 'the great liberation'; and the last words of his last letter to Vita from Berlin were: 'How glad I shall be when the train moves out of the Friedrichstrasse!' In his diary, when that day came (20 December 1929), he wrote: 'I am presented with a cactus. It symbolizes the end of my diplomatic career.'

Their marriage had now lasted seventeen years. Vita was to live another thirty-two, Harold another thirty-eight. It may be wondered why I should devote only a thirtieth part of a book entitled *Portrait of a Marriage* to an account of two-thirds of it. There are two reasons: first, because the remainder of the story has already been told in the three published volumes of Harold's diary, which he began to keep regularly in 1930; second, because there was no change in their relationship from that time forward, no threat to their married happiness. It simply deepened. I can summarize the events of those years quite shortly.

For eighteen months Harold compiled the Londoner's Diary for the *Evening Standard*, hating it. After the Foreign Office, with its pride in itself, its lofty intellectual aspirations and its discretion, daily journalism appeared to him trivial and squalid. He became closely involved with Sir Oswald Mosley's New Party in 1931, editing its newspaper *Action*, and stood unsuccessfully for Parliament in its name. It was the most depressing period of his life. On 'descending to the market place', as he put it, he had made two false starts. He found himself obliged to part in quick succession first with Beaverbrook, then with Mosley, and was left without a job, without money, and his reputation (so he believed) shattered. It was no consolation to him that during those same years he achieved sudden notoriety by his weekly talks on BBC radio under the title *People and Things*; nor that Vita was able to keep their home together and us at Eton by writing three best-selling novels, *The Edwardians, All Passion Spent* and *Family History*. Harold made his contribution with *Public Faces*, a brilliantly amusing novel about the Foreign Office, and together in 1933 they went on a joint lecture tour of the United States. On their return, Harold settled down to more serious books, *Peacemaking*, and *Curzon, the Last Phase*, and a biography of the American financier and statesman, Dwight Morrow, but he still believed himself to be a failure. Privately, without telling Vita, he bitterly regretted his resignation from the Foreign Office. His worst fears had been justified: he was 'lotus-eating'. Then in 1935, everything changed. He was elected to Parliament as National Labour member for West Leicester, and remained there for the next ten years.

Too little has been made of Harold's years in the House of Commons by potted accounts of his career. It has been tempting to write him off as a political lightweight because he gained no Government office higher than Parliamentary Secretary to the Ministry of Information in 1940–1, and could never bring himself to engage in party in-fighting. He should have been a Liberal, it was said, or sat for one of the University seats. But he had two great advantages in the House. He was almost the only back-bench Member to have had direct experience of the higher conduct of foreign policy; and he was exceptionally astute and personally very popular. His diffidence, his apparent lack of ambition, his geniality, his wit made his cleverness acceptable in a place where dexterity is usually more honoured than intelligence. He never advertised himself at Question-time, never snubbed the less well educated Members, and spoke rarely and shortly on the subjects he knew best. He had the courage to stand up to the Conservatives with whom his tiny splinter-party was nominally allied, protesting eloquently against their refusal to recognize the Nazi danger. He found himself in the pre-war years aligned with Churchill and Eden against Chamberlain, and reached the peak of his Parliamentary career in his speech against the Munich settlement of 1938.

When war came, and his friends were in power, he should have been rewarded for the stubborn rightness of his judgement, but his year of junior office was abruptly ended by Churchill, not because Harold had been found wanting, but because the Parliamentary Secretaryship was needed for someone else in the Party share-out of offices, and Harold was considered dispensable because he was not formidable. For the remainder of the war he was a Governor of the BBC, and devoted his Parliamentary gifts mainly to reconciling the British Government to the Free French. What an Ambassador to Paris he would have made when the war ended! But he did not have that sort of push. In the General Election of 1945 he lost his seat, and never returned to public life.

Vita all this time was gardening and writing books. If in the early years of their marriage things happened to Vita more than they happened to Harold, in the late years it was the other way round. She became solitary – a recluse would be too strong a description – finding happiness in country things and the periodic company of her family and a few close friends. She played no part whatever in Harold's political life, visiting Leicester on only one occasion during his ten years as its Member, and as far as I know never set foot in the House of Commons. She went to London as seldom as possible, but often abroad on holiday, to Italy and in later years to the Dordogne district of France. After the American tour of 1933 she appeared rarely in public, for she was a nervous lecturer though she enjoyed broadcasting, and social functions became increasingly abhorrent to her. She accepted one or two semi-public positions such as membership of the National Trust's Gardens Committee, and she became a Justice of the Peace, more because she liked the medieval sound of the title than the twentieth-century actuality of the work involved. During the war years she lived at Sissinghurst under the umbrella of the RAF, and helped to organize the Women's Land Army, whose history she wrote.

After the war Harold divided his time between weekends

writing at Sissinghurst and week-days in London, where he served on many committees and enjoyed a dazzling social life as an eligible single man, his hostesses having long given up hope that Vita could be induced to come too. Once he tried to re-enter politics by joining the Labour Party and standing as its candidate at the Croydon by-election in 1948, but he was not elected, and the mortification of the experience ('I was certainly not intended by nature or by training for one of the central figures in a harlequinade') decided him to abandon politics for literature. Soon after Croydon he was invited to write the official biography of King George V, and this was the most massive literary undertaking of his career, earning him a knighthood which he felt it ungracious to decline. Vita hated being Lady Nicolson even more than she hated being Mrs Nicolson, and anyone who addressed her as such would be startled by a freezing look.

To end the factual part of this narrative, a word should be added about my brother and myself. Both of us went to Balliol College, Oxford, after Eton, and both served in the army in North Africa and Italy during the war, from which we emerged unscratched by the enemy. Ben thereafter dedicated his gifts to the history of art, becoming in 1947 Editor of the *Burlington Magazine*, the leading journal of the history of the fine arts, a position which he still (1973) retains, and wrote major books on the painters Terbrugghen, Wright of Derby and Georges de La Tour. I entered publishing as George Weidenfeld's partner in 1947, and politics as MP for Bournemouth East in 1952, losing my seat seven years later mainly because I differed from most of my constituents about the Suez crisis. Ben and I both married and had children, but our marriages (in spite of the example which this book records) did not succeed, nature having endowed us with a greater talent for friendship than for cohabitation, for fatherhood than for wedlock.

The centre of our lives during later boyhood and adolescence was Sissinghurst Castle, near Cranbrook in Kent, where both our parents lived for more than thirty years and where both died. I remember well (but my memory is perhaps gilded by too frequent recital of the event) my first visit there in April 1930. I went with my mother and Dorothy Wellesley, the poet, to view 'an estate' recommended by a local agent. Vita and Harold had been disturbed by the rumour that the meadows around Long Barn were about to be sold to a chicken-farmer who intended to raise a cantonment of huts within view of the terrace, and were looking for another place where they could live in peace and make a new garden. Sissinghurst appeared to my eyes (aged thirteen) quite impossible. It was the battered relic of an Elizabethan house in which not a single room was habitable. The future garden was a rubbish-dump. The day was a wet one, and I trailed my mother between mountains of old tins and other unexplained humps from one brick fragment to another, each more derelict than the last. She suddenly turned to me, her mind made up: 'I think we shall be very happy here.' 'But we haven't got to live *here?*' I said, appalled, 'Yes, I think we can make something rather lovely out of it.'

My father came down with Ben next day, and recorded in his diary, 'I am cold and calm, but I like it.' But it was Vita who pressed the audacious plan, she who had the money to buy Sissinghurst, she who organized the rehabilitation of what had once been the finest architectural ornament of the central Weald. They repaired the surviving buildings, making two bedrooms for themselves in one of the cottages, one for Ben and me in another (which we shared until we were both at Oxford), and most important of all, separate sitting-rooms for each of us. There were no guest-rooms, deliberately, and only one common sitting-room, a room like Long Barn's fifty feet long, which we used only occasionally. They had achieved by the accident of the physical separation of the buildings the perfect solution to our communal lives. Each of us could be alone most of the day, and we could unite for meals.

Vita's own sitting-room was on the first floor of the

Elizabethan tower which rose slim and solemn from the centre of this disjointed compound. It had been the room in which we all four slept at weekends on camp-beds until the cottages were ready, breakfasting off sardines and honey on a packing-case. One morning my father took the butter-knife and prised loose a brick in the wall which sealed off the neighbouring turret-room, and Vita, peering through the hole, at once exclaimed, 'That will be my libary; and this', waving a teaspoon around the wall, 'will be my sitting-room.' Within a month or two it was, and it remained hers for the next thirty-two years. Few were ever admitted to it. We would go to the foot of the staircase in the opposite turret and shout that lunch was ready or that she was wanted on the telephone, but by an unspoken rule we never mounted it. She filled the room with her books and personal mementoes – a stone from Persepolis, a photograph of Virginia, one of Pepita's dancing slippers – and as the wall-paper peeled and faded, and the velvet tassels slowly frayed, she would never allow them to be renewed. Her possessions must grow old with her. She must be surrounded by evidence of time. When after a short absence I returned with her to inspect the repairs to her bedroom in the South Cottage, we found the workmen applying a skin of white plaster to the Elizabethan bricks. She stopped them immediately (she could be imperious, like Bess of Hardwick), and ordered them to undo all that they had done so far. 'But surely, madam, you don't want to have bare brick in the mistress's bedroom?' 'That's exactly what I do want.' To this day the room remains as she rightly ordered it, the red and purple bricks forming a tapestry against which hang the mirrors of a later age. Her sitting-room too is quite unchanged. For a week or two after her death, I tried to use it as my own. I could not endure it. I ceased to be myself: I became a ghost of her.

One day, perhaps, a book may be written about the making of the garden at Sissinghurst, and it could well bear the same title as this book, for the garden is a portrait of their marriage. Harold made the design, Vita did the planting. In

the firm perspectives of the vistas, the careful siting of an urn
or statue, the division of the garden by hedges and walls and
buildings into a series of separate gardens, the calculated
alternation between straight lines and curved, one can trace
his classical hand. In the overflowing clematis, figs, vines
and wistaria, in the rejection of violent colour or anything
too tame or orderly, one discovers her romanticism. Wild
flowers must be allowed to invade the garden; if plants
stray over a path, they must not be cut back, the visitor
must duck: rhododendrons must be banished in favour of
their tender cousin, the azalea; roses must not electrify, but
seduce; and when a season has produced its best, that part
of the garden must be allowed to lie fallow for another year,
since there is a cycle in nature which must not be disguised.
It is eternally renewable, like a play with acts and scenes:
there can be a change of cast, but the script remains the
same. Permanence and mutation are the secrets of this
garden.

Let the author of the future book understand well that it
emerged from their leisure hours. They created it in the
intervals of earning enough money to create it. The garden
was an extravagance. For both of them it was an accom-
paniment to their books, like the left hand on a piano to the
right. When Harold returned to Sissinghurst each Friday
evening, he would look round the garden in London suit
and with swinging briefcase, the first of all his concerns, a
sump to drain off the week's despair, a wineglass to hold the
weekend's delights. She, alone all week, would plan and toil,
committing to a vast notebook (for ink and paper were her
adjutants) her plans, her self-interrogation, and when he
came back, she put to him her ideas, her worries, her
triumphs and disappointments. 'Come: come and look.
What shall we do?'

Vita, I have said, withdrew into preferred solitude. Before
the war, because of it, and after it, she retreated to Sissinghurst. In her young womanhood she had been vigorous,
alert for new excitement. She had constantly made fresh
friends, and was anxious to make more. She searched for

experience, gambled with life. Now she was content with what was familiar, people and places, and her new adventures were tuned to a gentler key, measured by a slower tempo. Her loves lasted five, seven, years, not one or three; they were no longer rockets, but slow-burning fuses with no explosive at the end. She loved more deeply, less passionately, as she became more contemplative. Religion, which had hitherto meant little to her, began to puzzle and worry her. Why had she not reflected more? In *Saint Joan of Arc* and *The Eagle and the Dove* she explored the mysteries in which she could not believe, finding at the end of her long inquiries only a greater question mark. To her, nature was the dumb expression of what she could never satisfactorily explain – flowers and cattle, crops and birds – and her poem *The Garden*, a profounder commentary than *The Land*, was her attempt to reconcile the known with the unknowable, probing ever deeper and never reaching the bottom of the well.

This was her secret life, the life of the tower, into which we never attempted to penetrate. Often we would not know the title or subject of her latest book until we saw it advertised, while Harold would discuss his work-in-progress over lunch. More superficially she was very companionable. Occasionally her two worlds overlapped, and we became aware how easily, how deeply, we could wound her by an unconsidered remark. It was Christmas Eve 1933. I was sixteen. I came early to the dining-room, switched on the radio, and listened to the bells of Bethlehem which were being broadcast live by the BBC for the first time. I leant casually against the mantelpiece, munching a banana. My mother came in. 'What's that?' she asked. 'Oh, it's only the bells of Bethlehem,' I replied. It was the word 'only', my stance, the banana, which cumulatively shocked her. How could her son be so indifferent? She rushed out of the room, in tears, and it took an hour for my father to persuade her to return.

Such was the gap between her and us. It had been there since we were babies. When we were at school she dutifully tore herself away from her work to visit us on half-terms at Summer Fields and Eton, and was always sweet to us, but she could not disguise the effort which it cost her to find new subjects to talk about when we had exhausted the garden and the dogs, and she was touchingly different from the other mothers, dressed (as my father once said) in the sort of clothes that Beatrice would have worn had she married Dante, and at a complete loss to keep her end up in their smart society gossip. Later she always took an interest in what was happening to us, and during the war wrote to us very regularly, but her letters were more constrained than those which she wrote to Harold. Her pen had needed pushing, we felt, instead of keeping pace with her thoughts. She was guiltily conscious that she never managed to establish an intimacy with her sons, and thought herself a failure as a mother, but it was as much our fault as hers. We never made the necessary effort to know her well.

With our father it was quite different. I can express our relationship in no better words than those I used in the Introduction to the first volume of his Diaries:

His attitude ... was one of open enthusiasm for anything that we were doing. He read, for instance, the whole of Aeschylus' *Seven against Thebes* because it was my set-book at school. He hired a boat to visit the islands which I bought in the Outer Hebrides [the Shiant Islands]. He encouraged us to discuss with him anything that amused, interested or worried us. I once wrote to him from Eton about the problem of switching from surname to Christian-name terms with my close friends. He replied from the United States in a six-page letter of advice, the gist of which was to smother the explosive word: 'Don't begin by saying, "James, have you borrowed my Latin dictionary?" Say, "Oh, by the way, James, have you borrowed my Latin dictionary?"' This was exactly the sort of problem that delighted him. He always claimed that it was impossible for a father to transmit experience, but in fact he did so, for his advice was always very practical, and by understanding the exact nuances of our dilemmas, he dissipated them.

I do not think that it will unbalance these concluding pages if I quote a complete letter which he wrote to Ben at Eton in 1931, when Ben was seventeen, for Harold has been overshadowed in this book by Vita, just as he overshadowed her in his Diaries, and his whole nature is contained in this letter:

My darling Benzie,

I thought your sonnet excellent – really good. And the absurd thing is that the 'swallow' passage, which you made up yourself, was far the best passage in the whole thing. The rest was a clever imitation and adaptation. But the swallows were observed.

I think that your weakness in writing is not technique but originality. You need not bother about writing well. That comes naturally to you. But you must bother about thinking well. That has not come to you yet. I sometimes wish that you did not agree with Mummy and me so much. Of course, *of course*, we are always right. But a boy of your age should sometimes think us wrong.

It is no use *trying* to be original. That ends by being merely contradictory – and people who are merely contradictory are the worst of all sorts of bore. But you should think things out for yourself. Do not start merely by disagreeing in principle with whatever other people think. They are probably right. But work out slowly, carefully, quietly, your own ideas about everything.

I think in some ways you have an original and courageous mind. You were very good indeed about confirmation and Holy Communion. That was the real Ben. It was not *just* trying to be original: it was a deliberate and perfectly sensible attitude or gesture of thought. Now that you are becoming less bothered about what Hanbury thinks, or Sevelode thinks, or Tiddliumpty thinks, you might begin to be bothered about what Ben thinks.

My darling, I am so glad that you are less bored at Eton and less unhappy. Seek out the things you enjoy and forget the things you hate. You are beginning to realize that your independence is not just because you are a freak, but because you are a person. The same idea is occurring to your contemporaries. Go on being the same, only with a smile on your lips. They may tease you about it, but at the bottom of their hearts they respect you. Being 'odd', being 'different', is a sign of individuality. It exposes you, when a young boy among other young boys, to the jeers of the herd. But the herd is growing older even as you are growing older. They will come to look on you with a 'vague surmise' (or is it 'a wild surmise'?). They will begin to wonder whether after all Nicolson *ma* is not Benedict Nicolson – a person, who in spite of much suffering, has emerged as himself from the crude machinery, the crushing uniformity, of the lower boy ideals. You may find that the stand you have taken, which seemed so odd to them at first, seems to them now a rather courageous thing – a thing far finer than their own subservience to the course of the stream.

I repeat, be nice to the lower boys. I know that this may expose you to misunderstanding, and I do not wish you to flaunt intimacy with the more handsome youths of fourteen. But I beg you, when you see a person as shy and as unhappy as you were yourself, to give him a kind word, a look of understanding. You will answer, 'Daddy doesn't know the conditions at Eton'. I reply, 'Yes, I do.' They were just the same in my day at Wellington. Human nature doesn't change. And I know that in my case I found that when I got to your position in my house, the opportunity of being kind to little miseries, made up for all the unkindness and cruelty which I had received myself.

Boys are generally insensitive. You are far too sensitive. One act or word of kindness on your part will compensate you for all the jeers of the worthless people who have laughed at you in the past. Try it and see. It will give you a warm feeling inside, in place of that cold sore feeling which you know.

Bless you, my own darling. Your very loving,

H.G.N.

This was the person Harold had become in his maturity. His virtues are self-evident from what has already been said and quoted. His faults were that he had a slight insensitiveness (in spite of what he wrote about lower boys) to people who were not born with his advantages. His dislike of Jews and coloured people, the persistent 'bedint' prejudice, were characteristics which he shared with Vita, and against which Ben and I later reacted. It could also be said that he lacked mettle, which Winston Churchill once defined as the most estimable quality in a man, and he would smooth his path by concessions to a stronger will unless his deepest beliefs or emotions had been aroused by a political event like Munich of Suez, or a personal one like an act of cruelty. I have already mentioned the streak of sentimentality in him, which occasionally distorted his view of people, and its opposite, an acidity which could creep into his judgements. It seems strange that someone of so loving a disposition could cause pain, but there are people who knew him slightly who still think of him as rather formidable, a verdict which would have astonished him. He wanted always to repay, like a debt, the pleasure which he had gained from work and friendship. When he reached the age of fifty, he wrote in his diary:

I have dispersed my energies in life, done too many different things, and have no sense of reaching any harbour. I am still very promising and shall continue to be so until the day of my death. But what enjoyment and what interest I have derived from my experience! I suppose that I am too volatile and fluid, but few people can have extracted such happiness from fluidity, and when I look back upon my life, it is as gay as an Alpine meadow patinated with the stars of varied flowers. Would I feel happier if I had stuck to a single crop of lucerne or clover? No!

He and Vita had long ago reconciled their different temperaments, and they created for themselves a life which suited both perfectly – separation during the week, reunion at weekends. She when alone would garden all day, and write half the night: he in London, first at King's Bench Walk in the Temple, and after the war at Albany, Piccadilly, was busy, social, industrious. He would carry up from Sissinghurst on Monday baskets of flowers, bring down on Friday the London news which still entertained her so long as she was not involved, and in between, every day, they wrote to each other, and each kept all the other's letters. Few marriages can be better documented. What cannot be preserved except in memory is the gentleness of their reunions. They did not 'leap together like two flames', as when Violet returned from Holland, but berthed like sisterships. There was always a certain bustle, the business of unpacking and tea, the tour of the garden and the changing of clothes, but soon they settled down to their easy companionship, allowing words to trickle into the crevasses of the other's mind, feeding each other with impressions of what they had read or heard, stimulating, reassuring, teasing by turns – a process which was half solicitous, half provocative, always tender. It was the alternation of excitement and calm in their lives, the 'succession of privacies' as Harold described the charm of Sissinghurst itself, the sense that each was always available to the other though neither would intrude unasked, which made the later years of their marriage so consecrated and serene. When Virginia drowned herself in 1941, Harold came down to Sissinghurst at once to be with Vita, but during the whole of that long evening, Virginia's name was never mentioned by either of them. In 1960 Vita wrote to him:

I was always well trained not to manage you. I scarcely dare to arrange the collar of your greatcoat, unless you ask me to. I think that is really the basis of our marriage,

235

apart from our deep love for each other, for we have never interfered with each other, and strangely enough, never been jealous of each other. And now, in our advancing age, we love each other more deeply than ever, and also more agonizingly, since we see the inevitable end. It is not nice to know that one of us must die before the other.

It was she who died first. In January 1962, at the outset of the last of several winter cruises which they made together, she had an internal haemorrhage, but managed to conceal it from Harold throughout the voyage. On her return she could do so no longer, and underwent an operation which revealed advanced cancer. She barely survived the operation, but regained sufficient strength to return to Sissinghurst in late May. There she died on 2 June 1962.

I ended the last volume of my father's Diaries with Vita's funeral. During his lifetime I did not wish to dwell on his agony. 'Oh Vita, I have wept buckets for you', he wrote three weeks later. And he did, quietly at the dinner-table, clamorously when he thought himself out of earshot in the garden. I was awed by his desolation, giving him the comfort of my familiar presence, but fearing to increase his flow of tears by attempting to staunch them by words of consolation or remembrance. He never recovered from Vita's death. His gaiety gradually subsided into gentle good humour, his intellectual vitality to vague contemplation. He had two strokes in quick succession, which further dulled his mind. He gave up writing, then reading, and became very silent in his last two years. His decline was more painful to us than for him, for I do not think he was aware of it. When the earlier volumes of his Diary became unexpected best-sellers, he remarked to me with a flash of his old humour, 'It's sad to think that of all my forty books, the only ones that will be remembered are the three that I didn't realize I'd written.' But when I gave him the typescript of the third volume, he did not have the interest or energy to glance at more than half a dozen pages. Sometimes I would ask him about the past, but his responses became fewer. He told me that he had no wish to live longer, and I believed him.

The end was sudden and merciful. He died at Sissinghurst on 1 May 1968, of a heart attack, as he was undressing for bed.

Index

Berlin, 222; Lady Sackville tells about Violet affair, 190; later career, 226; marriage, 226; later relations with Vita, 231; and with Harold, 232-4

Nicolson, Harold: first meets Vita, 41-2, 92; in Monte Carlo with her, 42, 93; falls in love with her, 45-6, 93; proposes to her, 45, 94-5; her hesitant response, 46, 95-7; half-engaged, 46; Sackville attitude, to 95-6, 98-9; engaged, 50; married, 51; honeymoon, 51; first years of marriage, 51-2, 54; tries to reconcile Sackvilles, 109-10, 164; prevents Vita eloping, 123-4, 165-6; operation to knee, 127, 174; Vita tells him of elopement plan, 128-9, 173-4; pursues her to Amiens, 135, 181; terrible scene there, 135-6, 181-2; takes Vita to Paris, 137-8; at Paris Peace Conference, 151; tries to recall Vita to sanity, 165-6, 171-2; debates marriage with Vita, 197-8; at Long Barn, 200-201; attitude to Vita's affairs with G. Scott, 203, 206; and to her love for Virginia Woolf, 211-13; in Teheran, 214-19; writes *Some People*, 218; parting with Vita at Rasht, 216; returns to England, 219; in British Embassy, Berlin, 220-23; thinks of leaving diplomacy, 215, 220-22; leaves, 223; on *Evening Standard*, 223; joins Sir O. Mosley, 223; Member of Parliament, 224-5; Minister, 225; loses seat, 225; stands at Croydon by-election, 226; knighted, 226; at Sissinghurst, 228-9; in later life, 235; decline after Vita's death, 236; his own death, 237

Character: summary, 93, 151-2, 198-9, 234; in youth, 93; attitude to marriage, 196-8; to sex, 148-9, 196; not jealous of Vita, 150, 236; attitude to Violet affair, 152-3, 156, 165-6, 187-8; generosity of spirit, 165-6, 231-4; his love for Vita, 166, 276-7, 199-200, 216, 235; allows her complete freedom, 195-6, 203; emotionalism, 198-9, 218-19; as a politician, 224-5; social figure, 226; attitude to sons, 202, 231-4; ambition, 221-2; dislike of Jews, 234; love of gardening, 199, 219, 228-9, 235

243

Woolf, 207–14; with Harold in Persia, 215–19; parting with him at Rasht, 216–17; walks over Bakhtiari Mountains, 219; love for Mary Campbell, 220; lecture tour in US, 224, 225; during Second War, 225; buys Sissinghurst, 227; restores it, 227–8; makes garden there, 228–9; in older age, 229–30, 235; death, 236 **Her marriage:** summary, 13, 147–9, 195–201; her love for Harold, 28–9, 107, 155–6, 172, 174–6, 187, 199–201, 217, 235–6; attitude to marriage in general, 117–18, 162; homosexuality, 117–18, 161; dislike of 'normal' love, 147; attitude to her children, 155, 167, 230–31; uninterested in Harold's career, 151, 220–22, 225; indifference to scandal, 173–4, 195; mutual tolerance in marriage, 195–6; her 'little creed' for Harold, 196; their only quarrel, 199; sadness at separation from him, 200, 215–17, 219, 221; her later love-affairs, 230; relations with Harold in old age, 235–6 **Character:** summary,

153–4; as a child, 20–1, 27–8, 34–6, 71–4; as adolescent, 90–91; her 'dual nature', 47–8, 115–16, 118, 140, 154; attitude to men, 77, 147, on position of women, 154; recklessness, 154, 183; Wanderlust, 72, 153, 162; love of sailing, 20; and animals, 27, 72; and nature, 27, 153; and Italy, 37, 88–9; gardening, at Knole, 73, 97; at Constantinople, 107; at Long Barn, 108, 199, 201; at Sissinghurst, 228–9; a snob, 91; religion, 230; clothes, 231; love of seclusion, 218, 221, 225, 229; taste, 227–8 **Books:** Autobiography, 11–15, 117–18, 186; *The Dragon in Shallow Waters*, 28, 177–8, 185; unpublished juvenile books, 34, 74–7, 88; *Chatterton*, 41, 76; *Pepita*, 61, 68, 70, 109; *The Edwardians*, 91, 222, 224; *Passenger to Tehran*, 106, 215; *Poems of West and East*, 105, 107; *Orchard and Vineyard*, 182–3; *Challenge*, 124, 159–61, 162; *Grand Canyon*, 147; *Heritage*, 150, 154, 170; *The Land*, 202, 204, 211, 214, 217, 218, 219, 230; *Seducers in Ecuador*, 209;